THE BIRTH OF SOCIAL WELFARE IN IRELAND, 1922–52

To Maureen, Hannah and Evie

The Birth of Social Welfare in Ireland, 1922–52

Mel Cousins

FOUR COURTS PRESS

Set in 10.5 on 12.5 point Ehrhardt for
FOUR COURTS PRESS LTD
7 Malpas Street, Dublin 8, Ireland
e-mail: info@four-courts-press.ie
and in North America
FOUR COURTS PRESS
c/o ISBS, 920 N.E. 58th Avenue, Portland, OR 97213

A catalogue record for this title
is available from the British Library.

ISBN 1–85182–704–8

Printed in Great Britain
by Antony Rowe, Chippenham, Wilts.

Contents

Preface

THIS IS THE FIRST detailed, published account of the politics and policies of the social welfare system in Ireland in the period to the establishment of a unified system in 1952. It seems appropriate to publish this study to mark the fiftieth anniversary of the formal birth of the social welfare system.

It aims to shed light on the broader political history of Ireland, and on the political parties and the key figures of the time through an examination of one of the country's major social policy areas. For, as Peter Baldwin has argued, the development of social welfare 'conceals questions of utmost importance under matters that may at first seem merely technical and abstruse'. While the details of social welfare development policy may not seem the 'stuff of dramatic narrative' I agree with Baldwin that 'the nuts and bolts of social policy testify to the heated struggles of classes and interests'. It is indeed true that the 'battles behind the welfare state lay bare the structure and conflicts of modern society'.

As this is the first published account based on archival research, I have attempted to set out the 'nuts and bolts' of policy development to assist others in future research and to allow readers to judge for themselves whether or not they agree with my analysis of the story. I hope that my account will not be found to be too technical nor abstruse.

Over the several years of this study, a very wide range of people assisted in my research. I would, in particular, like to thank Tony McCashin who read the entire manuscript and provided numerous helpful comments and references. Adrian Kelly kindly allowed me to read his PhD thesis on 'Social Security in an Independent Ireland' while Gerry Hughes provided historical material from his own PhD thesis on 'The Irish Payroll Tax: Effects on Labour Supply and Incidence'.

I would like to thank the staff of the following libraries for their assistance: the National Archives (in particular Caitriona Crowe), the UCD Archives, the Irish Labour History Archives (and I must thank the trustees of the Norton papers for permission to examine them), the National Library of Ireland, Trinity College Library, and the staff of the library of the Department of Social and Family Affairs.

Bishop John Kirby kindly allowed me to examine the archives of the

Clonfert diocese for relevant papers of his predecessor Dr Dignan (unfortunately to little effect) and took the time to discuss Dr Dignan and his views.

A number of people assisted through the provision of material, comments
and discussion for which I am very grateful including Sophia Carey, Séamus
Ó Cinnéide, Eoin Ó Seaghda, Dr T.K. Whitaker, and Gerry Whyte.

Parts of chapter 5 originally appeared (in earlier draft) in *Irish Economic
and Social History* and were greatly improved by the comments of the editor
and referees.

Finally, I would like to thank Michael Adams and Anthony Tierney of
Four Courts Press for their assistance and support.

Introduction

> The workmen's discussions, he said, were too timorous; the interest they took in the question of wages was inordinate . . . No social revolution, he told her, would be likely to strike Dublin for some centuries.[1]

THIS CHAPTER SETS OUT briefly the context in which social welfare developed in an independent Ireland. In particular, it outlines the development of the Poor Law and the range of new 'income maintenance' schemes established at the turn of the twentieth century and in the period up to Independence – workmen's compensation (1897), old age pensions (1908) and national insurance (1911). It looks in more detail at the reforms of the Poor Law system which took place under the Dáil Ministry in the 1919–21 period. One of the difficulties of writing the history of the development of a new institution or set of policies is to avoid making it look as though this development is the result of an inevitable evolution. This is particularly true in the case of the 'birth' of social welfare as the social welfare system developed from a wide range of different policies – policies that were often seen by contemporaries as unrelated. However, to find the genesis of our social welfare system, it is necessary to trace the history of the different measures which ultimately came together to form this new institution. Readers should, however, bear in mind that the various 'income maintenance' policies described in this chapter were rarely seen by contemporaries as forming a related set of policies.

INTRODUCTION

The future directions for what was to become known, in Ireland, as social welfare policy had been signalled in the ferment of ideas arising from the

---

1 James Joyce, 'A Painful Case' in *Dubliners* (Penguin, London, 1992 [1914]).

French Revolution. Condorcet, a revolutionary himself but in hiding from his former colleagues, speculated on the future form of society shortly before his own death.[2] He proposed the establishment of a system of insurance against social risks such as old age and death. In furious response to this and other revolutionary ideas, the Reverend Thomas Malthus argued that social spending was counter-productive and encouraged the gradual abolition of the Poor Laws – an approach which has been argued to have a significant relationship to the subsequent reform of the Poor Law in the early 1830s.[3] At the same time, Tom Paine, another supporter of revolution, was proposing yet a third approach.[4] Paine proposed the payment of £15 to each person reaching the age of 15 'to enable him or her to begin the World' and £10 per annum to each person over 50 'to enable them to live in Old Age without wretchedness and go decently out of the World'. These three authors foreshadowed the three basic approaches of social insurance, means-tested and universal payments which will feature strongly in this book. However, in nineteenth-century Ireland there simply was no social welfare system as we know it today. Up to 1838, there was very limited state support for the poor in any form. As we will see in 1838 a national Poor Law was introduced by the United Kingdom government modelled on the 1834 reforms in England and Wales. It was only in the late nineteenth and early twentieth century that policy began to adopt a shape which is more familiar to us today with the establishment of a whole range of, initially unrelated, payments which could broadly be described as being connected to income support.

THE POOR LAW

The Elizabethan Poor Laws did not apply in the Kingdom of Ireland and only limited measures to deal with the poor, primarily applying to the main towns and cities, were adopted prior to 1800.[5] However, after the Union and faced by a rapidly growing population, a number of public commissions were

2 J.-A.N. Condorcet, *Esquisse d'un tableau historique des progres de l'esprit humain* (Flammarion, Paris, 1988 [1795]). 3 T.R. Malthus, *An Essay on the Principles of Population* (Routledge, London, 1992 [1798]). See M. Dean, *The Constitution of Poverty* (Routledge, London, 1991). 4 T. Paine, *Agrarian Justice* in *Rights of Man, Common Sense and Other Political Writing* (Oxford University Press, Oxford, 1995 [1796]). 5 On England see P. Slack, *The English Poor Law, 1531–1782* (Cambridge University Press, Cambridge, 1990); *Poverty and Policy in Tudor and Stuart England* (Longman, London, 1988). On the position in Ireland, see D. Dickson, 'In Search of the Old Irish Poor Law' in R. Mitchison and P. Roebuck (eds.), *Economy and Society in Scotland and Ireland 1500–1939* (John Donald, Edinburgh, 1988); F. Powell, *The Politics of Irish Social Policy* (Edwin Mellen, Lewiston, 1992), chapter 1.

appointed to consider the relief of the poor and related issues in the first decades of the nineteenth century. Reflecting the position in England and Wales, where public debate eventually led to the establishment of the 'New Poor Law' in 1834,[6] one of the most extensive public debates in the history of Irish social policy developed around these issues. Ultimately, however, the United Kingdom government rejected 'Irish solutions to Irish problems' such as that proposed by the Royal Commission for Inquiring into the Condition of the Poorer Classes in Ireland (the Whately Commission) and instead opted to implement the proposals of George Nicholls, an English Poor Law Commissioner who was appointed by Lord John Russell, then Home Secretary, to carry out a speedy review of the need for a Poor Law in Ireland.[7] The Whately Commission had, in 1836, rejected the application of the English Poor Law to Ireland and had recommended a policy 'calculated to promote the improvement of the country and so to extend the demand for free and profitable labour'.[8] In contrast, Nicholls strongly recommended the application of the workhouse system to Ireland as a necessary precedent to economic development. Legislation to this effect was adopted by the Whig government under Lord Melbourne in 1838. This divided the country into 130 Poor Law Unions which were to be responsible for the relief of poverty in their own areas. Each Union was governed, subject to the overall supervision of the United Kingdom Poor Law Commissioners, by a Board of Guardians, partly appointed ex officio and partly elected. Unlike the position in the United Kingdom where outdoor relief was allowed in certain circumstances, relief was to be provided only in workhouses which were to be established in each Union. The Poor Law was established on an almost nation-wide basis by the mid 1840s – an enormously impressive administrative achievement with workhouses being built or adapted across the country.[9] Without attempting to glorify the Poor Law or hide its many failings, it was, in many ways, a comprehensive and coherent institution for dealing with the

6 *The Poor Law Report of 1834*, S.G. and E.O.A. Checkland (eds.) (Penguin, London, 1974); J.D. Marshall, *The Old Poor Law 1795–1834* (Macmillan, London, 1968); K.Williams, *From Pauperism to Poverty* (Routledge and Kegan Paul, London, 1981); G. Himmelfarb, *The Idea of Poverty* (Faber and Faber, London, 1984); M. Dean, *Constitution of Poverty*; A. Brundage, *The Making of the New Poor Law 1832–39* (Hutchinson, London, 1978) and *England's 'Prussian Minister'* (Pennsylvania State University Press, University Park, 1988). 7 See Powell, *Politics of Irish Social Policy*, chapter 2; R.D.C. Black, *Economic Thought and the Irish Question* (Cambridge University Press, Cambridge, 1960), pp. 86–133. 8 *Third Report* (1836), p. 8. 9 G. O'Brien, 'The establishment of poor-law unions in Ireland, 1838–43' *Irish Historical Studies* (1982) XXIII, pp. 97–118. And see generally V. Crossman, *Local Government in Nineteenth Century Ireland* (Institute of Irish Studies, Belfast, 1994); H. Burke, *The People and the Poor Law in 19th Century Ireland* (Women's Education Bureau, Littlehampton, 1987); J. O'Connor, *The Workhouses of Ireland* (Anvil, Dublin, 1995).

poor. In addition to providing support (in cash or in kind), the Poor Law also ultimately provided health care services, catered for maternity, children, 'lunatics' and a whole range of other policy areas. However, the Irish Poor Law had hardly even been established when it was hit by a disaster of a scale with which it had never been designed to deal.

With the onset of the Great Famine in 1845, the British Conservative government under Sir Robert Peel originally opted for relief primarily outside the Poor Law through relief work and soup kitchens. However, as the Famine continued and worsened, the new Liberal government under Lord John Russell decided that the Poor Law system must play the main role in relieving poverty. The story of the Poor Law during the Famine lies outside the scope of this book.[10] However, one enduring legacy of that period was that, in 1847, the restriction of relief to those in workhouses was abandoned and the law was amended to allow outdoor relief in certain circumstances. In addition, an Irish Poor Law Commission was appointed as a separate body in that year.

After the Famine, the overall position of the Irish population improved significantly – largely from the fall in the population – and the numbers relying on the Poor Law fell up to the 1870s. In 1872, the powers of the Poor Law Commisioners were transferred to the Local Government Board. At the height of the Famine, there were over one million people in receipt of support from the Poor Law institutions, one-eight the pre-Famine population. But by 1861 the numbers dependent on the Poor Law had fallen to under 10 per 1,000 in the population.[11] From the 1870s on there was an intensified struggle between Irish tenants and their landlords. And, as Feingold has shown, the Poor Law Boards of Guardians formed a key locus for that struggle with tenants taking over electoral control of the Boards over the period.[12] From a position in 1877 when landlords and their agents controlled almost 90% of the officerships of boards, by 1886 this had fallen to 50% (and under 40% outside Ulster). The numbers dependent on the Poor Law also began to increase steadily. As can be seen in table 1, in the 1860s Ireland, despite its greater poverty, had a lower overall level of dependence on poor relief than England and Wales – very significantly so in the case of outdoor relief. However, in the 1870s and 1880s, while outdoor relief declined in England and Wales, both indoor and outdoor relief increased in Ireland.

Indeed the workhouses which dotted the country from the mid-century on

---

10 See C. Kinealy, *The Great Calamity* (Gill & Macmillan, Dublin, 1994). 11 T. Guinnane, 'The Poor Law and Pensions in Ireland' *Journal of Interdisciplinary History* (1993) XXIV, pp. 271–91. 12 W. Feingold, *The Revolt of the Tenantry* (Northeastern University Press, Boston, 1984).

Table 1: Daily Numbers on Poor Relief
(per 1,000 population), 1861–1901

	Ireland		*England and Wales*	
	Indoor	*Outdoor*	*Indoor*	*Outdoor*
1861	7.8	0.6	5.4	35.6
1871	8.6	4.0	6.2	37.5
1881	10.4	11.8	6.3	21.8
1891	8.9	13.3	5.7	17.9
1901	9.3	13.0	5.8	15.2

Source: Guinnane, op. cit.

were just one part of a 'carceral archipelago' which played a vital role in policies to respond to 'the poor' in Ireland. In addition to the Poor Law system which by the turn of the century supported 76,000 people (of whom 36,000 were in workhouses), these included lunatic asylums which housed 120,000 people, and the industrial and reform schools which accommodated 8,000 children.[13]

In the 1880s, arising both from economic conditions and from the increasing political agitation, the cost of outdoor relief increased significantly in nationalist dominated Connacht and Munster and the Local Government Board dissolved several boards of guardians.[14] Under Arthur Balfour's administration as Chief Secretary in the late 1880s and early 1890s, Poor Law relief was tightened up and a programme of largely successful relief works was initiated instead with the Congested Districts Board being established in 1891 with a long-term, developmental role. The 1896 Women's Poor Law Guardians Act allowed women to vote in Poor Law elections and to sit as Poor Law guardians. The 1898 reform of local government led to substantial changes in the structure of the boards of guardians with the ex officio membership being abolished and membership of the boards became the same as that of the newly established local authorities with separate boards of guardians being retained in urban areas – elected on the same franchise as the new urban district councils. The democratisation of local government

13 M. Finane, *Insanity and the Insane in Post-Famine Ireland* (Croom Helm, London, 1981); J. Barnes, *Irish Industrial Schools 1868–1908* (Irish Academic Press, Dublin, 1989).   14 M. Daly, *The Buffer State: The Historical Roots of the Department of the Environment*, Institute of Public Administration, Dublin, 1997), p. 21.

marked a further step in the nationalist take-over of the day-to-day operation of the boards of guardians.

By the turn of the century the need for reform of the Poor Law system was becoming apparent although there was a lack of consensus about the shape such reform should take. In Ireland, a Viceregal Commission was established by the Lord Lieutenant, the earl of Dudley, to recommend 'how, if at all, a reduction could without impairing efficiency be made in the expenditure for the relief of the poor, and at the same time to show, if possible, how an improvement in the method or system of affording relief might be effected'. Commissioner of the Irish Local Government Board William Lawson Micks and the Board's medical inspector Edward Coey Bigger were members of the Commission as was George Murnaghan, MP for Mid-Tyrone.

The Commission, which reported in 1906, first outlined the development of the Poor Law in Ireland reviewing, favourably, the approach of the 1836 Whately Commission and, much more critically, the government's response. The Commission echoed the 1836 Commission's view that poverty could not be dealt with by the Poor Law but only by development of the country's resources.[15] However, the Commission went on to carry out a detailed review of the existing Poor Law. It proposed 'the breaking up of the workhouse system of gathering together all the various classes . . . into the same institution'. General workhouses were to be reallocated or closed. Instead the different classes were to be segregated into different institutions appropriate to their needs – the sick to hospitals and medical institutions, the aged and infirm to 'almshouses' and vagrants and tramps to 'labour houses'.[16] Mothers of illegitimate children were 'on the occasion of their first lapse' to be sent to a special institution but 'more depraved cases' were to be separated from their children and boarded in religious houses or the labour houses to which vagrants were also to be committed. The Commission reported that the general view of witnesses was in favour of extending outdoor relief as better for the poor and more economical for the ratepayers. The Commission, however, was doubtful of the wisdom of this approach. It recommended a reduction in the number of guardians and that the area of charge should be changed from the union to the broader electoral division for outdoor relief and (George Murnaghan dissenting) to the county in the case of indoor relief.

The Commission's report was, to some extent, overshadowed by the fact that, as one of its last acts in late 1905, the Conservative government, then led

---

15 *Report*, p. 77.   16 However, 'genuine ballad singers' were to be exempt from the general restrictions on the itinerant poor.

by Arthur Balfour, appointed a Royal Commission to investigate the Poor Laws.[17] The Royal Commission was chaired by the veteran Conservative politician Lord George Hamilton and included the O'Conor Don (replaced after his death by Bishop Denis Kelly, bishop of Ross) and Sir Henry Robinson, Vice-President of the Local Government Board.[18] The Commission included both a number of the key figures in the Charity Organisation Society who helped to shape the 900-page majority report (published in 1909) and Beatrice Webb who, with her husband Sydney, largely wrote the minority report. In brief the majority favoured a reform of the existing Poor Law, voluntary aid committees and a national system of labour exchanges whereas the minority favoured breaking up the Poor Law into discrete services to support children, the sick, the mentally defective, the aged and infirm and so on.[19] The minority argued that the approach should also broadly apply to Ireland.

The Irish members, who formed part of the majority, drafted a much shorter report on Ireland which was agreed by the majority. This report largely applied the recommendations of the main report to the Irish situation. In particular, it recommended that guardians (of which there were 8,200 or an average of 51 per board) be abolished; that general workhouses also be abolished and replaced by classification by institution rather than in institutions; that public assistance authorities be appointed as committees of local authorities with elected and appointed members; that appointed public assistance committees take over the day-to-day administration of relief; that the system of voluntary aid committees be applied to Ireland; and that labour colonies be established for the able-bodied.[20] Given the large scale nature of agricultural self-employment in Ireland it found that the labour exchanges proposed for England and Wales did not seem adapted to the conditions of Ireland. It also recommended that outdoor relief be renamed as home assistance but shared the Viceregal Commission's reservations in this area and recommended that such assistance be granted only after thorough enquiry. The minority in a brief report praised the approach of the Viceregal Commission and concurred with the main principles of that report. In fact, both majority and minority claimed that their approach was in line with the principles of the Viceregal Commission;[21] both accused each other of

17 See M.E. Rose, *The Relief of Poverty 1834–1914* (Macmillan, London, 1972), pp. 43–4. 18 The Chief Secretary for Ireland was the President of the Board and Robinson was the executive head of the Board. 19 For a more detailed discussion see A.W. Vincent, 'The Poor Law Reports of 1909 and the Social Theory of the Charity Organisation Society' in D. Gladstone (ed.), *Before Beveridge: Welfare before the Welfare State* (Institute of Economic Affairs, London, 1999). 20 *Report on Ireland*, p. 81 *et seq.* 21 Majority, for example, at p. 48, Minority at p. 84. While the Minority could point to the Viceregal Commission's advocacy of

removing relief from democratic control;[22] and both criticised each other's lack of knowledge of Irish conditions and disregard for Irish opinion.[23]

In 1908, the Ulster Unionists had introduced a private member's bill in Westminster to give effect to the Viceregal Commission's report.[24] John Redmond, leader of the Irish Party, expressed his utmost sympathy with those who desired to reform the Poor Law but declared his inability to vote for this bill because of its 'inadequate and unsuitable' approach. Irish Chief Secretary Augustin Birrell promised to do his best to see that a bill implementing the report became a government measure but the government voted down the bill (the Irish Party abstaining).[25] Despite the fact that the matter was raised regularly by Irish parliamentarians (from both sides) no government measure appeared and in 1911 the Chancellor of the Exchequer, Lloyd George, stated that the introduction of national insurance legislation had changed the context of Poor Law reform (although he did not rule out the continued need for reform).[26] No action had been taken to implement the reports of these Commissions when war broke out in 1914 and while considerable reform was to occur in the period from 1908 to 1913, it followed neither the main lines recommended by the conservative majority nor by the Fabian minority of the Poor Law Commission. The 'New Liberal' governments chose instead to follow (various) paths of their own.[27] However, we will turn first to the earliest social policy measure of the period which came not from the Liberals but from Lord Salisbury's Conservative government.

WORKMEN'S COMPENSATION

The workmen's compensation legislation was introduced in 1897 by Joseph Chamberlain to reform the existing procedures whereby workers injured in the course of their employment had to seek compensation under tort law from their employer.[28] The courts had construed employer's responsibilities

economic development and its recommendation that hospital services be removed from the Poor Law, the latter's approach in relation to poor relief was surely more in line with reform based on classification and segregation as recommended by the Majority report – albeit without the COS influenced emphasis on the role of voluntary organisations. **22** Minority at p. 84; majority in a comment by the bishop of Ross and Sir Henry Robinson at p. 87. **23** A number of members of the Commission did not feel competent to sign the reports on Ireland. **24** *Parliamentary Debates*, vol. 187 col. 818 *et seq.*, 3 April 1908. **25** Redmond at col. 830 *et seq.*; Birrell at col. 836 *et seq.* **26** *Parliamentary Debates*, vol. XXV col. 431, 3 May 1911. **27** J.R. Hay, *The Origins of the Liberal Welfare Reforms 1906–1914* (Macmillan, London, 1975). **28** P. Marsh, *Joseph Chamberlain: Entrepreneur in Politics* (Yale University Press, New Haven, 1994), pp. 397–400; P.W.J. Bartrip, *Workmen's Compensation in Twentieth Century Britain* (Avebury, Aldershot, 1987).

in a very narrow manner and, in contrast, the workmen's compensation legislation provided that compensation at a set amount was automatically payable by the employer where an injury arose 'out of and in the course of employment'.[29] Only a narrow range of hazardous industries was originally covered but this was extended to agricultural workers in 1900 and subsequently to most manual and lower paid employments by the Liberal government in 1906. Compensation was to be paid directly by the employer and there was no obligation on the employer to insure against liability, although many did. Compensation was payable during incapacity for work as a proportion of previous earnings or, in the case of a fatal accident, as a lump sum to a person's dependants. The state was only involved to a limited extent in supervising the scheme and in providing the main forum for the adjudication of disputes through the courts.

With the exception of Bartrip's detailed historical account, workmen's compensation has received surprisingly little attention in British recent historiography.[30] This may be because workmen's compensation in the United Kingdom was incorporated into the overall social insurance system in the late 1940s but also because this was originally a Conservative rather than Liberal reform. However, workmen's compensation was of considerable importance at the turn of the century in the context of overall social policy. Of course, the introduction of the legislation had a significantly different impact in Ireland where less than half of the workforce was employed as opposed to Great Britain where 80% of the workforce were manual workers.[31] The workmen's compensation scheme was consistent with Chamberlain's view of the need for a paternalist approach by the State to social policy issues – combined with an emphasis on economy as the costs fell on employers rather than the Exchequer. However, the Conservatives proved unable or unwilling to extend this approach to other recognised areas of need, in particular old age pensions.[32]

---

29 Commission on Workmen's Compensation, *Reports*, Stationery Office, Dublin, 1963, chapter II.   **30** For example, Thane's *Foundations of the Welfare State* (Longman, London, 1996) contains only two passing references while Fraser's *Evolution of the British Welfare State* (Macmillan, London, 1984) gives no detailed account while devoting a chapter to 'Liberal Social Policy'. Gilbert's *Evolution of National Insurance in Great Britain* (Michael Joseph, London, 1966) dismisses workmen's compensation in a footnote as 'not a departure in the direction of true social legislation' but rather 'a continuation of the tradition of industrial protective measures begun by the Factory Acts'.   **31** Thane, op. cit. table 3.1.   **32** D. Steele, *Lord Salisbury: A Political Biography* (Routledge, London, 1999), pp. 304–5.

OLD AGE PENSIONS

Old age pensions constituted the first major 'New Liberal' welfare reform being introduced by the Asquith government in 1908. There had been considerable debate in the United Kingdom in the previous decades about the need for a state pension and different options had been canvassed.[33] These included both universal and contributory social insurance based approaches.[34] However, ultimately the Liberal government opted for a means-tested pension of 5s. per week funded out of taxation and paid at the age of 70, the relatively high age being chosen to reduce the cost of the pensions. Macnicol has pointed out that the non-contributory and tax-funded nature of the payment meant that it was both highly redistributive and that the majority of pensioners were women.[35] The pension as originally introduced included a number of clauses excluding claimants of bad character including those in receipt of poor relief, 'lunatics' in asylums, persons sentenced to prison for ten years after their release, persons convicted of drunkenness (at the discretion of the court), and any person who was guilty of 'habitual failure to work' according to one's ability.[36] The entitlement to pension was to be assessed by Inland Revenue officials who then reported to a local Pension Committee which was subject to appeal to the Local Government Board. Pensions were paid through the local post office.

The Old Age Pensions Act was particularly advantageous to Ireland given that the rates were set at a uniform basis for the entire United Kingdom (although wages and the cost-of-living were significantly lower in Ireland than in parts of Great Britain).[37] The decision to opt for a means-tested approach also benefited poorer Ireland. And the massive outflow of younger people since the Famine meant that Ireland had a greater proportion of older people in the population. The proportion of pensioners to the total population was much higher in Ireland (4.62%) than in England and Wales (1.85%).[38] In general historians of old age pensions have made little reference to Ireland and historians of the period in Ireland have made little reference to pensions. Therefore, it is not clear whether these favourable outcomes were a fortuitous result of decisions made for other reasons or a part of a Liberal

33 See J. Macnicol, *The Politics of Retirement in Britain, 1978–1948* (Cambridge University Press, Cambridge, 1998), chapters 2–6; P. Thane, *Old Age in English History* (Oxford University Press, Oxford, 2000), chapters 10 & 11; A.S. Orloff, *The Politics of Pensions* (University of Wisconsin Press, Madison, 1993). C. Carney, 'A Case Study in Social Policy: the Non-Contributory Old Age Pension', *Administration* (1985) 33, p. 483 *et seq.*; Gilbert, *Evolution*, chapter 4. **34** See, for example, H. Samuel, *Liberalism* (Grant Richards, London, 1902), pp. 135–44. **35** Macnicol, op. cit., p. 162. **36** Macnicol, op. cit., pp. 157–8. **37** Weekly earnings for Irish agricultural labourers were 10s. 9d. compared to 17s. 5d. in England. **38** Ibid., p. 161.

continuation of the policy of 'killing Home Rule with kindness'. One largely unanticipated reason why Ireland benefited disproportionately was the unexpectedly rapid ageing of the Irish population after the introduction of old age pensions. The fact that civil registration became compulsory in Ireland only in 1864 meant that there was no formal record of the age of many people. Ó Gráda has shown that farmers with the smallest holdings, and more likely to benefit from the pension, aged more rapidly than did larger farmers.[39] The exclusion clauses were substantially modified in 1911 and 1919. And arising from the considerable increase in the cost-of-living during the War years, the pension was increased as a temporary measure during the War and then doubled to 10*s*. per week in 1919 following the report of the government appointed Ryland Adkins committee.[40]

Guinnane has shown that the introduction of the old age pension appears to have increased household co-residence – presumably on the basis that the pension both allowed older people to remain in the community and made them more attractive co-residents.[41] He also shows that the pension had a significant impact on the Poor Law. Although by 1901 Ireland had a higher level of reliance on the Poor Law than England and Wales, this was not the case for older people where there was a lower incidence of both indoor and outdoor relief for those aged 70 and over. Guinnane refers to contemporary suggestions that this was due to the deterrence factor of the Poor Law. The introduction of the old age pension led to a significant reduction in the numbers on indoor relief from 10.2 per 1,000 in 1908–9 to 8.5 by 1913–14 and outdoor relief fell from 13.5 to 8.7. He finds that the pension removed large numbers of older people from the Poor Law, allowed Unions to reduce the poor rate, and to increase support to more non-aged people. However, this did not effect any fundamental change in poor relief practices in the short-term.[42]

NATIONAL HEALTH INSURANCE

The next major Liberal reform came in the National Insurance Act, 1911. While the old age pension had dealt with one of the great causes of poverty,

39 C. Ó Gráda, *Ireland – Before and after the Famine* (Manchester University Press, Manchester, 1993), p. 169. And see J.W. Budd and T.W. Guinnane, 'Intentional Age Misrepresenting, Age-Heaping and the 1908 Old Age Pension Act in Ireland', *Population Studies* (1991) XLV, pp. 497–518. **40** Macnicol, op. cit., chapter 7. The committee's membership included Sir Henry Robinson, vice-president of the Irish Local Government Board and Joe Devlin MP. **41** Guinnane, 'The Poor Law and Pension in Ireland,' *Journal of Interdisciplinary History* (1993) XXIV, pp. 271–91. **42** Guinnane, op. cit. p. 290.

issues such as unemployment, sickness and disablement still remained largely unaddressed outside the Poor Law. Both national health insurance and, unemployment insurance were to be provided for in the same 1911 Act but the two schemes were, in fact, quite separate. In Great Britain, but to a much lesser extent in Ireland, friendly societies already provided sickness benefits to their members and industrial insurance companies also provided insurance and, in particular, life cover. In England and Wales, Gilbert has estimated that about 50% of workers were members of friendly societies. In contrast he describes friendly society membership in Ireland as 'negligible'.[43] The evolution of national insurance was a complicated story as Lloyd George steered his proposals though the conflicting interests of the friendly societies, the industrial insurance companies and the medical profession.[44] Lloyd George originally envisaged a limited scheme to cover sickness, invalidity and widowhood (but not medical care). The level of benefits would be kept low at 5s. per week to encourage continued friendly society cover. However, widows and orphans pensions were dropped due to the opposition of the industrial insurance companies who felt that this would impinge on their lucrative life assurance business. Conversely, the money released by dropping the widows pensions was used to increase the remaining benefits and to include medical benefit (i.e. general practitioner care) thereby effectively replacing the existing friendly society services. However, the new scheme was to operate through the friendly societies and, after some controversy, through industrial insurance companies.

The scheme as finally adopted provided for sickness benefit for up to 26 weeks at a rate of 10s. for men and 7s. 6d. for women, disablement benefit of 5s. per week payable after the initial 26 weeks (possibly up to the pension age of 70 when benefit ceased), and maternity benefit of 30s. Contributions were paid by employers and employees (5½d. for a man and 4½d. for a woman of which 2½d. was paid by the employer) by purchasing insurance stamps through the post office and affixing them to the workers insurance card. The State undertook to pay two-ninths of all benefits and of administrative costs. A complicated system of funding was adopted with a notional reserve fund (to cover the actuarial cost of future benefits) being redeemed from ongoing contributions.[45] Subsequently each society was required to have a contingency fund and a central contingency fund was established to support societies in difficulties.

43 Barrington estimates that only about 40,000 people were members of friendly societies, of whom half were in the friendly society section of the Ancient Order of Hibernians, _Health, Medicine and Politics_ (Institute of Public Administration, Dublin, 1987), p. 35. 44 See generally Gilbert, _Evolution_, chapter 6 and 7. 45 See generally A.S. Comyns Carr, W.H. Garnett and J.H. Taylor, _National Insurance_ (Macmillan, London, 1912).

In most of the United Kingdom, national health insurance also covered medical benefit, i.e. the services of a general practitioner. However, as Barrington shows, the application of medical benefit to Ireland generated a major controversy. Unlike the 1908 period, when the Liberals were in a significant overall majority and not dependent on Irish votes, by 1910 the Liberals were now a minority government and relied on the support of the Irish Party. But equally, the Irish Party and its leader John Redmond relied on Liberal support for Home Rule. As Barrington points out, many in the Irish Party would have been unsympathetic to New Liberal welfare policies – although others, such as the West Belfast MP Joe Devlin, strongly supported the measure.[46] The Party approved the Bill in principle but set about drafting amendments on its application to Ireland. The main amendment was to result in the non-application of medical benefit. The details of the exclusion of medical benefit relate more to the history of the health services and have already been outlined in detail by Barrington. Suffice it to say that reaction to the Bill in Ireland was not supportive, with the William Martin Murphy-owned *Irish Independent* leading opposition on the basis of 'the burden of contributions on Irish industry, the potential insolvency of a Home Rule government, and the inappropriateness of its provisions to Irish conditions'.[47] The Irish medical profession was split in its response with a significant proportion opposed to the medical benefit proposals on the basis that they would lead to a loss of private patients while others sought increases in the rates of payment proposed. Then in June 1911, the Irish Catholic hierarchy issued a statement opposing the bill's application to Ireland and urged the Irish Party to seek a scheme more suitable to Irish needs. In July, the Irish Party decided that while it would support the Bill's application to Ireland, it would seek amendments, the most important of which was the exclusion of medical benefit. With little option, but also with little apparent regret, the Liberal government agreed to this amendment. Belatedly in November, the Irish medical profession sought the re-inclusion of medical benefit for Ireland and dropped its immediate demand for an increase in rates of payment. But it was too late and neither Redmond nor the government were prepared to change the legislation. As a result of the Irish Party's proposals a separate Irish Insurance Commission was established to oversee the operation of the legislation. The Commission, including Joseph Glynn as chair, Walter Kinnear, Dr William Maguire and Mary Dickie, was appointed in January 1913.[48] The legislation came into operation in 1913 and by April

---

46 P. Bew, *Ideology and the Irish Question* (Clarendon, Oxford, 1994), pp. 75, 125–7. **47** Barrington, p. 42. Interestingly, Arthur Griffith also opposed the measure. **48** Glynn was chairman of Galway County Council and a home rule supporter, see L. McBride, *The Greening*

1913, 700,000 workers were insured under the Act. While further consideration was given to the extension of medical benefit to Ireland by a govern-
ment-appointed committee in 1913 and by the Irish Public Health Council in
1920, both of which supported some extension, no change had been made by
1921.

UNEMPLOYMENT INSURANCE

While the problem of lack of or insufficient work had existed for centuries,
'unemployment' and 'the unemployed' were terms invented in the late nineteenth century.[49] Unlike the old age pension which had been canvassed for
decades, unemployment as an issue was of more recent provenance and
policy proposals were heavily influenced by key figures in the Liberal government and civil service including Winston Churchill, President of the Board
of Trade, and Hubert Llewellyn Smith and William Beveridge, civil servants
of the Board.[50] The solution adopted to unemployment involved both deca-
sualisation of the unemployed, putting unemployed persons in contact with
employers seeking workers, and the payment of financial support during
periods of unemployment. Labour exchanges were to play a key role both in
requiring men to register as unemployed and in matching them to available
work. A Labour Exchange Act was adopted in 1909 to provide for such a
system on a nation-wide basis. This was also intended as a structure through
which a system of unemployment insurance could be operated.

Unemployment insurance proposals were developed at this time but were
only published in 1911 in conjunction with the national insurance proposals.
The friendly societies and industrial insurance companies did not provide
insurance against unemployment. And, although some trade unions did,
their scope was quite limited. Accordingly, in contrast to the national insurance proposals, the unemployment insurance legislation provided for a
national system of insurance administered though the employment

of Dublin Castle (Catholic University of America Press, Washington DC, 1991), pp. 165–6.
49 C. Topalov, *Naissance du chomeur* (Albin Michel, Paris, 1994); W. Walters, 'The discovery of
'unemployment': new forms for the government of poverty', *Economy and Society* (1994) 23,
pp. 265–90. **50** See generally J. Harris, *Unemployment and Politics 1886–1914* (Oxford
University Press, Oxford, 1972); Gilbert, *Evolution*, chapter 5; N. Whiteside, 'Welfare
Insurance and Casual Labour; A Study of Administrative Intervention in Industrial
Employment, 1906–1926', *Economic History Review* (1979) XXXII, pp. 507–22. Both the
majority and minority reports of the Royal Commission on the Poor Laws had recommended
the establishment of labour exchanges and unemployment insurance (albeit that the minority
recommended that this be operated by trade unions rather than the state).

exchanges and branch employment offices. Only seven major trades were to be covered initially. Contributions were paid by employers and employees (2½d. each) by purchasing insurance stamps through the post office and affixing them to the workers insurance card. The State added one third of the employers' and workers' contribution. Unlike the national health insurance, no reserve fund was established. Benefit was payable at a rate of 7s. per week for up to 15 weeks in any period of 12 months – distinguishing neither on grounds of sex nor region. In order to qualify, unemployed workers had to have been employed in an insured trade for at least 26 weeks and be capable of and unable to obtain suitable employment. In addition workers who had lost employment through misconduct or who had voluntarily given up their job without just cause were disqualified. Trade unions were encouraged to administer unemployment benefits for their members and to pay larger unemployment benefits than payable under the legislation. However, this had only a limited impact in Ireland.

The scope of unemployment insurance was expanded during the war.[51] After the war, a non-contributory 'out-of-work donation' was introduced for demobilised soldiers and subsequently extended to civilian workers. This was payable at (relatively high) subsistence rates and, unlike the unemployment insurance scheme, included payments for dependants. The unemployment insurance scheme itself was effectively remade in 1920. Unemployment insurance was extended to all manual workers and to non-manual workers earning less than £250 p.a. although a number of specific groups including agricultural workers and domestic servants were excluded. Most civil and public servants, who were in permanent employment and therefore not subject to the risk of unemployment, remained outside the scheme. Payments were set at 15s. for men and 12s. for women – much lower than the out-of-work donation. However, the extended unemployment insurance scheme came into effect at a time when unemployment was rising sharply which led, in Fraser's words, to 'the grafting-on to the insurance scheme of a series of devices which sought to preserve the fiction of insurance but in reality were a system of thinly disguised outdoor relief'.[52] In 1921, dependant additions were included in the unemployment insurance scheme.

51 B. Gilbert, *British Social Policy 1914–1939* (Batsford, London, 1970), chapter 2. 52 D. Fraser, *Evolution of the British Welfare State*, p. 184. See also Thane, *Foundations*, pp. 137–9; W. Garside, *British Unemployment 1919–1939* (Cambridge University Press, Cambridge, 1990) chapter 2.

THE TROUBLES

The course of social policy development in Ireland was significantly affected by the outbreak of the Troubles in 1916 and the renewed conflict from 1919 on. One of the key objectives of Sinn Féin was to establish a *de facto* state. And one of the main areas in which they succeeded in doing so was in relation to the take-over of local government including the Poor Law. The other income support areas were more centralised and despite local involvement in all four areas there is little indication that Sinn Féin succeeded (or even attempted in any coherent way) to take control of unemployment, national insurance or old age pensions. The main impact of the Troubles in these areas appears to have been increased default in the payment of contributions by employers and robberies by the IRA of monies intended to pay pensions and benefits. In the area of the Poor Law, however, three issues came together, viz., Sinn Féin's desire to create a real state, the long recognised need for Poor Law reform, and the need for economy in local government caused by the withdrawal in 1920 of British financial support to local authorities.

Sinn Féin (in its pre-1917 guise) had found its first democratic forum in the new local authorities – particularly on Dublin Corporation – and a number of its key figures were experienced local authority members (including two future Ministers for Local Government, W.T. Cosgrave and Seán T. Ó Ceallaigh). While Arthur Griffith had certainly expressed unfavourable views about the Poor Law, it could not be said that Sinn Féin had developed any coherent policy about what might be put in its place. The Democratic Programme of the First Dáil, adopted in 1919, had promised to replace the 'odious, degrading and foreign' Poor Law with a 'sympathetic native scheme of support of the Nation's aged and infirm' (it is worth noting that its unemployed were not explicitly included). But as Farrell has shown this was little more than window-dressing to placate labour interests and when de Valera was questioned in the Dáil in April 1919 about what was being done to implement the Programme he had little to say.[53]

A Dáil ministry had been formed in 1919, with Ministers appointed to various policy areas, but this had relatively little impact in the absence of real control on the ground. However, the local government elections in 1920 (in January for towns and boroughs and June for county and rural district councils) led to Sinn Féin taking over democratic control of the great majority of local authorities in what was to become the 26 counties. This meant that the Department of Local Government, led by W.T. Cosgrave with Kevin

53 B. Farrell, *The Founding of Dáil Eireann* (Institute of Public Administration, Dublin, 1971), pp. 57–61; *Miontuairisc an Chead Dála 1919–21*, p. 78, 11 April 1919.

O'Higgins as assistant Minister, now had the opportunity to implement real policies. In June 1920, O'Higgins, who was effectively in charge for much of the period, wrote to newly elected county councils, rural district councils and boards of guardians asking them to pass a resolution acknowledging the authority of Dáil Éireann. Many local authorities did so but continued to receive funding from, and to report to, the Local Government Board. O'Higgins was aware of the serious financial implications of a total break with the British State and Dáil Éireann established a Commission, chaired by him, in July 1920 to consider the practicalities of a total break with the Local Government Board.[54] The question of local authorities breaking with the Local Government Board was, in effect, determined by the British government which instructed the Board in July 1920 that no funding was to be provided to any local authority without a definite assurance that it would submit accounts to and comply with the rules and orders of the Local Government Board. This was backed up by legislation in August 1920 denying funds to any local authority which in any respect failed or refused to perform its duties, thereby forcing the issue of a break on republican local authorities. Faced with this direct ultimatum from the British authorities, many local authorities largely severed all connections with the Board, thereby leading to a reduction in British grants of over £1,500,000 and making the question of finances even more urgent.

The Commission submitted a final report to the Dáil in September 1920 recommending a total break with the Local Government Board.[55] In order to address the withdrawal of British funds which this would involve, it proposed a range of local government economies including the abolition and amalgamation of workhouses. The Dáil Commission estimated that economies in a range of areas could produce annual savings of £370,000 of which the abolition and amalgamation of workhouses would contribute a significant £50,000. In particular the Commission recommended that the number of workhouses in each county be reduced and as many inmates as possible be placed on outdoor relief.[56] The Commission also recommended economies in other social policy areas including dismissing large numbers of asylum inmates to their homes, increasing the maintenance contribution from relatives and putting able-boded inmates to work; removing TB patients not in an advanced stage of the disease to district hospitals or their own homes; and

---

54 Ibid. p. 185, 29 June 1920. 55 Commission of Enquiry into Local Government, *Final Report*, NAI DE 2/243 published in H. O'Sullivan, *History of Local Government in the County of Louth* (Institute of Public Administration, Dublin, 2000), p. 318 *et seq. Miontuairisc an Chead Dála 1919–21*, p. 218 *et seq.*, 17 September 1920. 56 The details of proposed reforms are discussed in a memorandum by Dr Richard Hayes TD published as an appendix to the report, O'Sullivan, op. cit., pp. 341–4.

reducing expenditure on the treatment of venereal disease and child welfare schemes. It is clear that the main focus of the Commission was to effect reductions in spending rather than to improve services although O'Higgins argued that the economies were to be achieved through the elimination of waste and corruption rather than through disimprovements in the quality of service.[57] The report of the Commission was discussed by the Dáil in September and there was considerable debate on some of the proposed economies. A young Sinn Féin deputy for Monaghan South, Seán MacEntee, successfully opposed the proposed cut in child welfare services.[58] But the Dáil approved the report in principle and on 30 September Cosgrave wrote to local authorities proposing the establishment of county schemes to replace the existing Poor law system.

Schemes were drawn up by most local authorities over the period from March 1921 to 1922. While the details of these schemes varied from county to county,[59] they shared a number of key principles. In place of the existing workhouses, ranging from 3 to 4 in smaller counties to 10 or 12 in large counties, a central county home and county hospital was to be established (although several counties retained subordinate institutions). Indoor relief was in general replaced by outdoor relief (often renamed as home assistance). And the local Boards of Guardians and Unions were abolished with control transferring to the local authority. The politics and policies involved have been discussed in detail by Barrington, by Mitchell in his study of revolutionary government in Ireland and in Daly's history of the Department of Environment.[60] At a local level there was considerable local politicking as to which town or towns were to retain institutions. The spirit of the times is well-captured in Kevin O'Higgins' subsequent account which is worth quoting in some detail. O'Higgins recalled how he had been present at the birth of a great many of the county schemes when 'drastic schemes of retrenchment and economy had to be entered upon'.[61] He found 'a good deal

---

57 *Dáil Debates* vol. 2 col. 1434, 9 February 1923. 58 *Miontuairisc an Chead Dála 1919–21*, pp. 220–1, 17 September 1920. However, this simply resulted in the deletion of child welfare from the list of proposed cuts with the result that the proposed cut of £25,000 attributed to reductions in treatment of venereal disease and child welfare services now stood to the former service alone. 59 The schemes are published as appendices to the Local Government (Temporary Provisions) Act, 1923. 60 Barrington, *Health, Medicine and Politics*; A. Mitchell, *Revolutionary Government in Ireland* (Gill and Macmillan, Dublin, 1995); Daly, *The Buffer State*. There are also a number of local studies including Fitzpatrick's study of Clare, *Politics and Irish Life, 1913–1921* (Gill and Macmillan, Dublin, 1977), p. 194–5, O'Sullivan's account of the period in Louth, op. cit. chapter 3; and Farry's study in Sligo *The Aftermath of Revolution* (University College Dublin, Dublin, 2000), pp. 24–6. 61 *Dáil Debates* vol. II col. 1434 *et seq.* 9 February 1923. See also W.T. Cosgrave's contemporary complaint that some members of the

of waste and a moderate amount of corruption existing in the local adminis-tration'. A workhouse industry had grown up with Unions in which 'the staff outnumbered the inmates'. O'Higgins and the Dáil inspectors (who included a young Dr James Ryan, later to become the first Minister for Social Welfare) had fallen foul 'of vested interests in particular localities' and had faced 'intense local dissatisfaction where a particular institution was being closed'. O'Higgins quoted a representative cry of 'Are you going to rob us of our only remaining industry?' However, the circumstances of the time, including the financial shortage, the 'high standard of selfishness [*sic*] and self-imposed discipline', had allowed the amalgamation policy to be imposed where in normal times a government would have found it very difficult to carry through the new policy.[62] O'Higgins explained how there had often been 'an interchange of views between the local people and the Dáil Local Government Department' before a scheme had been agreed but that they had finally been agreed on and had worked fairly well.

Thus the Dáil ministry, in a relatively short period of time, carried though the most fundamental reform of the Poor Law system, significantly reducing the number of workhouses, switching the emphasis from indoor to outdoor relief, and replacing the system of local Unions and Boards of Guardians with a county-based system. The approach of amalgamation and closure of Poor Law institutions with an increased emphasis on outdoor relief (in line with public opinion as expressed to the Viceregal Commission) was signifi-cantly different to that proposed by the Viceregal Commission and the majority of the Royal Commission both of which had favoured segregation of institutions rather than amalgamation and both of which were doubtful of the merits of increasing outdoor relief. However, the basic principles of the Poor Law, such as less eligibility, still applied, and whether the county schemes would develop into a 'sympathetic native scheme' could only be decided when normality returned to Ireland.

CONCLUSION

Over a period of less than two decades, United Kingdom governments had introduced no less than four separate schemes designed to provide income support to people who were injured at work, sick, unemployed or elderly.

Dáil had provided 'very considerable opposition' to local reform, *Miontuairisc an Chead Dála 1919–21*, p. 375, 10 May 1922. **62** Indeed the United Kingdom government did not implement a similar 'break-up' of the Poor Law until the late 1920s, Thane, *Foundations*, pp. 173–7; Gilbert, *British Social Policy*, p. 203 *et seq.*

And each scheme had followed quite a different logic. The workmen's compensation scheme imposed responsibility for occupational injuries directly on the individual employer. Insurance against the risk was not compulsory and, if chosen, was actuarially related to the risk involved. Thus there was a transfer of risk from the employee to the employer but the most limited pooling of risk after that. National health insurance, in contrast, was a scheme of national insurance but one operated through a myriad of quasi-private societies. Here there was a pooling of the risk involved within the societies but significant variations between the risks to which the membership of different societies were exposed. Unemployment insurance took risk-pooling one step further being a wholly national scheme, albeit one originally limited to a narrow rage of industries. With the broadening out of the scope of insurance in 1920, the risk of unemployment, from the viewpoint of compensation, was shared among a broad insured population. Finally, broadest of all was the old age pension scheme. Here the risk of an impecunious old age was broadly imposed on the whole community by being tax-funded. And this approach was clearly most beneficial to women. The old Poor Law, the original basis of a system of income support in Ireland, has been significantly reformed by the revolutionary Dáil ministry in 1920 and 1921. In the following chapter we will see whether and to what extent the new government of an independent Ireland advanced social policy reforms in its first decade.

2

'Letting the rest go to the devil': social policy under Cumann na nGaedheal, 1922–32[1]

'People may have to die in this country and may have to die through starvation.'[2]

IN THIS CHAPTER WE LOOK at the development of various 'social welfare' schemes in the first decade of Independence: from the appointment of the Provisional Government in 1922 to the general election of 1932 which saw the return of the first Fianna Fáil government. The *dramatis personae* of the governments show incredible stability – both in personel and party – for that period. Cumann na nGaedheal[3] was in office for the entire decade.[4] Following the deaths of Collins and Griffith in 1922, W.T. Cosgrave became President of the Executive Council and remained in that position through three elections and four changes of government. A small number of leading Cumann na nGaedheal politicians, in particular Ernest Blythe, Richard Mulcahy and Paddy McGilligan, held the key portfolios of Finance, Local Government and Public Health, and Industry and Commerce for much of this period.[5] As

1 The phrase is Patrick Hogan's, Minister for Agriculture (1922–32) who defined his policy as 'helping the farmer who helped himself and letting the rest go to the devil', F. MacManus (ed.), *The Years of the Great Test* (Mercier, Cork, 1967), p. 72. 2 Paddy McGilligan, *Dáil Debates*, vol. 9 col. 562, 30 October 1924. 3 Although it was not formally established until March 1923, for the sake of brevity I will use the term Cumann na nGaedheal for the ruling party of this period. The Sinn Féin opposition did not serve in either the Dáil or Provisional Governments after de Valera's resignation over the Treaty vote in January 1922 and the decision to form Cumann na nGaedheal was made in late 1922. 4 In contrast, for example, the United Kingdom (one of the more stable countries in the period) was ruled, from the Bonar Law government in 1922, by Labour (twice), Conservatives (again twice) and from 1931 by a National government. 5 Blythe was Minister for Local Government from 1922 to 1923 and Minister for Finance to 1932. Mulcahy was Minister for Local Government and Public Health from 1927 to 1932. McGilligan was Minister for Industry and Commerce from 1924 to 1932. In addition W.T. Cosgrave was Minister for Local Government in the Dáil and Provisional Governments until he became President on the deaths of Griffith and Collins in August 1922. He served as President of the Executive Council for the entire 1923–32 period and also as

we saw in the previous chapter, the key 'income maintenance' payments in this period were (in order of introduction) the Poor Law, workmen's compensation, old age pensions, national health insurance and unemployment insurance. Any unified study of this diverse range of schemes is in many ways anachronistic, as contemporaries did *not* generally see them in any (even potentially) unified way. National health insurance was, in general, seen as more closely related to the general health system than as part of a system of social security; the Poor Law included a range of medical and other services as well as home assistance. However, as argued above, such a unified study is necessary if we are to trace the path by which these diverse schemes came to be united. In this chapter, we look first in chronological order at developments over the period. Subsequently we examine a number of key themes that emerge from this examination.

1922–4 – THE POLITICS OF NATIONAL RETRENCHMENT[6]

'National' was a particularly (although not exclusively) Cumann na nGaedheal adjective.[7] With their political opponents in Sinn Féin (and subsequently Fianna Fáil) having appropriated the 'republic', Cumann na nGeadheal emphasised the nation. But indeed an emphasis on Ireland as a nation rather than a republic predates the 1922 spilt and was an underlying tension between the different strands of 'nationalist' thought in early twentieth-century Ireland.[8] 'Retrenchment' was also a concept dear to the hearts of key Cumann na nGaedheal leaders, including Cosgrave (once described by Keynes as 'a nineteenth century liberal'), Blythe and O'Higgins.[9] Indeed, I would argue that several of these politicians – perhaps informed by their local government experience in the formative 1920–21 period – saw Ireland's

Minister for Finance from August 1922 to September 1923. 6 Such a title is common to authors writing about this period: R. Fanning, *The Irish Department of Finance* (Institute of Public Administration, Dublin, 1978) refers to the 'Campaign for Retrenchment'; F. Powell, *The Politics of Irish Social Policy 1600–1990* (Edwin Mellen, Lewiston, 1992) to 'The Politics of Austerity'. In this case, the phrase is inspired by the title of Blythe's November 1923 speech to the Dáil 'National Finances: Retrenchment Proposals'. Such a title is in itself unusual in the normally sober Dáil Debates and is not found on what appears to be a copy of Blythe's speech, NAI D/Finance 826/6. 7 See, for example, the Cumann na nGaedheal advertisement for the 1923 election which referred to putting *national* finance and *national* credit on a sound basis, developing education in accordance with the *national* tradition, restoring the *national* language, organising *national* defence, establishing a *national* judiciary, and providing the *Nation* with an organised civil service (my emphases), *Irish Times*, 27 July 1923. 8 R. Davis, *Arthur Griffith and Non-Violent Sinn Féin* (Anvil, Tralee, 1974). 9 R. Skidelsky, *J.M. Keynes: The Economist as Saviour 1920–1937* (Macmillan, London, 1992), p. 479.

nationhood as implicitly involving retrenchment.[10] Cumann na nGaedheal's approach to income maintenance payments in the initial 1922–24 period is clearly tied to these twin concepts of nation and retrenchment.

Old age pensions

On old age pensions, the emphasis on retrenchment was most prominent. Pensions were one of the largest financial burdens on the new state – some £3.3 million out of total spending for 1922–3 of £20 million.[11] While senior Cumann na nGaedheal figures were obviously concerned with the cost of pensions from late 1922,[12] no action was taken until after the 1923 elections which saw Cumann na nGaedheal elected to office with 42% of the seats. In theory the party was a minority government, but in practice because of Sinn Féin abstention and support from farmers and independents, it had a massive majority. Joseph Brennan, secretary of the Department of Finance, was very concerned about overall government spending and, in particular, about the cost of old age pensions. As early as March 1923, Brennan issued a circular to all Departments warning that the condition of public finances was a matter of 'very serious concern' and seeking economies.[13] After the August election, Brennan returned to the fray. In a memorandum on the Budget position, he argued that Exchequer expenditure would significantly exceed income in the coming year. He found 'great objections' to increasing taxation and accordingly he argued that it was necessary to concentrate on bringing down expenditure. He proposed cuts in relation to the army, the administration, education and a cut in old age pensions of 2s. 6d. per week.[14] It would appear that Finance eventually proposed a cut of 2s. per week.[15] However, the government chose a reduction of 1s. combined with a range of other pension cuts which achieved broadly the same level of savings. These cuts were calculated to save some £5–600,000 per annum. This was announced by Ernest Blythe, Minister for Finance, as part of a range of reductions also affecting the civil service, national schoolteachers' salaries and the army, in a speech to the Dáil on 2 November 1923.[16] This speech very much followed Brennan's concerns about overspending, his opposition to increased taxation and consequent emphasis on retrenchment. It must also be seen in the context of the impending National Loan. Given difficulties in raising finance from the

---

10 See, for example, Cosgrave at *Dáil Debates*, vol. V col. 1313–5, 21 February 1924; O'Higgins *Dáil Debates*, vol. II col. 1434 *et seq.*, 9 February 1923.   **11** J. Meenan, *The Irish Economy since 1922* (Liverpool University Press, Liverpool, 1970), p. 369.   **12** See, for example, Cosgrave and Blythe's comments on the pensions estimates: *Dáil Debates*, vol. I col. 2127–8, 16 November 1922; *Dáil Debates*, vol. III col. 1112 *et seq.*, 18 May 1923.   **13** NAI D/Finance 826.   **14** NAI D/Finance 826/5.   **15** Fanning *Finance* p. 111. The file to which he refers is not in the National Archives.   **16** *Dáil Debates*, vol. V col. 661 *et seq.*, 2 November 1923

banks, the government was keen to launch a National Loan and saw a commitment to sound finance as essential to the success of this project. The cuts announced in November 1923 were an indication of its commitment in this regard.[17]

The Old Age Pensions Bill was introduced in the Dáil in February 1924. It provided for a reduction from 10s. to 9s. in the weekly pension and altered the means test rule so that, *inter alia*, whereas people with means of up to 11s. formerly got a full pension and up to £1 got a minimum amount, in future these figures were reduced to 7s. and 16s. respectively. Blythe argued that because the cost-of-living had fallen significantly since the pension had been set at 10s., the reduction was justified rather than pursuing an inflationary policy that would leave the pension at 10s. but reduce its real purchasing power. The means test changes meant, however, that the reductions were much more significant (up to 4s. per week) in many cases. Despite vigorous opposition from the Labour party and some independents,[18] the bill passed both Houses with only minor concessions to the parliamentary opposition.[19] The effect of the measures was that average pensions dropped from 9s. 8d. in 1923/4 to 8s.7d. in 1925/6 while expenditure fell from £3.2 million to £2.6 million over this period.[20] The proportion of the population over 70 entitled to a pension fell sharply from an estimated 76% in 1922 to 66% in 1926.[21]

The old age pension cut is one for which the Cumann na nGaedheal government has become infamous. But contemporary response was also highly negative. Even the *Irish Independent* and the *Freeman's Journal* – staunch government supporters – while arguing that it was 'absolutely essential' that the Budget be balanced had reservations about the prioritising of cuts on teachers and pensioners.[22] In September 1924, Seamus Hayes, the

---

17 See generally Fanning, *Finance*, pp. 88–98. For the level of work put into promoting the Loan see UCDA P24/350. The link between the two issues is nicely illustrated in a letter from Blythe to Governor General Tim Healy asking him to use his influence with Lord Beaverbrook to get good publicity for the Loan in the Beaverbrook papers. Blythe referred to his forthcoming speech which would announce 'drastic cuts which will be painful to those affected but which the Government will not shirk carrying out' Blythe to Healy, 31 October 1923, UCDA P24/350. 18 With a better grasp of rhetoric than of history Teachta Padráig Ó hOgáin argued that 'deirtear go bhfuil Riaghaltas na nGall imithighthe, agus gur Riaghaltas Gaodhalach atá againn anois. . . . Tá aon rud amháin cinte – tá rud ceapaithe ag an Riaghaltas seo nar cheap Riaghaltas na nGall riamh; 'sé sin daoine bochta na tíre seo do chur chun bhais.' *Dáil Debates*, vol. V col. 1292, 21 February 1924. 19 On the financial impact of concessions, see NAI D/Finance 958/7. 20 Note on OAP Estimates 1931/2, no date, UCDA P24/272. 21 Department of Social Welfare *First Report*, 1950, table IV. 22 *Irish Independent* 3, 7, 8 and 9 November 1923; *Freeman's Journal* 3 and 11 November 1923. Some support for the Cumann na nGaedheal position may perhaps be gained from recent comparative research which suggests that the Irish old age pension was, at that time, one of the more generous in Europe as a

secretary of Cumann na nGaedheal, wrote to Blythe on behalf of the Coiste Gnótha (standing committee) stating that they had received resolutions from five areas concerning the pension cuts and that 'our members everywhere regard the present revision of payments as most inopportune' (i.e. in the context of pending bye-elections). The Coiste were at a loss to know if Ministers took 'any account of the political effect produced and of the possible consequences on the stability of the State of continuous public displeasure'. An unabashed Blythe found it 'somewhat deplorable that responsible people [were] so unwilling to defend the reduction and make clear the causes which rendered it necessary'. Unsurprisingly this did not placate Hayes who claimed that he had yet to meet a single government supporter who approved of the measure.[23]

Poor Law
On the Poor Law, the key elements of policy had already been implemented (as set out in chapter 1) in 1921. Blythe, then Minister for Local Government and Public Health, introduced legislation to give formal legal effect to these reforms in the Local Government (Temporary Provisions) Bill, 1923. A draft of the bill was circulated in January 1923.[24] This proposed to make it compulsory for local authorities to prepare a 'county scheme' which the Minister could confirm modify or reject. Where a local authority failed to act, the Minister would be empowered to establish a scheme. Each scheme was to provide that every person unable to support himself and his dependants by his own industry or other lawful means should receive sufficient assistance. Assistance could be provided in a county home if this was less costly or if it could not be effectively provided otherwise. Each local authority was to provide for a county home for the aged and infirm, invalids and expectant mothers. The draft allowed (but did not require) schemes to abolish the boards of guardians. In contrast to the draft, the bill, published in February 1923, simply confirmed existing schemes and allowed (rather than required) counties that did not already have a scheme to adopt one. The Minister was not given power to impose a scheme where none was adopted. The effect of this was to allow Dublin city and county to continue to operate under the old Poor Law (a situation that continued until 1930). The bill allowed the abolition of boards of guardians, and in fact all the published schemes (implicitly

proportion of average industrial earnings. This arose, as we have seen, from the fact that the pension was set at the United Kingdom rate despite the generally lower standard of living in Ireland. See W. Korpi, *Welfare State Development in Europe since 1930: Ireland in a Comparative Perspective* (ESRI, Dublin, 1992), p. 4–5.   23 UCDA P24/453. See J.M. Regan, *The Irish Counter-Revolution 1921–1936* (Gill and Macmillan, Dublin, 1999), pp. 209–11.   **24** NAI S. 3491.

or explicitly) did so. Unlike the draft, the bill did not set out the specific basis of entitlement to assistance and simply (in section 10) allowed the payment of outdoor relief 'notwithstanding anything in any enactment'. This meant that the legal provisions concerning relief remained those of the old Poor Law (as amended by section 10). Twenty-two county schemes were published as a schedule to the bill. These make fascinating reading and vary considerably from one to the other. Blythe explained that the bill was intended 'to regularise the position temporarily of the various county schemes' which had been introduced under the Dáil government. As the existing Poor Law had been 'blown sky high' and as there was no legal basis for the existing schemes, 'the Oireachtas should pass legislation of a temporary nature regularising the position'. He added that '[l]ater on, and as soon as possible, permanent legislation will be put before the Dáil'.[25] The bill was adopted largely as published with most of the debate centring on issues other than the structure of the system.

However, a very significant reform of the administration of relief was implemented by way of Ministerial regulation in 1923.[26] In place of the wide range of approaches set out in the original County Schemes, Blythe amended all the existing schemes in June 1923 to bring them into a uniform order. This provided that County Boards of Health were to be established. Each area was to have a County Home for the Aged and Infirm and a County Hospital for medical, surgical and maternity cases and such other institutions as might be approved by the Minister. No person was to be relieved in an institution unless could be done at less cost than in any other lawful way. A person eligible for relief was defined as 'any poor person who is unable by his own industry or other lawful means to provide for himself or his dependants the necessaries of life . . .'. Any new schemes subsequently approved also followed this standard approach so that by 1925 all counties except Dublin were now following a broadly uniform approach, at least in theory. A further standardisation of the administration of outdoor relief (or what was becoming known, in line with the recommendation of the Royal Commission, as home assistance) was introduced in 1923 and 1924. The county schemes provided for a wide variety of different arrangements for deciding applications for home assistance. Many of the schemes abolished the position of relieving officer and established alternative procedures. Decisions were generally to be made by the County Board of Health or its subcommittee often on the recommendation of a local subcommittee. Initial applications often had to be recom-

---

25 *Dáil Debates*, vol. II col. 723–4, 12 January 1923. The Act was, in fact, to remain in place until 1942. 26 During debate on the 1923 bill, Blythe had indicated that something along these lines was to occur, *Dáil Debates*, vol. II, col. 1419, 9 February 1923.

mended by an authorised person or persons, for example by a local councillor (Laois, Longford), a member of the relevant subcommittee (Cavan), three 'recognised' persons (clergy, doctor, councillor or brehon: Clare) or a parish committee consisting of the parish priest or in parishes with a conference of St Vincent de Paul, the conference might be appointed as the committee (Galway). However, Blythe provided that each Board of Health was to appoint a superintendent assistance officer and assistance officers whose duty it was to receive and investigate applications for assistance which the super-intendent then submitted to the Board for its decision.[27] Questioned in the Dáil as to the abolition of the local committees, Minister for Local Government James Bourke, who succeeded Blythe on his appointment as Minister for Finance in October 1923, argued that 'wasteful and unnecessary expenditure frequently arose' where subcommittees had had direct power and 'deserving cases did not always receive impartial consideration'.[28]

Unemployment

Unemployment increased rapidly in the early 1920s although accurate meas-urement of unemployment (and underemployment) in the period is extremely difficult.[29] The period was a highly unstable one from an employ-ment perspective. Not only was there considerable disruption arising from the War of Independence and subsequent Civil War, there was also the general post-World War rise in unemployment, demobilisation of the greatly expanded Free State Army and also a sharp fall in wage rates which led to considerable industrial unrest in the early 1920s.[30] The Cumann na nGaedheal government had, in effect, no *employment* policy. Employment creation was seen as part of a broader fiscal or tariff policy. The problem of unemployment was not, in general, seen as being capable of short-term reso-lution through the creation of employment in the private sector. So, policy on *unemployment* tended to rotate between three alternative poles: supporting the unemployed through unemployment insurance (on the assumption that unemployment was reasonably short-term and likely to improve within the

27 County Boards of Health (No. 1) Order, 1924. This was subsequently replaced by the County Board of Health (Assistance) Order, 1924 which provided further details as to the administration of relief. It is, of course, difficult to gauge the impact of these rules in practice. For example, Longford Board of Health was dissolved and its powers transferred to a Commissioner in 1924 on the basis that it had 'wilfully neglected' to appoint assistance officers. 28 *Dáil Debates*, vol. VII col. 2934, 25 June 1924. 29 Ó Gráda *Ireland: A New Economic History* (Oxford University Press, Oxford, 1994), p. 437; Department of Industry and Commerce, *The Trend of Employment and Unemployment in the Saorstat, passim* (Stationery, Office, Dublin, 1935). 30 E. O'Connor, *Syndicalism in Ireland* (Cork University Press, Cork, 1989). On the situation in the UK, see W. Garside, *British Unemployment 1919–1939* (Cambridge University Press, Cambridge, 1990).

next six to 12 months), the provision of relief work (on the assumption that unemployment was likely to persist into the medium term) and (effectively a residual option) financial support through the Poor Law system. All three of these options existed in 1922. As we have seen, unemployment insurance had been established in a limited way under the 1911 Act and substantially extended in 1920. Unemployment, however, had reached levels unplanned for in the original unemployment insurance scheme and so 'uncovenanted' benefit had been introduced in 1921. This involved the payment of benefit without contributions on the assumption that contributions would be paid in the future. On relief, the Provisional Government was already providing funding for relief schemes to local authorities in 1922 and many local authorities operated direct labour schemes with the objective, at least in part, of reducing unemployment.[31] In addition, there were several thousand able-bodied males on the Poor Law at any given time. The debate as to the appropriate balance between these measures waged throughout the 1920s. The Department of Industry and Commerce was, from an early date, convinced that extending unemployment insurance was not the way to go and that relief work was a more productive use of resources. Finance, however, tended to favour extension of unemployment insurance as a lesser use of resources than unproductive relief work.[32] The general Finance view was that expenditure to relive unemployment was 'financially unsound'. Brennan wrote that '[t] the economic evil of unemployment is generally less hurtful to the State than the evil of inflationary finance'.[33] In the absence of any resolution of this dispute, by default pressure remained on poor law relief.

On unemployment insurance, the Provisional Government had, by decree, extended the provisions of the United Kingdom Unemployment Insurance Act, 1922 to Ireland. This provided for an extension of uncovenanted benefit given the continuing high levels of unemployment and made permanent the increases for dependants which had been introduced on a temporary basis the previous year.[34] Despite the estimated Exchequer cost of £1.15 million, Finance agreed to the extension.[35] Subsequently, the Provisional Government again extended the scheme in line with a British extension of the period of entitlement to benefit.[36] Again, Finance agreed that it would not be possible

---

31 NAI S. 921. See also NAI D/Finance 165/2 and 165/4.   32 See, for example, *Dáil Debates*, vol. XXIV col. 2210, 5 July 1928.   33 'Financial Situation after the Loan', Memo by J. Brennan 12 December 1923, UCDA P24/350.   34 Provisional Government Decree No. 4. Section 16 of the Unemployment Insurance Act, 1922 allowed for its application to Ireland and this was achieved by Order in Council (Provision Government (Unemployment Insurance) Order, 1922) and by Decree No. 4 which largely repeated the wording of the British Order. See Gilbert, *British Social Policy*, chapter 21.   35 NAI D/Finance 165/2.   36 Decree No. 6. See NAI D/Finance 165/4 and 34/16.

to adopt a less generous line and approved the proposed approach. In December, at the proposal of Industry and Commerce, the government established a Commission on Reconstruction and Development to develop proposals for the relief of unemployment.[37] In March 1923, Joseph McGrath, Minister for Industry and Commerce, submitted a memorandum to government outlining proposals for an Unemployment Insurance bill.[38] About 33,000 people were then drawing unemployment benefit, of whom 18,000 would exhaust their right to benefit in April, 8,000 in May and the remaining 7,000 in June. About 22,000 would requalify for benefit in July at the start of a new benefit year. Industry and Commerce argued that it was necessary to extend entitlement to benefit. However, rather than a further extension of uncovenenated benefit (as in the United Kingdom), they argued for an ingenious arrangement to retain (at least in theory) the contributory nature of the benefit. Uncovenanted benefit, it was argued, was open to abuse and had been called a 'dole'. It was proposed that, rather than paying uncovenenated benefit on the (possibly notional) assumption of the payment of contributions in the future, the value of existing contributions paid should be enhanced by a factor of up to three. The Exchequer cost of the measure was estimated at £250,000 up to October 1923. The bill also contained provisions in relation to unemployment insurance cover for members of the Defence Forces who had previously been insured. The proposals were approved by government and adopted largely unchanged by the Dáil.[39] Interestingly, an Industry and Commerce proposal to allow unemployment insurance to be used to support the *employment* of persons unemployed or threatened with unemployment was withdrawn at Committee stage because of the objections of the Labour party.[40]

However, the unemployment crisis did not improve in the short-term and in November 1923, Gordon Campbell, secretary of the Department of Industry and Commerce (and previously of the Irish department of the Ministry of Labour) submitted a memorandum to government on 'Unemployment this Winter'.[41] Campbell predicted that by mid-February 1924, three quarters of those then on unemployment benefit would have exhausted their entitlements leading to a 'serious outcry' for further relief. He argued that it was 'undesirable in the extreme' to revert to the payment of

---

37 NAI S. 1906, S. 3185. 38 NAI S. 2168. Industry and Commerce stated that a recommendation had been received from the Commission on Reconstruction and Development that legislation on the subject of unemployment benefit should be introduced at once. See also NAI D/Finance 828. 39 *Dáil Debates*, vol. III col. 477 et seq., 2 May 1923. 40 *Dáil Debates*, vol. III col. 702, 9 May 1923. On the rejection of similar proposals in the UK, see Garside, *British Unemployment*, pp. 206–9. 41 NAI S. 3417 on S. 4278 (which amalgamates a number of files concerning unemployment and relief in the 1922–32 period).

benefit unsupported by contributions and called instead for a road building scheme as recommended by the Commission on Reconstruction and Development in its interim report.[42] The Executive Council decided in November that McGrath should consult with builders' organisations on a housing programme while the Minister for Local Government should proceed with a scheme for the relief of unemployment by road work at a cost of £1.25 million in the period to March 1925. In December, Campbell submitted a further memorandum arguing that the situation was rapidly becoming critical. Of the 39,000 in receipt of benefit in October, 8,000 had already exhausted their right to benefit and three-quarters of the remainder would do so by February 1924. Including demobilised soldiers and agricultural workers (not covered by unemployment insurance) there would be 80,000 unemployed people within two months with 'no work, no benefit, and little or no prospect of any private employment'. This was a 'serious, if not dangerous problem'. Campbell pointed out that any proposed road scheme would not provide work for more than 10,000 people and that it was doubtful if a housing scheme was practicable. He argued that it was imperative to allocate £500,000 to other constructive works and suggested duties on selected commodities to stimulate employment. By this time, even Brennan was prepared to admit that 'from the law and order point of view serious unemployment in the Spring is a matter specially to be feared'. However, any support for unemployment relief should be 'only for a brief period'.[43] At the Executive Council of 18 December 1923, President Cosgrave submitted a report (not on file) on government schemes for the relief of unemployment including work on roads and housing which was approved 'in its general principle'. By mid 1924, however, the government decided to extend further unemployment insurance and Paddy McGilligan introduced the Unemployment Insurance Bill, 1924 in June. McGilligan continued to defend the Industry and Commerce line that such an extension was not a 'dole' because beneficiaries would, in future, repay their contributions to the fund.[44]

However, Winter 1924 again saw no improvement in the position. In October, McGilligan announced that the unemployment figures were no longer being published as 'the figures were not being properly understood.'[45]

42 See the *Interim Report* of the Commission on Improvement of Roads, 31 May 1923 on NAI S. 3185. Interestingly the Commission recommended that its proposals to develop the road network at a cost of over £1.6 million, while providing work for about 10,500 people, 'should not be looked on as relief work'. It appears that the report was effectively rejected by government, the Labour members withdrew and the Commission was wound up in January 1924, J.A. Gaughran, *Thomas Johnson* (Kingdom, Dublin, 1980), p. 243. 43 'Financial Situation after the Loan', Memo by J. Brennan 12 December 1923, UCDA P24/350. 44 *Dáil Debates*, vol. VII col. 2217, 12 June 1924. 45 *Dáil Debates*, vol. IX col. 549, 30 October 1924.

In a debate of an unemployment motion proposed by the Labour party, he argued that '[p]eople may have to die in this country and may have to die through starvation.'[46] In November, Campbell circulated a memorandum on unemployment arguing that 'the Winter now beginning may be the most critical in all the early years of the Free State'.[47] Serious economic depression was the main cause. Campbell argued for a bold policy for relief of distress and unemployment. He rejected the Labour party call for the further extension of unemployment insurance This was the cheapest option but, he claimed, was unpopular with all sections of the public and was 'non-constructive'. Given the previous extensions on entitlement, any further extension would bring unemployment insurance nearer and nearer in approach to the dole. He proposed a range of measures including a building programme and national preference in relation to public contracts and materials. On 20 November, the Ministers for Finance, Industry and Commerce, Local Government and Lands were appointed by the Executive Council to act as an Economic Committee to make recommendations on the unemployment problem. However, it appears that the Committee met only once and on 2 December the Executive Council agreed that a bill be introduced to extend further unemployment insurance and to make provision for ex-Army members. This was provided for in the Unemployment Insurance (No. 2) Act, quickly adopted in December 1924, which provided special benefits for demobilised soldiers who were not insured contributors.[48] McGilligan explained that the further extension of insurance arose because relief schemes could not be started sufficiently early.

National health insurance
In relation to national health insurance, the main reform was the National Health Insurance Act 1923 which was intended primarily to 'nationalise' the existing health insurance system.[49] Under the 1911 Act, British societies operated in and had members in Ireland and vice versa. The Act, despite initial opposition from the Association of Approved Societies, effected a 'full severance' between the Free State and the United Kingdom and provided that only societies based in Ireland could be approved under the scheme.[50] The legislation also provided for insurance cover for members of the Army

---

46 *Dáil Debates*, vol. IX col. 562, 30 October 1924. In fairness to McGilligan, he immediately went on to say that this was not what he desired to see. **47** NAI S. 4278. **48** As McGilligan accepted, this represented a 'complete departure' from the insurance principle. He stated that about 30,000 soldiers had been demobilised of whom half had previously been insured. Of these, about 10,000 had claimed unemployment insurance. He estimated that the legislation would involve about the same level of additional claims. *Dáil Debates*, vol. IX col. 2025–6, 4 December 1924. **49** NAI S. 3083. **50** See *Dáil Debates*, vol. III col. 1520, 6 June 1923.

who had previously been member of an Approved Society and, in view of the high level of unemployment, continued in force national health insurance provisions maintaining insured persons' coverage up to 1924.

1924–7 – A TIME FOR ENQUIRY

Following the plethora of initial legislation to nationalise the health insurance scheme, to put the 'sympathetic native' Poor Law scheme on a legal basis, to retrench old age pension costs and to respond to the continuing crisis of unemployment, the next period saw a deluge of official enquiries into the operation of most schemes. Commissions (under varying titles) were set up to examine the Poor Law, workmen's compensation, the administration of old age pensions and the national health insurance scheme.

Unemployment insurance
Unemployment insurance was the only area in which a major review was not carried out.[51] McGilligan had reconsidered his 1924 position in favour of extended unemployment insurance and by June 1925, he was of the opinion that any further extension of insurance 'must be looked upon as dole, because contributions having been exhausted and having been multiplied five times over, any further multiplication . . . would be nothing more or less than complete charity'.[52] He was now of the opinion that any further response should be by way of relief schemes rather than a further extension of insurance.[53] Finance, however, did not agree and consistently opposed relief expenditure as a solution to unemployment.[54] The only legislation in this period was the Unemployment Insurance Act, 1926 which involved primarily 'administrative changes designed to secure economy' and implemented a recommendation of the 1923 United Kingdom Watson Committee report.[55] The Cumann na nGaedheal refusal to extend unemployment benefits, whatever its immediate impact may have been on the unemployed, certainly avoided the sort of

51 In April 1922, Joseph McGrath, then Minister for Labour, stated that he personally was 'not satisfied that the present scheme is the best that could be fixed for the needs of this country and it is my intention to get together as early as possible a small committee to go into the whole matter' NAI D/Finance 165/2. However, McGrath does not appear to have proceeded with this plan and his resignation in March 1924 over the 'Army Mutiny' may have put an end to any possibility of a review. There is little indication that either his Department or successor, Paddy McGilligan, had any interest in a public review. From the few extant Industry and Commerce policy files, the Department appears broadly satisfied with the scheme and to be keeping a close eye on relevant developments in the United Kingdom. 52 *Dáil Debates*, vol. XXII col. 1770, 30 June 1925. 53 Ibid., 1798. 54 See Blythe's comments at *Dáil Debates*, vol. XXIV col. 2210, 5 July 1928. 55 S. 4922.

policy difficulties which emerged in the United Kingdom in the early 1930s when the government tried to terminate the provision of uncovenanted benefit.[56]

Employment and unemployment figures for the 1920s and 30s are notoriously difficult to interpret. The numbers claiming unemployment insurance dropped from over 30,000 in 1924 to 28,000 in 1925 and, sharply, to 17,000 in 1926. It is unclear, however, whether this relates to falling unemployment or the failure to further extend entitlements after 1924. Interestingly unemployment insurance claims did not rise significantly in the late 20s and early 30s. However, home assistance claims increased dramatically from 1927 on with over 6,000 able-bodied men on home assistance by March 1931. The Department of Industry and Commerce's own assessment was that the growth in unemployment insurance fund income after 1925 and in persons insured from 1927 reflected a genuine increase in employment rather than merely improved compliance. It was felt that up to 1927, the increase in employment related to greater continuity in employment and after that to greater numbers in work.[57]

Poor Law

Given the promised 'temporary' nature of the Poor Law reforms, detailed proposals for a permanent system were obviously required. A Commission on the Relief of the Sick and Destitute, including the Insane Poor (hereafter Commission on the Relief of the Poor) was appointed in March 1925 to devise 'permanent legislation for the effective and economical relief of the sick and destitute poor'. Chaired by Charles O'Connor and including five Oireachtas members, two religious, Sir Joseph Glynn and Padraig Ó Siochfhrada (who acted as Commissioner in place of a number of dissolved boards), the Committee held oral hearings on 32 days between May 1925 and December 1926, hearing evidence from a wide variety of bodies and individuals. The report, concluded in August 1927, examined the full range of the then Poor Law services including medical services and those for the 'mentally defective' but we focus here primarily on the recommendations relating to home assistance/outdoor relief. The Commission's view of the new system was less than positive. While accepting the switch from indoor to outdoor relief as a *fait acompli* and approving of this in so far as it had resulted in the 'closing of unnecessary workhouses and placing the poor law on a county basis', the

---

56 Gilbert, *British Social Policy*, chapter 3; Garside, *British Unemployment*, chapter 3; F.M. Miller, 'National Assistance or Unemployment Assistance: The British Cabinet and Relief Policy 1932–33' *Journal of Contemporary History* ((1974) pp. 163-84; *id.*, 'The Unemployment Policy of the National Government 1931–36,' *Historical Journal* 19 (1976) pp. 453–76; *id.*, 'The British Unemployment Assistance Crisis of 1935,' *Journal of Contemporary History*, 14 (1979) pp. 329–51.   **57** Note to Minister on Unemployment, 2 October 1930, UCDA P35A/28.

Committee was 'convinced that the schemes . . . have in some counties . . . operated prejudicially in the interests of the poor, while the saving in cost has been negligible'.[58] The Commission had grave reservations in relation to the operation of county homes. They found these to contain a wide variety of different categories of person including the aged and infirm, lunatics, idiots and imbeciles, unmarried mothers and their children, in others married mothers and their children, orphans and deserted children (and in a number TB and cancer cases). The Commission was convinced that county homes were 'not fit or proper places for the reception of the various classes which we have found in them and, therefore . . . the schemes . . . must . . . be deemed inadequate and unsatisfactory'. They found the standards of accommodation in some to be 'extraordinarily bad'.[59] The Commission found that the cost of outdoor relief had tripled between 1913 and 1925, reflecting the switch from indoor relief. However, overall, and taking account of changes in the value of money, the Commission found that the Boards of Health 'whilst perhaps acting with more liberality than their predecessors, still fall far short of discharging their full obligations in regard to persons eligible for relief who cannot be sent to institutions'. In many cases, the amounts paid were 'altogether inadequate to provide the necessaries of life.'[60] While highly critical of the standards of indoor relief, the Commission revealed a lingering attraction for the workhouse test arguing that 'it might not prove wise to prevent altogether the relief of some classes in institutions'.[61] Unlike the 1909 Royal Commission, the Poor Law Commission did not favour the disbursement of public monies though private charities nor was such a role favoured by the Society of St Vincent de Paul which gave evidence before it.[62] As can be seen, the report of the Commission did not reflect well on the existing Poor Law system. Its recommendations, which in some areas reflected those of the Viceregal Commission twenty years earlier, involved a more effective and efficient implementation of the existing system; some shift back towards institutional support particularly for unmarried mothers; and a greater role for central government in specific areas such as support for widows.[63] These would inevitably have had significant cost implications. As such, it is unsurprising that little was done to implement the recommendations.

National Health Insurance
The origins of the review of national health insurance lay in a letter from Joseph Brennan to Joseph Glynn, chair of the National Health Insurance Commission, in October 1923.[64] As part of his retrenchment campaign,

---

58 *Report* p. 16.   59 Ibid., pp. 17–18.   60 P. 56.   61 p. 53.   62 pp. 58–9.   63 Recommendations in relation to widows and lone parents are discussed below, p. 51.   64 The NHIC was

Brennan wrote that it would 'be essential for the government to effect heavy reductions in the cost of normal government services in order that the maintenance of a sound financial situation may be assured.'[65] He pointed out that the system of health insurance involved a heavy burden of the State and asked for Glynn's personal views as to whether 'without serious detriment to the public interest, a substantial economy could be effected by radical alteration of the present Health Insurance system even to the extent, if necessary, of abandoning the scheme of compulsory insurance altogether.' Glynn, unsurprisingly, did not believe that the system could be abandoned without grave injury to the public interest. He pointed out that Labour would be sure to oppose such an approach. Glynn suggested that some economies were achievable through removing the cost of medical certification from the State (something which was subsequently implemented in part) and effecting drastic reduction in the numbers of approved societies by compulsorily winding-up all mismanaged societies. He also proposed an inquiry into the system. Brennan was quickly convinced of the merits of an inquiry and in February sent draft terms of reference to Glynn. In April, the Executive Council approved Blythe's proposal that a Committee of Inquiry be established and the Committee, chaired by Deputy Magennis[66] and including representatives of the NHIC (Glynn and Maguire), the Departments of Local Government and Finance (J.J. McElligott) and the medical profession, was appointed in May 1924. Its remit was to inquire into and report on the advisability of the continued maintenance of the national health insurance system in its present form, to consider whether it was desirable to establish a system of medical treatment on a contributory basis and to examine whether medical services assisted by state or local funds could be improved.[67] The Committee received extensive written and oral submissions from interested parties and in February 1925 produced an interim report which found that the overwhelming body of evidence was in favour of the continuation of the existing insurance system. The Committee's recommendations in its interim

one of the few survivors of the range of pre-Independence administrative bodies which had made up the Irish administration. Many became part of the new departmental structure but the NHIC, while operating under the auspices of the Department of Local Government and Public Health retained a considerable degree of autonomy while, at the same time, operating as part of the civil service. The Revenue Commissioners are today one of the few bodies to combine this degree of autonomy and centrality. **65** Brennan to Glynn, 19 October 1923. NAI F 46/1/24. **66** Magennis was a Cumann na nGaedheal TD who subsequently resigned from the party in 1925 over the Boundary Commission affair and set up a small (and unsuccessful) party called Clan Éireann. **67** Again we focus on the insurance payments aspects of the report. For the broader medical issues see Barrington, *Health, Medicine and Politics*.

report focused on reform of the existing health insurance system. It set out a range of recommendations the most controversial of which were to prove those in relation to 'unification' of approved societies and the introduction of a medical benefit.[68] The NHIC had argued strongly for unification while the societies themselves were strongly opposed. The Committee considered the options of 'nationalisation', i.e. bringing the operation of the system within a government department, unification of the societies and a reduction in numbers. It considered that unification, if feasible, afforded the best method of simplifying the existing system.[69] The Committee recommended, in principle, the introduction of medical benefit (McElliggott dissenting). Its final report, published in 1927, set out detailed recommendations for the introduction of a contributory system of medical benefit linked to the existing health insurance scheme with contributions to be increased by 1d. for both employers and employees. McElligott and Hurson, a Local Government nominee, dissented.

Workmens's compensation
A Departmental Committee was appointed by Paddy McGilligan, Minister for Industry and Commerce, in May 1925 to enquire into the workmen's compensation system and to consider what changes were necessary. It was chaired by Alfred Dickie KC and included representatives of employers and employees. Again, it took evidence from a range of key bodies. A number of significant alternatives to the existing system were proposed to the Committee including compulsory public accident insurance or a state insurance fund for workmen's compensation. 'Labour interests' pressed for fundamental change whereas the Law Society, Chambers of Commerce, business groups and the insurance industry opposed modification. The Committee concluded that the only way to ensure payment of compensation was by compulsory insurance. However, it somewhat weakly decided not to recommend compulsory insurance but that the matter be re-examined when more evidence became available.[70] The Committee recommended a range of relatively minor improvements to the scheme to expand its scope (by raising insurance thresholds) and improve benefits.

---

68 The Committee's recommendations in relation to married women are considered in more detail below. 69 *Interim Report*, p. 12. The government subsequently sought clarification of the term 'if feasible'. The Committee explained that they were referring to the possible political opposition and the possibility of a financial liability on the State to guarantee benefits in the case of unification. 70 *Report*, p. 19.

Old age pensions
In response to much public criticism in relation to the administration of old age pensions, Blythe agreed to appoint a Committee of Inquiry in November 1924. The Committee originated in a Dáil motion by Patrick McKenna TD in October 1924, calling for a parliamentary inquiry into the administration of old age pensions.[71] Brennan opposed in principle the investigation by the Oireachtas of matters of administration and argued that no case had been made for an enquiry. But Blythe agreed to set up a Committee albeit that he indicated that he did not want a preponderance of Deputies on it. The Committee was appointed in December 1925 and was chaired by T.S. McCann and included a number of Oireachtas members and civil servants. The remit of the Committee was tightly confined to the administration of pensions and it focused on the system for processing claims and decisions. Many of the disputes in relation to claims related to age as the absence of a system of birth registration up to 1863 meant that there was, in effect, no system of proving the age of many claimants. The report of the Committee, published in February 1926, made a series of recommendations to improve the operation of the system.

As we have seen, following a period of some activity in 1923–4, the government saw out the remainder of the Fourth Dáil though establishing a series of enquiries in most of the key social services areas. The Dáil ran almost its full term and in the elections of the June 1927, Cumann na nGaedheal was narrowly returned to office with only 30% of Dáil seats. The newly established Fianna Fáil party won almost as many seats but its deputies were not allowed to take their seats in the Dáil because of their refusal to take the oath. With the support of the Farmers Party and Independents, Cumann na nGaedheal returned to government with an increased Labour party as the token opposition. However, following the assassination of Kevin O'Higgins in July 1927 and the subsequent introduction of public order and related legislation, Fianna Fáil decided to enter the Dáil on the understanding that a motion of no confidence in the government to be tabled by Labour would be carried with Fianna Fáil and other support – leading to a Labour-led government supported by Fianna Fáil from outside cabinet. In the event, the motion was defeated on the casting vote of the Ceann Comhairle. Recognising that their continuation in government was extremely tenuous, Cumann na nGaedheal called a further election and were returned with a significant increase in their vote and seats won (41%). With the support of the Farmers Party and Independents, Cumann na nGaedheal now had a slim majority.

71 F 66/3/24.

Despite a major increase in Fianna Fáil seats to 38%, a fall in the Labour representation meant that the opposition (even if combined) could not defeat the total votes of Cumann na nGaedheal and its supporters.

1928–31: INERTIA

Despite the range of reports available to the government and despite the greatly increased tempo of parliamentary opposition on social issues, the Cumann na nGaedheal government did little in most areas during the life-time of the Fifth Dáil from 1927 to 1932. The government's obsession with economy continued. In 1927, the government established an Economy Committee to recommend cuts (which is considered in more detail below) and in October 1928, the President met all heads of Department in an attempt to achieve 'large savings'.[72] The government showed less than willing to implement any of the more substantial recommendations of the Old Age Pensions Committee, although some administrative changes were intro-duced.[73] The pensions issue remained a contentious one[74] and in November 1927 Labour Deputy Dan Morrissey submitted a Dáil motion calling for the restoration of the pension cut. This was debated in the Dáil in February 1928. Arising from this and earlier representations, both Finance and the Revenue gave detailed consideration to different ways on increasing pension rates.[75] While, as we have seen, the 1924 cut involved both a 1s. reduction in the pension and other reductions, the main public outcry related to 'restoring the shilling' and ultimately, the government decided to opt for a restoration of the 10s. maximum rate but only for those with no or minimal means.[76] The Old Age Pensions Act, 1928 gave effect to this decision. It reversed, in part, the 1924 cuts by restoring the maximum level of pension to 10s. (but only for some pensioners). It did not reverse the means changes which meant that the old age pension system remained less generous than on Independence. The limited nature of the 1928 Act is shown by the fact that, whereas the 1924 cuts reduced the average pension by over a shilling, the 1928 move only

72 O'Hegarty to members of the Executive Council 10 October 1928 enclosing a statement made by President Cosgrave at this meeting on 4 October 1928, UCDA P35/152. This followed on a letter from McElligott arguing that '[t]he real remedy for the present financial emergency is a rigid and unswerving policy of retrenchment' 17 September 1928, ibid. 73 NAI. S88/7/26. 74 See letters and resolutions from trade unions, pension committees and county councils on Finance file NAI S88/4/26. The file includes a letter from the Chairman of the Cumann na nGaedheal Dublin City North Constituency Committee who describes cutting off the shilling as a 'sad mistake'. 75 UCDA P24/38; NAI S88/4/26. 76 It appears that a Mr. Robert Kelly, builder of Bantry, may have been the originator of this idea, Kelly to Blythe, 20 March 1927, NAI S88/4/26.

increased average pensions by 4½d. to 9s., at an additional cost of about £150,000 and there was no increase in the proportion of persons over 70 entitled to a pension.[77] A Fianna Fáil bill to improve further the position of pensioners led to the defeat of the government on the Second Stage vote in March 1930. However, it would appear that this took the Opposition by surprise as much as the government rather than reflecting a fundamental change in political support.[78] The Cumann na nGaedheal government decided to resign but was re-elected by the Dáil shortly afterwards. De Valera's nomination as President was soundly defeated with the Labour party voting against. Nonetheless, the incident is symptomatic of both Fianna Fáil's increased emphasis on social policy and Cumann na nGaedheal's increasing precarious hold on power.

The National Insurance Act, 1929 finally gave effect to the (politically) non-controversial recommendations of the 1925 Interim Report of the Health Insurance Committee. These related to the operation of the existing national health insurance scheme and legislation had been in preparation for some time. However, the two key outstanding issues from the reports of the Commission were shelved. The Executive Council decided to postpone any decision on the proposed establishment of a system of medical benefits.[79] And, under strong lobbying from the Approved Societies Association, the Executive Council also decided not to proceed with the Commission's proposed unification of insured societies.[80] However, arising from a Fianna Fáil amendment calling for unification of societies, Mulcahy announced on the second stage of the bill that he would introduce an amendment to facilitate unification and require it if a voluntary approach did not work.[81] When this was ruled out of order by the Ceann Comhairle, Mulcahy decided to introduce separate legislation to this effect[82] and Glynn met with the National Health Insurance Advisory Committee in January 1930 to discuss this with the societies.[83] While a proportion of societies were prepared to consider the issue, the Association of Approved Societies remained 'entirely opposed to any form of compulsory limitation or amalgamation of societies' and the matter did not proceed. However, around this period, the NHIC drew up a detailed scheme for the unification of the approved societies.[84]

77 Note on OAP Estimates 1931/2, no date, UCDA P24/272.   78 *Irish Independent*, 29 March 1930.   79 NAI S. 4677.   80 See NAI S. 4767 and F46/4/25. Minister Bourke informed Glynn in early 1926 that the Executive Council had found it difficult to agree to amalgamation due to the opposition to this and the inadvisability at that late stage in the life of the then Dáil of introducing controversial legislation, Glynn to Bourke, 5 March 1926.   81 *Dáil Debates*, vol. 32 col. 76, 23 October 1929.   82 *Dáil Debates*, vol. 32 col. 232, 24 October 1929. 83 Minutes of meeting of National Health Insurance Advisory Committee, 24 January 1930, UCDA P7/C/89.   84 'Unification or Amalgamation of Societies' undated NAI IA 85/53C;

Given government inaction in relation to the Workmen's Compensation report, a private members bill was introduced in 1929 by Vincent Rice TD to give effect to some of the recommendations of the Committee.[85] The government decided not to oppose the bill and it passed second and third stages. However, at report stage, Paddy McGilligan proposed that the Workmen's Compensation Committee be recalled to reconsider its recommendation in the light of more up-to-date statistics. Although this appears to have been nothing more than a blatant delaying tactic, Deputy Rice agreed to this suggestion. The Committee reconvened to no great effect. The majority of the Committee reaffirmed its recommendation on the level of benefits although three employer members now opposed this. The chairman clearly saw this an opportunistic opposition declaring that he could see no basis for altering their recommendations on the basis of the new statistics. However, the bill was subsequently withdrawn and no replacement had emerged from the Department of Industry and Commerce when the government fell in 1932.

In the area of home assistance, again little effort was made to implement the relevant recommendations of the Commission on the Relief of the Poor. The major activity in this area was the legislation which finally brought Dublin broadly into line with the remainder of the country as regards the operation of the home assistance system.[86] In May 1929, Mulcahy submitted proposals to the Executive Committee for Public Assistance legislation. Mulcahy gave a highly complacent, and quite inaccurate, gloss on the Poor Law Commission's findings stating that it had 'approved of the principles of the county schemes and ha[d] made a number of recommendations mainly of an administrative nature but on the whole little fault ha[d] been found with the system of poor relief that ha[d] been established thereunder and no radical change [was] proposed in its report'. Nonetheless, the confused state of the law relating to poor relief meant that consolidation was necessary and Mulcahy proposed to bring forward legislation to this effect. Interestingly, Mulcahy noted that this would also involve the preparation of a further general bill to deal with changes in local government law. The Executive Committee approved this in June 1929 but again no legislation appeared by the fall of the government.[87]

Thus of the three major inquiries into health insurance, home assistance and workmen's compensation, nothing publicly was done to implement the

'Draft Scheme for a Unified Society', undated NAI IA 85/53E. **85** Rice was a former National League TD who had voted with the government on the 1927 confidence motion and subsequently joined Cumann na nGaedheal. **86** Poor Relief (Dublin) Act 1929. This led to a significant increase in the numbers in Dublin on home assistance, Department of Local Government and Public Health, *Fifth Report 1929–30*. **87** NAI S. 2886.

workmen's compensation report, little in relation to home assistance and only the non-controversial recommendations of the health insurance report were brought into effect. The government belatedly attempted to give the impression of reversing the old age pensions cuts in 1928 and introduced relatively minor changes in the administration of pensions arising from the Committee report. However, pensions clearly remained a highly contentious issue as evidenced by the (albeit temporary) fall of the government on this issue in 1930.

The main area of activity in this period was in relation to unemployment with the establishment in November 1927 – arising from a Dáil motion on unemployment – of a Committee on Unemployment chaired by Vincent Rice.[88] The Committee, in its final report, recommended a range of short-term measures to increase employment and, in particular, a national housing programme. Although President Cosgrave stated that the government had accepted all the Committee's recommendations and although he personally launched two conferences in 1928 on the proposed housing programme in Dublin and Cork, little appears to have happened as a result of the Committee's work.[89] Subsequently, the government – again arising from a Dáil Motion – agreed to the establishment of an Economic Committee, largely consisting of Oireachtas members. However, having produced two interim reports, divided on party lines, the Committee decided that further meetings 'would not be justified by the results which might be anticipated therefrom'.[90] While figures are again lacking, it does appear that the perception of unemployment as an issue increased in the late 1920s. However, the dramatic rise in unemployment figures which occurred in the United Kingdom was not replicated in Ireland and it has been argued that as late as 1931 the worst effects of the world-wide depression had not been felt in the Free State.[91] Nonetheless there was considerable agitation in relation to the lack of work with unemployment protests being dispersed by the police outside Dáil Éireann in November 1929.[92] Unemployment insurance claims did not increase significantly in this period. In fact, the unemployment insurance system moved into the black with income exceeding outgoings and began to liquidate the debt against the fund which had been built up earlier in the decade. In late 1929, the Department of Industry and Commerce proposed to the Minister, Paddy

88 Mr. Rice had not been re-elected to the Dáil in September 1927. 89 NAI S. 5553E. J.A. Gaughran, *Thomas Johnson* (Kingdom, Dublin, 1980), p. 352. 90 NAI S. 5768B. 91 B. Girvin, *Between Two Worlds: Politics and Economy in Independent Ireland* (Gill and Macmillan, Dublin, 1989), p. 84. 92 Eoin O'Duffy, the Garda Commissioner, subsequently complained that the police tried to persuade the demonstration to disperse when 'force should have been used to clear the streets' and 'it was clearly case for . . . a baton charge. '[P]ersuasion' O'Duffy opined ' . . . is absolutely lost on such people', 8 November 1929, NAI S. 5972.

McGilligan, that legislation be introduced in line with a recommendation of the 1923 United Kingdom Watson Committee to deal with an administrative problem in relation to claims for benefit.[93] Gordon Campbell also proposed that, as it was anticipated that unemployment fund would be solvent in two years, the legislation should allow the Minister to reduce contributions by order should this become appropriate at a later date. Displaying an impressive grasp of the intricacies of the unemployment insurance scheme, McGilligan declared that he had not heard much complaint about the amount of benefit and that he would not be in favour of any change in this area. However, he felt that the tax represented by contributions was excessive and decided to reduce this. This was provided for in the Unemployment Insurance Act, 1930 with a cut of 1*d*. off both employers' and employees' contributions and a cut in the State contribution.

A further issue which arose in this period was a campaign for widows and orphans pensions. This matter had been discussed by the Commission on the Relief of the Poor which had recommended the introduction of mother's pensions payable by the state (i.e. maintenance grants in respect of children under a fixed age to a widowed or deserted mother with inadequate means). A campaign had been run by the Irish 'Mothers Pensions' Society which lobbied throughout the 1920s for the introduction of pensions for necessitous widows and orphans.[94] A Labour motion calling for insurance pensions for widows and orphans in October 1928 was supported by Fianna Fáil.[95] In response Blythe undertook to examine the matter but, perhaps learning the lesson of earlier public inquiries which had not been implemented, this inquiry was to be a departmental matter.[96] After considerable delay, McElliggott requested costing from the British Government Actuary in June 1931.[97] Interestingly, in a rare burst of initiative, Finance requested costings not only on a widows' pension scheme but also on a full old age and widows' contributory scheme along the lines of that introduced in the United Kingdom in 1925. However, nothing had emerged when the government fell in 1932.[98]

Finally, Finance tried to end the decade as it had begun. As we have seen

---

93 NAI EB 114763. Although originally agreed to by McGilligan, this proposal was not proceeded with for reasons which are unclear. 94 NAI F 46/9/25. See J.P. Dunne, *The Meaning and Need of Mother Pensions* (Irish 'Mothers Pensions' Society, Dublin, 1925); *Waiting the Verdict: Pension or Pauperism – Necessitous Widows and Orphans in the Free State* (Irish 'Mothers Pensions' Society, Dublin, 1930). The vice-presidents of the Society included the ubiquitous Sir Joseph Glynn. 95 *Dáil Debates*, vol. XXVI col. 479 *et seq.*, 17 October 1928. 96 *Dáil Debates*, vol. XXVI col. 492 *et seq.*, 17 October 1928. 97 Committee of Inquiry into Widows' and Orphans' Pensions, *Report* (Stationery Office, Dublin, 1934), Appendix E. 98 See *Dáil Debates*, vol. XXXIX col. 1, 10 June 1931.

an Economy Committee, chaired by M.R. Heffernan TD, leader of the
Farmer's Party and Parliamentary Secretary to the Minister for Posts and
Telegraphs, and otherwise consisting solely of civil servants, was established
in 1927.[99] As Fanning points out, the Committee was heavily dominated by
Finance and was intended to investigate public expenditure and to recommend possible reductions. The work of the Committee appears to have
proceeded slowly. Nonetheless, by 1931, it was clear that the economic
depression would lead to a Budget deficit and Finance was, as usual, seeking
cuts from departments. Blythe reported to government in September 1931
that the response had been 'without exception, disappointing and unsatisfactory'. Finance predicted that the position for 1932 would be much more
serious. Given that an increase in taxation of the scale needed to balance the
Budget would be 'disastrous', drastic economies in expenditure were 'not
only possible but justifiable'. Finance recommended a reduction in wages due
to a fall in the cost-of-living and reduced incomes for 'non-producers'. It
particular, it recommended no new public expenditure, the adjustment of
police pay and pensions, teachers pay and pensions, old age pensions,
national health insurance, unemployment insurance and other payments on
the basis of the current cost-of-living, a thorough revision of all other expenditure, and additional taxation to bridge any small remaining deficit.[100] It was
in this context that the Economy Committee finally produced an interim
report to government. The Committee recommended a reduction in the rates
on old age pension in line with the cost-of-living, i.e. a cut of about 20% –
which would give a saving of about £540,000 – and the abolition of 1s. and
2s. pensions.[101] It also recommended reductions in teachers and Garda pay in
line with the drop in the cost-of-living.[102] Heffernan, who had signed the
report without reservation, nonetheless quickly let his colleagues know of his
political reservations. While he agreed 'in theory' with the pension cuts, he
pointed out that the recommendation was based on the assumption that the
pension rate when first introduced was equitable and sufficient. He saw no
sufficient reason why pensioners should be selected for a cut unless at the
same time reductions were made in other social services. He felt that a
pension cut should only take place 'when every other possible source of
retrenchment ha[d] been exhausted' and when no further taxation could be
justified.[103] This time the government showed far less enthusiasm for cuts,

99 *Dáil Debates*, vol. XIX col. 1355–58, 21 April 1927; NAI S. 5450 and see Fanning, *Finance*, pp. 198–201. **100** 'Financial Position', Finance memorandum to government, 9 September 1931, UCDA P24/99; P24/336. **101** This was on the basis that the cost-of-living index for May 1931 was 156 and that, therefore, people should get about 160% of what they got before the War (when the index was 100), i.e. 160% of 5s. **102** NAI S. 5450; UCDA P24/147; P24/333. **103** Heffernan to Blythe, 30 November 1931, NAI E. 121/2/27.

unsurprisingly given that a general election was imminent, and opted to raise taxes instead to reduce the Budget deficit.

PAUPERISING THE OLD

Kelly has suggested that Cumann na nGaedheal tended to blur the distinction between entitlement to state welfare and charitable provision.[104] There is certainly an element of truth in this but Kelly perhaps overstates the case. The essence of social policy is discrimination between one class and other. The key issues are the lines where distinctions are drawn and the reasons why they are drawn in these particular places. In the case of Cumann na nGaedheal, there can be little doubt that leading politicians attempted to 'pauperise' pensioners. The old age pension had been introduced in 1908 largely to take people off the Poor Law.[105] The tests for desert which existed under the original 1908 Act had been removed in the following decade. Nevertheless, the Cumann na nGaedheal government, whose concern about pension spending has already been seen, was clearly convinced that large numbers of pensioners were 'undeserving' and it made this view plain.[106] However, in relation to other classes of claimant, the government was not so quick to claim that large numbers were undeserving. In the case of unemployment, McGilligan did distinguish between unemployment insurance and the dole – but in order to protect the insurance system from the charge of being undeserved (and by implication those in receipt of benefit from the charge of being undeserving). The distinction between deserving and undeserving unemployed, of course, existed at that time. Pigou, for example, in a work which is quite contemporary in many ways in its emphasis on productivity and training, refers to 'the line which separates independent poverty from a shiftless and unworthy pauperism'.[107] But rather than trying to claim that unemployment insurance was a dole and its recipients 'shiftless and unworthy', McGilligan and his Department defended the system. Indeed, the Finance attitude to insurance payments (and

---

104 Kelly 'Social Security in Independent Ireland, 1922–52' (Ph.D. thesis, NUI Maynooth), chapter 3.   105 Carney 'A Case Study in Social Policy – The Non-Contributory Old Age Pension' *Administration* (1985) 33, p. 483.   106 See, for example, Blythe *Dáil Debates*, vol. I, col. 2130, 16 November 1922, *Dáil Debates*, vol. III, col. 1118–9, 18 May 1923; Cosgrave *Dáil Debates*, vol. III, col. 1112, 18 May 1923; Bourke *Dáil Debates* vol. VII, col. 3054–5, 25 June 1924. Displaying a grasp of history equal to that of Padraig Ó hOgain, quoted above, Bourke argued that the disaster arising from the Great Famine was 'mainly as a result of charity continually distributed at the expense of the provident and thrifty, who continually decreased in proportion as the destitute and the dependent increased, and owing to the system of charity and poorhouses and various charity institutions established . . .'.   107 A.C. Pigou, *Unemployment*, Williams & Norgate, London, 1913, p. 34.

by implication beneficiaries) was much more positive than was the case in relation to tax-funded pensions for older people (and indeed than was to be its attitude at many times in the future).[108]

MOTHERS AND FALLEN WOMEN

The various social service schemes established under the United Kingdom had assumed very different roles for men and women and had treated women, particularly married women, primarily as homemakers. It was hardly to be expected that Irish Independence would lead to a dramatic change in this area or to greater equality for women. In fact, in a number of areas Independence led to further inequality and a disimprovement in the treatment of women, something which was broadly accepted by all political parties. In the case of national insurance, the 1925 interim report of the National Health Insurance Committee recommended that women's membership of an approved society should terminate on marriage and they should be compensated by the payment of a marriage grant. Even if a married woman continued to work, she would not qualify for any benefit until she had worked for a further year. This proposal was implemented in the 1929 Act. In the case of the Poor Law, attitudes towards women – and, in particular, different categories of mothers – were strikingly displayed in the report of the Commission on the Relief of the Poor. The Commission divided unmarried mothers into two categories: those who were 'amenable to reform' and 'less hopeful cases'. The first group, referred to as 'first offenders,' required moral upbuilding. However, the 'women who had fallen more than once' should be housed in separate institutions. The Commission was concerned that there was no power to detain unmarried mothers in institutions 'even where it is clearly necessary' for their own protection and recommended that there should be power to retain a person, although this was to be in no sense penal but for the benefit of the woman and her child.[109] In contrast, as we have seen, the Commission took a much more positive view of widows and deserted mothers recommending a mothers' pension and commenting favourably on the United Kingdom widows' contributory pension as having 'many attractive features'. While members of the government may have shared the negative view of unmarried mothers, their views on financial stringency generally prevailed over the

---

108 While it is only speculation, it may well be that Brennan and some of his officials shared the United Kingdom Treasury's relatively positive attitude to social insurance. 109 *Report*, pp. 68–74. It will be recalled that this approach closely mirrored that of the Vice-Regal Commission of 1906.

Commission's recommendations. However, the recommendation for separate institutional accommodation for unmarried mothers was implemented, at least in part. The 1930–31 report of the Department of Local Government and Public Health related that four special institutions for unmarried mothers had already been formed.[110] However, the majority of unmarried mothers remained in general poor law institutions.

The government's discussion of the October 1928 motion calling for a contributory widow's pension shows an interesting combination of their views in relation to widows (generally favourable), public spending (invariably negative) and the use of discrimination (in the neutral sense of the term) to attempt to address the issue. Blythe, for example, argued that '[t]here is, undoubtedly, this to be said in favour of home assistance in a country which is poor, that there can be some measure of discrimination, and if only one could arrange to have that discrimination sympathetically exercised and remove objectionable features . . . we might be able to do a great deal of good . . . .'[111] Mulcahy rejected that charge that pauperism attached to home assistance and argued that '[t]he thing that will relieve the situation is a better way of dealing with widows through home assistance'.[112] In reality, however, as the Commission on Relief of the Poor showed, home assistance was tainted with pauperism and Cumann na nGaedheal's commitment to financial retrenchment meant that this was an integral part of the system. A sympathetically exercised discrimination was, therefore, impossible and there was 'no better way' of treating widows through home assistance.

CONCLUSION

The general assessment of the Cumann na nGaedheal government is that it achieved an impressive feat of statecraft by overseeing the establishment of a stable democratic system in an Independent Ireland.[113] This achievement then sets in context the government's prudent caution in relation to public expenditure or, alternatively, is somewhat tarnished by the government's 'campaign against the weaker elements in the community' (in contrast to its support for income tax cuts and derating of agricultural land).[114] This chapter's analysis of aspects of social policy under Cumann na nGaedheal

110 pp. 129–30. By the mid 1930s, about 500 unmarried mothers were in 'special institutions' administered by or supported by the poor law authorities compared to about 700 in general institutions. See the relevant annual reports of the Department of Local Government and Public Health. 111 *Dáil Debates*, vol. XXVI co. 497, 17 October 1928. 112 Ibid. col. 1883, 1888, 17 October 1928. 113 For example, J. Lee, *Ireland 1912–1985: Politics and Society* (Cambridge University Press, Cambridge, 1989), pp. 171–4. 114 Lee, *Ireland*, pp. 124–7.

does not call into question the facts underlying these assessments. However, it can throw some light on the politics of those involved.

It has, for example, been suggested that Cumann na nGaedheal were increasingly moving towards a relaxation of its free trade policy and that the 1930s would, even without a change in government, have seen a shift to protectionism.[115] Equally, Lee has criticised Cosgrave for his 'shift to the right' and for failing to seek Labour support.[116] While Lee is undoubtedly correct from a party political point of view, this study questions whether such a re-alignment was in the realms of practical politics. Whatever about free trade, there is no indication that Cumann na nGaedheal was changing its views on 'social welfare' policies in the early 1930s. The only change which appears is a recognition of the political unattractiveness of the 1924 pension cuts and a reluctance to proceed with the 1930s cuts proposed by Finance rather than any policy disagreement with them. The personal views of key Cumann na nGaedheal figures are plain. McGilligan's 'people may die' comment, Bourke's attribution of the famine to excessive charity, O'Duffy's apology for the use of insufficient force by the police, and Cosgrave and Blythe's attacks on pensioners were characteristic of their views and not unrepresentative comments. Most, if not all, these key figures were 'souls without remorse', at least insofar as remorse implied public policy measures to improve the position of the poor.[117] Given that Labour's key policies – other than support for a democratic polity – revolved around increased public expenditure on social policy measures, the wonder is not that Cumann na nGaedheal failed to coalesce with Labour but that Labour for so long supported (and indeed offered to coalesce with) Cumann na nGaedheal. It is a comment on the political instability of the times, Labour's commitment to parliamentary democracy, the absence of any real social policy alternative from Sinn Féin and Fianna Fáil in its early years and, perhaps, the fundamental conservatism of many of the key Labour figures that a Labour/Cumann na nGaedheal pact was even conceivable. More favourably for the future of welfare policy, however, key civil servants were committed to an expansion of existing services. The incoming Fianna Fáil government was to provide the political support for this approach.

---

115 Ó Gráda, *Ireland: An Economic History 1780–1939* (Oxford University Press, Oxford, 1994), p. 387; M. Daly, *Industrial Development and Irish National Identity* (Syracuse University Press, Syracuse, 1992), pp. 47–57. In contrast Girvin emphasises the redirection of policy under Fianna Fáil, *Between Two Worlds*, pp. 88–90. 116 Lee, *Ireland 1912–1985*, p. 171. 117 This is, of course, a comment on their public policy values not an assessment of their personal merits.

3

Fianna Fáil in government, 1932–38

[D]uring my whole time in struggling for the freedom of this country I had only one object and that was to get free so as to be able to order our life for the benefit of our own people. I never regarded freedom as an end in itself, but if I were asked what state-ment of Irish policy was most in accord with my views as to what human beings would struggle for, I would stand side by side with James Connolly.[1]

In the best, and in the original sense of that so often misused and misapplied word, we have been conservative. We have conserved every good thing which was passed on to us, and by prudent management and careful foresight have increased the national estate; so that to-day our little community is stronger in will, stouter in heart, more confident of its future, than it was this time five years ago.[2]

In the election campaign held in early 1932 Fianna Fáil concentrated heavily on social policy and economic issues as well as the more traditional national questions. Fianna Fáil criticised the government for its performance on unemployment, promised to direct economic affairs so as to create 85,000 extra jobs in industry (including the introduction of protection) and to build up a prosperous, self-reliant and self-supporting nation. It also gave specific commitments to amend the Old Age Pension Acts in accordance with the 1929 bill and to introduce pensions for necessitous widows and orphans.[3] The Fianna Fáil message was not, however, one of increased public expenditure. Instead it promised to reduce taxes by not less than £2 million per year and to effect substantial economies in expenditure without reducing the social

---

1 Eamon de Valera *Dáil Debates*, vol. XLI col. 906, 29 April 1932.   2 Seán MacEntee *Dáil Debates*, vol. LXVI col. 781, 14 April 1937.   3 *Irish Press*, 5, 11 February 1932.

services. The campaign featured a striking level of business support for Fianna Fáil with the National Agricultural and Industrial Association running a series of major ads promoting a 'buy Irish' solution to unemployment – a line implicitly supportive of Fianna Fáil's approach.[4] The Labour party also featured social issues promising to introduce widows and orphans pensions and pointing out that 'owing to there being a strong Labour party' in the House of Commons, widows pensions had been introduced in the UK in 1926.[5] Cumann na nGaedheal, in contrast, stood on its record, ran a virulent campaign against the 'communists' and 'gunmen' who were voting for Fianna Fáil and made few if any social commitments. The election returns made Fianna Fáil by far the largest part with 48% of the seats and it took office as a minority government with the support of Labour. The new government took office on 9 March 1932 with de Valera appointing Seán MacEntee as Minister for Finance, Seán Lemass as Minister for Industry and Commerce and the veteran Seán T. Ó Ceallaigh as Minister for Local Government and Public Health with Conn Ward as his Parliamentary Secretary.[6]

In what the *Irish Press* described as a 'sensational step' de Valera dissolved the Dáil in early January 1933 and sought a majority government.[7] His decision to call a snap vote pre-empted the *Irish Times'* hope that 'a solid and united National Party' would soon take the field in time for what it had predicted would be an early election.[8] Despite the snap decision, relations appear to have remained reasonably cordial with the Labour party with Fianna Fáil calling for second preference votes for Labour.[9] Fianna Fáil focused on the farming and working vote promising to half the land annuities payable by farmers and to abolish unemployment. Cosgrave responded by announcing that Cumann na nGaedheal would also half land annuities only for Fianna Fáil to gloat that it was 'Right All the Time'.[10] Fianna Fáil's bid for a majority was successful winning an absolute majority with 51% of the seats. The same ministerial team was re-appointed. Fianna Fáil took immediate action to implement its election commitments in the social policy area. In its first two years in office, it introduced reforms of the old age pension, established a new unemployment assistance scheme, unified national health

4 *Irish Press*, 16, 23, 30 January 1932; *Irish Times*, 16, 19, 23, 30 January 1932. See also the similar theme in the City of Dublin Assurance ad which asked 'Can Ireland afford this continuous drain of £5 million per year?' referring to expenditure on British insurance policies, *Irish Press*, 6 February 1932. 5 *Irish Press*, 12 February 1932 – a dubious interpretations of events given that the 1923 Labour government had failed to introduce such pensions and that the 1925 Act was very much a Conservative initiative. See Macnicol, *The Politics of Retirement in Britain, 1878–1948*, chapter 9. 6 On Ward, see Barrington, *Health. Medicine and Politics*, pp. 115–16. 7 *Irish Press*, 3 January 1933. 8 *Irish Times*, 2 January 1933. 9 *Irish Press*, 24 January 1933. 10 Ibid. 6, 10, 13, 14 January 1933.

insurance, passed a Workmen's Compensation Act and established a committee to report on widows pensions. In 1935 it introduced a widows and orphans pensions scheme which came into operation in 1936. In addition, it adopted a range of measures in relation to public housing, health and land distribution.

OLD AGE PENSIONS

Within a month of taking office in March 1932, Conn Ward submitted proposals to government to reform the old age pension legislation broadly in line with his 1929 bill.[11] Ward proposed a number of changes, in addition to the amendments already proposed in the 1929 bill, including the restoration of the rate of the pension to its pre-1924 position and the relaxation of the qualification conditions for blind pensions. De Valera had the proposals circulated to Ministers noting that they were the subject of discussions between Local Government and Finance but anticipating that agreement would be reached in time for the measure to be considered at the government meeting on 19 April. Finance were clearly taken by surprise by this – for one thing, pension legislation has traditionally come from Finance not Local Government – and had little opportunity to resist the proposals.[12] MacEntee estimated the cost of the proposals at an additional £900,000 per annum and stated that he could not see any possibility of finding this sum in 1932. In the circumstances, Finance suggested plenty of time should be given to consider the proposals in all their bearings. However, this was forlorn hope and on 19 April, the Executive Council authorised the introduction of the legislation. On the same day a conference was held between MacEntee and Ward to discuss the details of the proposal. Finance did subsequently succeed in altering some of the details of the proposals and for reasons which are unclear the proposal to restore the 10s. pension to its pre-1924 status was not proceeded with. The bill was approved by the Executive Council in May 1932 by which time the Revenue Commissioners had produced a more realistic estimate of the cost at an additional £367,500 per annum. The bill was introduced in the Dáil by Ward (not MacEntee) later that month and passed in August 1932. The Act involved a number of significant changes including the dropping of the benefit and privilege clause for pensions and the poor law disqualification. Previously, people entering a poor law institution were disqualified for pension. In a sharp contrast to the comments of Cumann na nGaedheal ministers, Ward argued that if old people 'after 70 years of

11 NAI S. 5958.   12 Codling to McCarron, 14 April 1932, NAI S. 84/8/32.

hardship, 70 years of service to the country . . . have to enter a poor law institution, it appears to me they should be enabled to enter that institution, not as paupers, but as independent citizens'. He went on to argue that 'there is no justification and cannot be any justification for labelling these poor old people as paupers, simply because they are destitute and have no one to look after them'.[13] The Act led to a significant increase in pension expenditure from £2.7 million in 1932 to £3.3 million in 1934 with an extra 17,500 people qualifying for pension. The proportion of persons over 70 entitled to a pension increased dramatically from under two-thirds in 1932 to three-quarters by 1935 – reversing the 1920s cuts.

One of the issues addressed in the Act was the transfer of land by older farmers. Under the 1908 legislation, property, including a farm, disposed of in order to qualify for a pension was taken into account as means. In general, a farm transferred to a child on marriage would be viewed as a bona fide transfer and would not affect pension rights but most other transfers were construed as being to qualify for pension. The 1924 Act had allowed small farmers to transfer land without this being assessed as means. However, difficulties had arisen in relation to transfers of property over that amount. The 1932 Act repealed the 1924 changes with a view to encouraging land transfers to younger farmers.[14] However, Ward's views as to what the legislation should allow went far beyond Finance's interpretation of the law. Ward issued a letter to pension committees stating that due weight should be given to evidence showing that a farm transfer was made bona fide for the better working of the farm or for a family settlement and instructed the appeals officers in his department along the same lines. Finance, in contrast, believed that marriage settlements were the only class of transfer which should be deemed bona fide and that a presumption should exist in all other cases of transfer by an elderly farmer that the transfer was made in order to qualify for pension. An interdepartmental conference in December 1932 failed to resolve the issue and Ward added fuel to the fire during the 1933 election campaign, by claiming that the 1908 provisions were retained solely to prevent fraudulent advantage being taken of the 1932 Act and not to prevent transfer of land by older farmers. He claimed that hundreds of pensions were being awarded weekly at a cost of an extra £500,000.[15] Finance, concerned at the additional cost involved, complained about Ward's approach to the Executive Council in June 1933.[16] Eventually a cabinet committee was appointed to report on the issue. The committee's report broadly favoured the Finance position and the OAP vote was reduced by £100,000 to come from savings from a review of existing claims.

---

13 *Dáil Debates*, vol. XLI, col. 2525–6 25 May 1932.   14 *Dáil Debates*, vol. XLI, col. 2527–30 25 May 1932   15 *Irish Independent*, 13 January 1933.   16 NAI S. 6440.

UNEMPLOYMENT

In the area of unemployment, one of the first debates in the new Dáil arose from a motion from Labour Deputy Dan Morrissey proposing that work or maintenance be provided to meet the immediate needs of the unemployed.[17] Lemass argued that unemployment could not be taken in isolation and that the essential steps necessary to solve unemployment included the removal of the Oath, so as to secure political stability, and the retention of Land Annuities.[18] However, the government accepted the principle of the motion. One of the first steps taken by the Fianna Fáil government in its first Budget in May 1932 was to announce funding of over £2m for unemployment relief works.[19] At the same time compulsory notification was required of jobs subsidised by public funds to the employment exchanges and branch employment offices.[20] Local officers of the Department of Industry and Commerce were given the job of filing these vacancies. While intended to ensure that the registered unemployed got jobs, its effect was to ensure that jobseekers had to register as unemployed. The measure led to a trebling in the number of vacancies notified. But it also led to a massive increase in the numbers on the Live Register from 32,000 in April 1932 to over 100,000 by the end of that year. If nothing else, the measure disclosed the extent of unemployment and underemployment in Ireland and highlighted the need for immediate measures to respond to this issue.

In November 1932, Lemass submitted a memo to de Valera outlining his views on the economic situation and the need for drastic remedies to address the position.[21] Lemass argued that the fullest possible industrial development could not employ 100,000 unemployed without an export market. Accordingly, he proposed the creation of a Ministry of Public Works, free of Finance control, to ensure the employment of all unemployed in public works pending their absorption into industry. It is not clear how serious Lemass was in this proposal since he went on to say that he could not see any alternative to this approach unless Ireland negotiated a trade treaty with Britain.[22] The proposal may perhaps better be seen as a criticism of the Economic War than as a serious proposal for massive public works. Supporting the view that the public works proposals were either not meant seriously or not expected to succeed, only a week later Lemass submitted a

---

17 *Dáil Debates*, vol. XLI col. 279 *et seq.* 20 April 1932.   18 Ibid. col. 284.   19 *Dáil Debates*, vol. XLI col. 1499–50, 1512–4, 11 May 1932.   20 Department of Industry and Commerce, *The Trend of Employment and Unemployment in the Saorstat* (Stationery Office, Dublin, 1935), p. 13.   21 On NAI F. 200/25/37.   22 Certainly Professor John Busteed, to whom MacEntee sent the proposals for comment, did not take them seriously, UCDA P67/102.

further memo to de Valera.[23] He recalled that they had 'frequently discussed the steps which must be taken to provide for the unemployed and [had], more or less, accepted responsibility for giving effect to the principle of 'work or maintenance' insofar as it may be practicable to do so'. Lemass now argued that the establishment of large-scale public works would take a considerable time and could not deal with the great numbers of unemployed. In the meantime the unemployed were dependent on home assistance and charity which was altogether inadequate. Lemass proposed, firstly, that landlords should not be allowed to evict unemployed tenants for non-payment of rent and, more importantly, the establishment of a system of unemployment assistance somewhat on the lines of that recently recommended by the British Royal Commission on Unemployment Insurance.[24] Lemass proposed that every unemployed person over 18 not in receipt of unemployment insurance who satisfied a means test should receive a weekly payment varying from 10s. per week in urban areas to 7s. in rural areas with additional payments for dependants. This payment would only be payable to persons capable of work and genuinely seeking it. He estimated that about 40,000 would qualify at a cost of about £1,150,000 per annum to be met by an increase in insurance contributions (£250,000), rates on county councils (£575,000) and the Exchequer (£325,000). He proposed the establishment of a committee from the relevant departments to 'hammer out the details'.

MacEntee sought the views of his Department on both proposals. McElligott strongly opposed any increase in public works and felt that the only option was a treaty with Britain. McEligott argued that rather than public works being increased, there should be a dramatic reduction. These required the state to provide work whereas the furthest it ought to go was to provide maintenance, they achieved little relief in unemployment, involved heavy local indebtedness, created useless or objectionable works, rendered it extremely difficult for Finance to control expenditure and diverted the energies of departments from their proper tasks.[25] He argued that '[i]t cannot be denied that it is cheaper to maintain somebody out of work than to maintain

23 NAI S. 6242A. **24** Royal Commission on Unemployment Insurance, *Report* (HMSO, London, 1931). In fact, although the Royal Commission had proposed a scheme of unemployment assistance this was more a modified form of poor relief without any set scale of means or benefits quite unlike the detail of Lemass' proposals. **25** NAI F. 200/25/37. As with the UK Treasury, the Finance opposition to public works was based both on economic theory and the perceived administrative difficulties caused by such expenditure. See G.C. Peden 'The "Treasury View" on Public Works and Employment in the Interwar Period', *Economic History Review* (1984) 38, pp. 167–81; R. Middleton 'The Treasury in the 1930s: Political and Administrative Constraints to the Acceptance of the "New" Economics', *Oxford Economic Papers* (1982) 34, pp. 49–77.

him in work when the work itself has no ultimate economic value'.[26] However, he objected to the unemployment assistance proposal because of the increase in rates and the change in the machinery, arguing that the new machinery proposed was 'likely to be out of touch with the traditional methods' – the latter view Lemass would, no doubt, have shared. The assistance proposal was discussed at a meeting of an Executive Council committee on the economic situation on 18 November (which most ministers attended). The meeting felt it would be inadvisable to carry out the proposals on rent but agreed to appoint a committee chaired by Finance and including Industry and Commerce and Local Government to examine the unemployment assistance proposal and to prepare a detailed scheme for putting this into effect, or if it was considered impracticable to devise an alternative scheme. This was approved by the full Council on 22 November and a committee chaired by J.L. Lynd of Finance and including J.J. Keane, chief employment officer of the Department of Industry and Commerce, was established.

The Committee reported in March 1933.[27] It presented an overview of the options for dealing with unemployment. The Committee argued that relief though the home assistance scheme was not satisfactory and that the taint of pauperism deterred many in genuine distress. It also took the view that putting the burden on local authorities was not prudent as their capacity to bear it was inversely related to the level of unemployment. Unemployment insurance was also dismissed as unable to meet the level and duration of unemployment facing the country. The Committee was unenthusiastic about relief work which, it argued, was often non-productive and non-commercial and which was of little psychological value to the unemployed. In contrast, cash assistance could be given where and when needed, could reach all classes and could give a greater amount of relief at a lower cost. Accordingly the Committee came down quickly in favour of the complete abandonment of relief works and, if the government was satisfied of the necessity for some scheme for the relief of distress caused by unemployment, for its replacement by a system along the lines recommended by Lemass. However, echoing the inconsistency which was to recur in this area over the 1930s, the Committee went on to say that work was preferable to maintenance and that assistance should be given to relief works, not exceeding the saving of maintenance, provided that the work would not be undertaken otherwise. It recommended that the Department of Industry and Commerce should

26 Echoing the views of the UK Ministry of Labour at the same time which wrote 'unemployment pay is the only way of maintaining a big proportion of the unemployed while the registers are so large. And it is far cheaper than any other system'. Quoted in F.M. Miller 'National Assistance or Unemployment Assistance' *Journal of Contemporary History* (1974) 9, p. 167. 27 NAI S. 84/38/33.

administer the new scheme which was to apply to all able-bodied persons of 18 and over who were unemployed, available for and genuinely seeking work. The Committee supported the principle that 'members of a family should look to each other for mutual support'. However a family means test would be difficult to administer and so it recommended that assistance not be granted to any person being maintained by their family or who would normally be so maintained. The Committee recommended rates varying from 7s. 6d. in towns to 6s. in rural areas with additions for dependants. Given its very rough estimate of those qualifying at 50,000 this gave an estimated cost of £1.4 million to be funded from an increase in unemployment insurance contributions, a reduction in the agricultural grant, and a special rate in urban areas, with the Exchequer meeting the balance.

Lemass immediately reported to the Executive Council that he was preparing the heads of a bill. UA would be payable to all unemployed people but excluding persons under 18 and over 70, persons on unemployment insurance, people maintained by their families or who would ordinarily be maintained by them and, for a period of six months, persons who refused suitable employment, voluntarily left employment or lost employment though misconduct. Lemass now felt that the Committee overestimated the numbers who would qualify which he felt would be 35,000. Given this reduction he proposed to increase the rate of assistance to between 7s. 6d. and 10s. (rural/urban) giving a total cost of £1.2 million. In MacEntee's absence, the Executive Council broadly approved this proposal in June 1933 but substituted three different rates of assistance ranging from 6s. 6d. in rural areas to 10s. in urban areas with an intermediate level for medium sized towns. Lower rates were also provided for single women and widows. It was decided that the scheme be administered by Industry and Commerce through the same machinery as unemployment insurance with the cost being shared by the state and a special rate on county boroughs and large towns. Lemass personally drafted heads of the bill which were then revised by J.J. Keane. Many of the key parameters were now settled and much of the remaining work was a matter of detailed administration. However, a number of key points were decided in the course of drafting the bill.[28] One key issue was the treatment of small farmers. Keane argued that there was 'a danger that as soon as unemployment assistance becomes available everybody who has or thinks he has a semblance of a claim will endeavour to obtain the money'. Keane proposed a number of alternative approaches: firstly, small farmers could be allowed to claim UA only in periods prescribed by the Minister, an approach which Keane rightly predicted would 'give rise to all kinds of controversy'.

28 NAI EB 144057.

Alternatively, unemployment could be defined in such a way as exclude all landholders on the basis that they were continuously following the occupation of farmer. A further possibility could be based on the valuation of the farm. However, Lemass opted for the first alternative which eventually became the option of allowing small farmers to claim UA unless excluded by a ministerial Employment Period Order (see below).

While the scheme on its face applied to all, subsequent clauses effectively excluded the vast bulk of women. While there is surprisingly little discussion of this issue, it appears to have been a shared assumption that married women should not qualify and they were specifically excluded in Keane's earliest draft of the legislation. In the case of married women, the assumption was that the normal state of affairs was that they were dependent on their husbands. Where the husband was unemployed he could claim an increase in UA in respect of a dependant wife. Ultimately it was decided that a married woman could only qualify for UA if she could show that her husband was dependant on her or that she was not dependant on her husband and had dependants. Single women (spinsters) and widows could only qualify if they had dependants or if they had been insured for at least one year in the four years prior to the claim. Lemass had originally intended to exclude all single women without dependants. As he put it 'the particular difficulty which necessitated the deletion of provision for single women without dependants [was] the absence of employment for such women outside certain very easily defined centres'.[29] And the government, Lemass unashamedly admitted was 'not anxious that [employment] should be specially made available to them, say, at the expense of adult male labour'. To include single women would increase the cost by an estimated 50%. However, in response to concerns raised by William Norton, Lemass subsequently brought forward an amendment at committee stage to include single women with a previous record of insurable employment.

Industry and Commerce moved quickly and a final draft of the heads of the bill was submitted to the Executive Council in September 1933.[30] The costs had now escalated to £1.9 million and Industry and Commerce proposed that this be met by £250,000 from the Unemployment Insurance Fund, reduction of £700,00 in the agricultural grant, special rates of £190,000 with the state meeting the balance of £800,000.[31] Predictably Local Government and Agriculture opposed such a large reduction in the agricultural grant while Finance argued that the state contribution was excessive

---

29 *Dáil Debates*, vol. LXIV col. 1772, 27 September 1933.   **30** The bill had already been introduced in the Dáil on 8 August 1933.   **31** NAI S. 6242B. The increase in cost arose largely from the change in rates which brought the average estimated payment up from 10s. to 13s. 3d.

and called for a drastic overhauling of the proposal to reduce the cost to £1 million.[32] However, exposing its lack of familiarity with the issues, Finance did not identify a number of key issues such as likely heavy claiming by small farmers. Given the strong opposition a Cabinet Committee was appointed to consider the bill including Lemass, MacEntee, Jim Ryan (Minister for Agriculture) and Ó Ceallaigh and on 18 September the Executive Council agreed the bill subject to further reductions in rates to a range of from 6s. to 9s. and changes in the means test. The bill was discussed in the Dáil later in September. Lemass still argued that the number of persons who would qualify for UA would be less than 40,000 on average for the year.[33] The recently formed Fine Gael party criticised the reliance on a 'dole policy' with Paddy McGilligan arguing that 'the idea of work has now been given up and we are back on maintenance'.[34] However, Labour strongly welcomed the bill. The bill allowed the authorities to require a person in receipt of UA to attend a course of instruction. Lemass described this as a 'merely a pious hope' at present but one which he hoped 'to translate into reality at some later stage'.[35] It was, however, to remain no more than a pious hope for many years.

The legislation came into effect in April 1934. However, Lemass' estimate of the numbers who would claim UA turned out to be widely optimistic. By the end of December 1934 there were almost 100,000 applicants for UA on the Live Register and this rose even further in early 1935. In response to the significantly greater level of claims and the consequent overrun in costs, a number of different initiatives were considered. These revolved around three poles

i) reducing entitlements – Lemass resisted proposals to cut the rate of UA but, as we will see, altered the means disregard in the 1935 Act.
ii) encouraging people to work by (a) disqualifying them under the Employment Period Orders (EPOs) and (b) taking a more pro-active approach to employment functions.
iii) providing alternative (public) work.

Reducing entitlements
In February 1935, in view of the serious cost overrun, McElligott wrote to John Leydon, secretary of Industry and Commerce, outlining Finance concerns about the additional costs.[36] He proposed that the rates of UA be

32 NAI EB 144057. **33** *Dáil Debates*, vol. LXIV col. 1663, 27 September 1933. This despite the fact that a committee including Keane and Roy Geary now estimated that 54,000 would be a more likely figure, NAI. S. 84/38/33. **34** Ibid. 1670–1. **35** Ibid. 1658. **36** NAI EB 172477.

reduced, the minimum means limit be reduced and the rural classes be excluded. However, Industry and Commerce were not prepared to reduce the rates of payment. These were, Keane argued, already too low, pointing out that the Labour party had sought an increase. Leydon agreed but was prepared to accept a change in the means test and the making of an Employment Protection Order excluding some farmers. In March 1935, having failed to secure agreement to the proposals, MacEntee brought the matter before the Executive Council. He argued that the overrun in costs had been largely due to the fact that the number of recipients in rural areas, mainly farmers and their sons and farm labourers, was much greater than anticipated.[37] It was agreed to make an EPO and Lemass was asked to submit proposals to alter the means disregard. Ultimately this proposal was proceeded with in the 1935 Unemployment Assistance (Amendment) Act. While Lemass made a valiant effort to portray the bill as a measure involving both additional spending and savings, William Norton eventually wrung out of him the fact that the key provision was the change in the means test which was expected to save £180,000 per year.[38] Despite all these efforts, costs in 1935 continued to overshoot the estimates but Industry and Commerce persevered in resisting Finance proposals to reduce the rates of UA.

Genuinely seeking work
It is clear that the process of bringing UA into operation and ensuring that claims were processed and put into payment affected the extent to which local offices could ensure that claimants were genuinely seeking work or assist them in finding work. However, in October 1932, the guidelines issued by Industry and Commerce went beyond any temporary administrative measure and discouraged local staff from stringent application of the work test.[39] The guidelines instructed that with the exception of certain well known classes 'unemployed persons generally are only too anxious to obtain work and that they are genuinely seeking it insofar as it possible to do so'. The contrary view should not be taken unless there was clear evidence that there was work available of which the applicant should be aware and which he had made no effort to obtain. This was especially true in the case of small farmers who could not be expected 'to abandon their farms and travel in an indefinite search for work' and workers in country districts where there was little work. It addition, the guidelines discouraged submission of cases for rejection to the chief employment officer (Keane) thereby encouraging local staff to grant border-

37 1 March 1935, NAI S. 84/38/33. 38 *Dáil Debates*, vol. LVIII, col. 1163–1180, 23 July 1935. 39 Assistance Circular 2/5, NAI EB 160720.

line claims. Only 'wasters', applicants of the itinerant class, and hawkers and peddlers should be carefully tested.[40]

Lemass' views on this were dramatically different. In November 1934 he told Leydon that he received many complaints about the administration of UA, particularly in rural areas, from 'responsible persons'.[41] He has been told that assistance was being granted to people who never worked and who had no intention of working, to people incapable of work, to people who refused work, and to people already working. He suggested that instructions be issued that people who were not genuinely seeking work, who were incapable of work or who refused work should have their UA stopped and that notification of vacancies by employers be used to test their bona fides. Industry and Commerce officials were less sanguine about the possibilities for tightening up administration pointing out that they were dependent on the co-operation of employers in providing information and that the work test could not be applied unless work existed.[42] Leydon broadly agreed but suggested that local offices be reminded of the importance of the genuinely seeking work rule, that employers be asked to co-operate and prosecutions be initiated against fraud cases. Lemass agreed and a circular was issued to local offices in January 1935.[43] This pointed out that the primary function of local offices was to place workpeople in employment. This important work had been lost sight of due to pressure of other work and local employers should now be reminded of the role of local offices in this area. Every vacancy notified should be used to test the fulfilment of the qualification conditions for UA and an intensive canvassing campaign should be run with employers both to seek vacancies and their general co-operation. 100,000 letters to employers were printed and 300,000 cards for notification of vacancies. The files do not indicate the outcome of this initiative. However, in 1941 Stores section pointed out that there had been little or no demand for either item since 1935 and asked whether remaining stocks could be disposed of. Employment Branch stated that these were intended to form part of a drive in 1935 and that 'it was not intended to make the procedure permanent'.[44]

Employment period orders
No EPO had been made in 1934 but in view of the dramatic rise in UA claimants, orders were made in 1935 prohibiting farmers with a rateable valuation over £4 from claiming UA from mid April to the end of September

---

40 The context suggests that the term 'itinerant class' is used to refer to all those who travel around in search of work rather than being specifically aimed at any ethnic group. **41** Lemass to Leydon, 7 November 1934, NAI EB 162851. **42** Note by Mr. Duffy, 4 January 1935 ibid. **43** RTT Circular 40/56 Registration and Placing of WorkPeople in Employment, ibid. **44** File note 19 May 1941, ibid.

and similarly disqualifying single men without dependants in rural areas from mid July to the end of September.[45] This was the period during which such men could be expected to have or find farm work. It is estimated that the first order disqualified about 6,600 people while the second affected 47,000, producing savings of £125,000.[46] Given the limited negative response to the EPOs and the fact that there had been no large increase in demands for home assistance, the Departments of Agriculture and Industry and Commerce proposed, in January 1936, to extend the period of the EPOs to March to September and the Executive Council accepted this for farmers while retaining a second EPO for single men operating from June. These EPOs continued in effect unchanged up to 1938.

Public works

The discussion on unemployment assistance had shown that while most senior figures – political and administrative – would have preferred to address unemployment by providing work, there was an almost universal view that public works were expensive and ineffective. While several key Fianna Fáil Ministers tended to refer to public works in reasonably positive terms, their private views were often considerably more negative.[47] However, the dramatic rise in recorded unemployment led to a further detailed consideration of the public works option. This was advocated, in particular, by Hugo Flinn, Parliamentary Secretary to the Minister for Finance, and one of the few senior figures who believed that public works could have a real role to play. In January 1934 the Executive Council appointed a committee of Ó Ceallaigh, Lemass, Ryan and Flinn to consider and report on schemes of public works which had been submitted by departments.[48] Subsequently in April, MacEntee, coinciding with a Dáil motion proposed by the Labour party calling for large-scale public works, proposed the establishment of an Interdepartmental Committee on Public Works. This committee was established in July 1934, chaired by Flinn, to consider the extent to which it was practicable to devise a scheme of 'useful and desirable' public works to be carried out over the next four years with a view to reducing expenditure on UA to a minimum. The Committee was in total to produce five reports in 1935 and 1936 and while these led to some increase in the level of public works, they failed to convince policy makers of the viability of a major

45 NAI S. 9537A.   46 NAI. EB 172477.   47 For example, in the May 1934 Budget speech, MacEntee stated that the aim of government policy was to provide work for the workless, *Dáil Debates*, vol. LII col. 635, May 1934; while in a contemporaneous debate Lemass stated that public works were the second line of defence against unemployment, behind industrial development but before assistance, *Dáil Debates*, vol. LI col. 2553, 27 April 1934.   48 NAI S. 6524.

programme of works and the money invested was significantly less than that proposed by the Committee.[49] MacEntee was later to describe the results of the Committee's work as 'very disappointing'.[50]

The first report in January 1935 focussed on possible measures in the coming financial year.[51] It recommended significant extra investment in a programme of public works, that those to be employed should be on UA, and that priority should be given to those on the highest rates of UA and the longest on the payment. However, of crucial relevance to the response its recommendations was to receive, it also found that to reduce spending on UA by £1 would require expenditure on public works of £4–5 of public money.[52] The Committee's proposals were submitted to the Executive Council in April 1935. However, MacEntee emphasised the additional costs involved arguing that 'any ambitious programme of public works seems, therefore, clearly a wasteful method of obtaining its objective'.[53] Joseph Connolly, Minister for Lands, supported MacEntee cautioning that US experience in the New Deal should act 'as a warning' as US Federal funding was, he argued, simply used by local bodies for work which would have been carried out anyway.[54] In August 1935, the matter was again considered by the Executive Council. MacEntee argued that the terms of reference of the committee were too restricted as they were confined to useful and desirable public works. In fact, the type of work which would maximise the use of unemployed men would be unlikely to be either useful or, in an economic sense, desirable. MacEntee was prepared to fund an experimental scheme of road works recommended by the Office of Public Works (OPW). One of the main objects of this would be 'to improve the moral of the unemployed' and the economic value of the work had not been the primary consideration. MacEntee appears to have

49 The first three reports are discussed below. See also NAI S. 9412 for the fourth interim report which relates to a farm improvement scheme and the brief final report which contains a useful index to the reports. See M. Daly, *Buffer State,* pp. 187–96. **50** Report of meeting with ITUC, 31 January 1940, NAI S. 11644. **51** NAI S. 8786. **52** The reports of the Committee, despite the membership from September 1934 of Professor T.A. Smiddy, are striking for their general avoidance of any discussion of the economic effects of public works. Discussion of such Keynsian concepts as the multiplier effect is nowhere to be found. They are in sharp contrast to the reports of the UK Economic Advisory Committee on related issues. See S. Howson and D. Winch, *The Economic Advisory Council 1930–1939* (Cambridge University Press, Cambridge, 1977). **53** Finance memo to the Executive Council, 15 April 1935, NAI S. 8786. Despite MacEntee's well-deserved reputation as a prickly customer, he appears to have established a good relationship with his Parliamentary Secretaries and to have given them considerable scope. The 'public works' episode suggest that MacEntee, despite reservations, toyed with the idea of public works and allowed Flinn to explore it before eventually deciding that the McElligott line was the correct one. **54** Connolly had visited the USA in 1933 and was supportive of the New Deal in an American context, see J. A. Gaughan (ed.), *Memoirs of Senator Joseph Connolly* (Irish Academic Press, Dublin, 1996).

been caught in two minds on the issue and while prepared to fund a pilot scheme he estimated the cost of a more general scheme at approaching £1 million and, given the negligible economic value, wondered whether the State could afford to spend that amount 'or even a smaller sum mainly for the purpose of improving the moral of the unemployed'.

A key issue was whether it was possible to 'rotate' workers in order to maximise savings on UA and decisions were postponed pending a second report of the Committee on 'rotational employment'. This was received in January 1936.[55] Flinn and the OPW pushed strongly for a rotational approach whereby men would be employed for part of the week, receiving somewhat more than their week's entitlement to UA, and be disqualified for UA for the entire week. Other departments were unconvinced by this approach. In particular, Industry and Commerce argued that this approach would lead to casualisation and also that it was unfair to deny workmen their right to UA. Their opposition was such that the departmental representative, William Maguire, refused to sign the report. The Committee's second report highlighted the fact that public works did not provide a solution to unemployment, that no scheme could be devised which would not include a high percentage of work of little or no economic value, and that UA spending could not be reduced without an overall increase in expenditure and taxation which might have a serious adverse effect on industry and agriculture and, in the long run, intensify the unemployment problem. Nonetheless the Committee went on to examine and recommend a rotational approach to employment schemes.

In April, the Committee delivered its third report.[56] It concluded, somewhat in contradiction of its earlier comments, that it had found it practicable to devise a scheme of useful and desirable public works which would appreciably reduce expenditure on UA. Their proposals consisted mainly of an intensification of expenditure on standard departmental services with the work being co-ordinated by the OPW. The Committee recommended that these additional costs be borne partially by savings on UA (estimated at between £1.5 and £4.5 million depending on the degree of rotation involved) and partially by ad hoc taxation. However, as the necessary funds could not wholly be obtained by taxation, advice should be sought on the possibility of raising a public loan. As part of its investigation, the Committee carried out an unemployment enquiry. They found that the numbers of skilled workers on UA were so small that it would be difficult to provide skilled work.[57] Accordingly the public works had to focus on unskilled labouring work.

---

55 NAI S. 8775.   56 NAI S. 8787.   57 Over two-thirds of those on UA were classified as general, agricultural or road labourers with a further 7% classified as 'other' or 'not stated'.

Responding to this report, MacEntee reminded the Executive Council of the negative conclusions of the second report on public works (outlined above).[58] MacEntee regarded these points as being of paramount importance. Later that month Finance submitted a further memorandum on public works, this time discussing the economic justification – or lack thereof – for this approach. Finance took an orthodox line on the issue and the publication of Keynes' *General Theory* two months earlier made little, if any, impact on the arguments. Finance argued that the first consideration was the extent to which public works, by increasing the purchasing power of the community, would create demand and bring about an improvement in the condition of the nation. However, if public works were funded from taxation, the amount involved was simply withdrawn from the community and the overall position was not improved. As for borrowing capital, it was argued that capital was scarce in Ireland and a loan for the purpose of public works might interfere with efforts to secure capital for future development. As for its effects on unemployment, Finance argued that it was 'extremely doubtful if on grounds of moral and physical fitness the public works system [had] any great advantage over a system of doles'. And it costed £150 per annum to keep a man employed as against £26 on UA. In an overwhelmingly negative review, Finance argued that public works might attract people from normal employment, that government policy on industrial development was, in any case, slowly but surely providing employment and, finally, that public works could only go a little way towards solving unemployment and works without a definite economic value should not be adopted. So, as the unemployment problem was being solved anyway, public works might only make it worse and even if they didn't they would not do much to make it better. Despite this condemnation, the Executive Council provided some additional funding for public works – but significantly less than envisaged by the proponents of a public works approach.[59] This was announced by MacEntee in the Budget of May 1936.[60] The average numbers employed on public works increased significantly from 7,400 in 1936 to 23,000 in 1937.[61] However, this represented the peak of public works employment and the numbers fell steadily thereafter as the underlying employment situation improved. A later review by the Department of Finance estimated that only £11.5 million had been spent on relief works over the seven year period from 1936 to 1944 compared to the Committee's recommendation of spending £13.1 million over four years.[62]

58 Memorandum to Executive Council 9 April 1936, ibid. 59 MacEntee to Seán Moynihan 1 May 1936, ibid. 60 *Dáil Debates*, vol. LXXV col. 28–33, 12 May 1936. 61 Department of Industry and Commerce, *The Trend of Employment and Unemployment in the years 1936 and 1937* (Stationery Office, Dublin, 1938), p. 10. 62 A subsequent review of employment schemes found a considerable degree of inefficiency and a very limited success 'in effecting any

One aspect of public works which led to a battle between MacEntee and Lemass related to the proposals for rotational employment.[63] In order to maximise savings on UA, it was necessary to amend the UA legislation. While an element of rotation was possible under the existing law, MacEntee argued strongly for an amendment to maximise savings. As outlined already, Industry and Commerce were strongly opposed to this approach. However, in June 1936 the Executive Council decided in principle that the Acts should be amended subject to consideration of the details by the relevant departments. In October 1936 Industry and Commerce submitted draft legalisation to provide for this. Finance sought to extend the principle to any work financed out of public monies (as opposed to simply work funded under the Employment Schemes vote) and this was approved by the Executive Council. The legislation was introduced in the Dáil in November 1936 but was not proceeded with.[64]

Fianna Fáil's policy of industrial development did bring a significant increase in employment with the numbers of those employed, insurable under national health insurance, increasing from 355,000 in 1933 to 415,000 in 1937.[65] The improving economy, the use of the EPOs from 1935 and the expansion of public works, all led to a sharp fall in the numbers on the Live Register from an average of 119,500 in 1935 to 81,800 in 1937. In November 1936, William Norton moved a Dáil motion condemning the inadequate rates of UA and calling for proposals to provide adequate maintenance.[66] While this was defeated, the rising cost-of-living in 1937[67] meant that increases in the rates of UA remained on the agenda. However, nothing was done before the General Election in June 1937. In September 1937, Lemass asked his officials to prepare proposals setting out the cost of increasing UA by between 10 and 20%.[68] However, both Keane and Leydon felt that it would be unwise to explicitly link any increase to the cost-of-living. In October 1937, Lemass submitted proposals for an increase in UA rates pointing to the increased cost-of-living and likely political pressure.[69] However, he accepted that any increase should not publicly be linked to the cost-of-living to avoid setting a precedent for such a link. He outlined the cost of an increase ranging from 10 to 20% as being £112–224,000 per annum. MacEntee predictably opposed

real improvement in the capability' of participants. It recommended the abolition of the rotation system. Inter-departmental Committee on State-Aided Employment Schemes (1945–6) *Report*, 1946, D/SCFA Library.   63 NAI S. 8993.   64 *Dáil Debates*, vol. LXIV col. 989, 26 November 1936.   65 *Trend of Employment and Unemployment* for the relevant years. This figure relates to the estimated average weekly number of persons employed.   66 *Dáil Debates*, vol. LXIV col. 931 *et seq.*, 26 November 1936.   67 After a period of relative stability between 1931 and 1936, the cost-of-living index rose to 170 in 1937 compared to 153 in 1932. 68 NAI EB 215667.   69 NAI S. 10202.

any increase arguing that it would lead to similar demands in all other social services. He argued that the introduction of UA had led to disinclination on the part of recipients in rural areas especially to seek employment and any increase could only aggravate this. Eventually in November the Executive Council decided that £150,000 be provided to increase the rates of UA, £80,000 from the Exchequer, £50,000 from the Fund and £20,000 from local authorities. In December, Lemass brought forward a proposal to increase rates by about 15% and included miscellaneous proposals which had been included in the 1936 bill which had not been proceeded with.[70] MacEntee agreed, subject to the inclusion of the rotational employment proposals from the 1936 bill which Lemass had deliberately dropped from the proposal. To include them now, Lemass argued, would delay the bill which was 'very urgently required' and would arouse considerable opposition. The Executive Council this time agreed with Lemass and the bill proceeded without the rotational employment proposals. However, the cabinet requested that Lemass consider reducing the increase from 15 to 10% in rural areas and it subsequently decided not to give any increase to men without dependants in rural areas. The legislation was also to provide that any town could opt for the higher (intermediate) rate of UA subject to agreeing to make the necessary contribution from the rates. The legislation was adopted in early 1938 but received a very lukewarm welcome from Labour.

WORKMEN'S COMPENSATION

In contrast, the reform of workmen's compensation was far less controversial. As we have seen, legislation had been prepared by the Department of Industry and Commerce based on the report of the Departmental Committee. Lemass brought this legislation to cabinet in July 1933.[71] This generally followed the recommendations of the Committee although Lemass did propose some changes including an increase in the level of compensation. He did not, however, reopen the question of making insurance compulsory for employers. The legislation was approved by the cabinet and discussed in the Dáil in October 1933.[72] The bill widened the scope of employment covered by the law by increasing the income threshold over which non-manual workers were not covered from £250 per annum to £350 (£100 higher than national health insurance and unemployment insurance thresholds). Compensation was increased generally with, for example, compensation in

70 NAI S. 8993. 71 NAI S. 4300. 72 *Dáil Debates*, vol. LXIX col. 2304 *et seq.*, 11 October 1933.

non-fatal cases being increased from 50% to 75–80% of previous earnings (although the maximum weekly payment was reduced from 35*s.* to 30*s.*). The bill was broadly welcomed by Cumann na nGaedheal and it became law in March 1934.

WIDOWS' AND ORPHANS' PENSIONS

Immediately on taking up office, Seán T. Ó Ceallaigh announced that the government would set up a Committee to inquire into pensions for widows and orphans.[73] The Committee was established in May 1932. Chaired by Mr Justice Meredith, it included Sir Joseph Glynn, Eamon Lynch and Louie Bennet of the ITUC, the campaigner J.P. Dunne, departmental representatives and others with Local Government official P.J. Keady as secretary.[74] It was required to inquire and report as to a scheme of widows' and orphans' pensions suitable for the country and as to the probable cost. The Committee did not report until September 1933. The majority of the Committee interpreted their remit as being to prepare a pension scheme rather than commenting on the desirability of the principle of widows' pensions or methods of support other than pensions. They also did not consider that support through local authorities or an improved system of home assistance would satisfy their terms of reference.[75]

The Committee sought costings for a contributory approach from the British government actuary Sir Alfred Watson. McElligott requested Watson to produce a separate report on the cost of widows' pensions in October 1932.[76] Watson prepared detailed costings for a scheme similar to the 1925 legislation in the UK. However, some members of the Committee objected to a contributory approach on the basis that it would apply to a comparatively small proportion of the population.[77] Only one third of the male population was insured as compared with three-quarters in the UK. And evidence given by the NHIC and relevant departments suggested that it would not be possible to include the smallholder class in a contributory scheme. Compliance costs would be high and the weekly burden on smallholders would be intolerable.[78] Accordingly the majority of the Committee felt that the only practical approach was a non-contributory one. This it felt should be payable only to widows with dependent children. Acknowledging that this

73 *Dáil Debates*, vol. XLI, col. 55 15 March 1932. 74 NAI S. 6233. 75 Committee of Inquiry into Widow's and Orphans' Pensions, *Reports* (Stationery Office, Dublin, 1934), p. 5. 76 Ibid. Appendix E. As will be recalled, McEligott had originally requested costings for a full scheme of old age and widows' pensions. It does not appear that the contributory old age scheme was pursued further. 77 Ibid., p. 19. 78 Ibid., pp. 20–1.

was in effect a scheme of mother's rather than widow's pension, the Committee argued that as, in a means tested scheme, the main test was necessity it would be difficult to defend assistance for necessitous widows as contrasted with necessitous spinsters or even necessitous males.[79] It is difficult to follow the Committee's logic on this point. Given its remit it is unclear why a necessitous widow without children should be seen as less deserving than a widow with children. But at the same time the Committee's proposal was not for a general scheme of mother's pensions but only for widowed mothers. So the status of widowhood both was, and was not, sufficient to ground a claim of desert. Balancing the advantages of a contributory scheme of its 'safeguard of self-respect' and more adequate pensions against the limited scope of such a scheme, the majority of the Committee concluded that such a scheme was not suitable to existing conditions and that the only alternative was a non-contributory scheme.[80] The ITUC representatives supported the non-contributory approach but only as 'a mere initial instalment of social justice for a deserving section of the community'.

However, two Committee members, Mrs M.J. McKeon and John O'Neill, wrote a minority report recommending a contributory scheme. They rejected the non-contributory approach on the basis that it would not establish a scheme of widows' pension but would 'fix as a permanent feature of our social system a form of State Poor Relief for a particular class'.[81] Insurance, they argued, encouraged thrift, forethought and prudence, recognised the responsibilities of workers and the duties of employers, safeguarded the self-respect of beneficiaries and provided an absolute guarantee of benefit. A non-contributory approach, in contrast, discouraged thrift, removed responsibility, and sapped and destroyed self-respect and self-reliance. They addressed the argument of limited scope by arguing that only about one third of the population *required* protection pointing out that 89% of widows in receipt of poor relief were widows of insured men.[82] Finally, John Herlihy, the Finance representative, rejected outright a contributory scheme as 'practically a scheme of gratuitous pensions, to be kept on foot at the expense of taxation, for the benefit of a section of the population'.[83] But Herlihy also argued that a non-contributory scheme was unjust and extravagant. He proposed a flexible scheme, basically an improved home assistance, whereby payments would be set by a local committee without any right of appeal. The report is an interesting overview of the different approaches then prevalent. However, none of the three schemes proposed was readily implementable from a political perspective and it is perhaps unsurprising that Fianna Fáil

79 Ibid., pp. 25–6. 80 Ibid., pp. 36–8. 81 Ibid., p. 42 *et seq.* 82 Ibid., p. 46. 83 Ibid., p. 51.

was never again to appoint a public committee on such an issue in the period to 1948.

Having received the report in October 1933, the Executive Council referred the report to Finance for examination.[84] In his Budget speech in May 1934, MacEntee was able to announce that a scheme would be introduced that year and set aside money to provide for it. The approach finally chosen by Local Government in July 1934 was a broadly contributory one with a non-contributory approach for the existing survivors of men who would have been insured under the legislation had it been passed earlier (often referred to, following UK practice, as 'pre-Act widows'), widows and orphans of insured men who had not paid sufficient contributions and small working farmers with a rateable valuation under £10.[85] However, only women over 60 and women with dependent children would qualify for the non-contributory pension. The scope of the contributory scheme was to be practically identical with that of the existing national health insurance scheme covering about 500,000 men and women.[86] Agricultural labourers were to be included but at a reduced level of contributions because of their low wages. Rates for the contributory pension were set at 10s. with lower rates for the non-contributory scheme which varied in urban and rural areas. Finance had concerns about the treatment of agricultural labourers and small farmers. Local Government argued that all classes should be 'compelled to contribute' for their pensions and that the whole trend of social legislation was in the direction of a contributory approach.[87] However, there was great difficulty in applying this approach to small farmers. On the other hand the low wages of agricultural labourers did not justify a departure from the general principle. In early August MacEntee, Ó Ceallaigh, McCarron of Local Government and Codling of Finance met to discuss the issues.[88] MacEntee asked whether smallholders could be brought in on a contributory, possibly voluntary, basis. McCarron argued that this was impractical and futile while Ó Ceallaigh took the view that the Dáil would oppose any such proposal. McCarron suggested that the only possible way of bringing in smallholders was to add the contributions to the rates but this time both Ministers dismissed the idea as 'quite impracticable'. By default the Local Government proposals were accepted as the only way forward. McCarron suggested that the concession to agricultural labourers be confined to 5 years

---

84 I have not, unfortunately, located files for the crucial period between October 1933 and the first draft of the legislation in July 1934.   85 NAI S. 6612; S. 84/47/34; *Dáil Debates*, vol. LVI col. 2234–6 4 June 1935.   86 Despite this there appears to have been little if any consideration of having the scheme administered thought the NHIS. Nor was the funding to be on a pre-funded basis.   87 Local Government memo, 3 August 1934, NAI S. 84/47/34.   88 Note of Conference, 7 August 1934, Ibid.

and MacEntee agreed. The proposals did not follow the recommendations of the Committee that 'moral conditions' be imposed. The Committee had proposed that only widows 'of sober habits and of good moral character' should qualify.[89] However, reflecting the assumption that a women should be supported by a man with whom she was cohabiting, cohabitation was a bar to payment (though not as regards the children's allowance in the case of contributory pensions).

Norton submitted proposals for modifications to the bill and MacEntee was amenable to making some changes.[90] Ironically, however, these were to lead to a reduction in the benefits payable under the bill. MacEntee was favourably disposed to reducing the age at which non-contributory widows could qualify from 60 to 50 and possibly even lower. In order to pay for this he proposed restricting eligible small-holders to those with a rateable valuation not exceeding £8 and reducing benefits to agricultural labourers.[91] Local Government, however, were opposed to reducing the qualifying age arguing that while it might be necessary to reduce the age to 55 (as in the UK) it would be better to see how the scheme operated first. McCarron accepted that it was reasonable that workers paying reduced contribution should receive reduced benefits although he pointed out that the original reason for the reduced contributions was that agricultural workers could not afford them and not that they did not need the benefits. Ultimately the Local Government view on the appropriate age was accepted in October 1934 but with the cost saving proposals of reducing the rate of pensions to agricultural labourers to 8s. per week and the limit for small holders to £8 valuation. Ó Ceallaigh pushed for publication of the legislation but in March 1935 the Council decided informally that it should not be published until after the Budget. The bill was finally approved in the Summer of 1935 and it came into operation in 1936. There was, however, a very high rejection rate in the claims for pensions. Up to October 1936, 27,000 claims had been submitted but only 14,200 claims had been awarded while 11,000 had been rejected.

In June 1936, the cabinet returned to the issue of broadening the widows' pensions scheme and agreed to extend the benefits of widows' pensions to the maximum number of destitute widows but without any extra costs to the state.[92] In November 1936 Local Government proposed to reduce the qualifying age for the non-contributory pension to 55 and to increase the age of dependent children from 14 to 16. The total cost involved was less than £100,000 and Finance did not object.[93] However, in November 1936, the Dáil debated a Fine Gael motion to remove the requirement that the deceased

89 *Report*, p. 28. **90** Norton's proposals are not on file. **91** MacEntee to Ó Ceallaigh 26 September 1934, NAI S. 84/47/34. **92** NAI S. 8964. **93** IA 87/53H.

spouse be in insurable employment for the purposes of the non-contributory pension. Labour, in contrast, argued for a broadening of the scope to cover independent contractors and for an increase in the non-contributory pension to the existing groups of claimant. Ó Ceallaigh outlined in broad terms the limited nature of the government proposals which were expected to bring in an additional 5,000 widows.[94] Opposition deputies argued for considerably broader measures and, subsequently, Fianna Fáil deputies made their views clear to Ó Ceallaigh 'pretty forcibly'.[95] As a result, the original proposals were withdrawn and a more extensive measure agreed by government. The new proposals, in addition to making the proposed changes in the age limits for widows, dropped the requirement, for the non-contributory pension, that the husband had been employed in insurable employment (or was a smallholder). This meant that rather than being a primarily contributory scheme with limited exceptions for pre-Act widows and smallholders, the scheme was now much more a dual scheme of contributory and non-contributory pensions. In addition, the means test was broadened to allow more widows to qualify. Ó Ceallaigh estimated that over 25,000 widows would qualify as a result of the changes at a further cost of £200,000 per annum. The bill was strongly welcomed by the opposition.

NATIONAL HEALTH INSURANCE

National health insurance was another area in which the incoming Fianna Fáil government took a different approach to its predecessor. However, unlike the old age pension and unemployment changes which were politically driven, the unification of national health insurance had already been strongly advocated by the civil service from the mid 1920s. Unlike his predecessors, Seán T. Ó Ceallaigh agreed with this approach, took on the societies and, with surprisingly little resistance, imposed unification. Indeed, as we saw in the previous chapter, Fianna Fáil had supported unification at the time of the 1929 bill. The reasons for this support are not clear although Fianna Fáil was obviously more supportive of state intervention and some of the largest societies – such as the Ancient Order of Hibernians – would hardly be seen as Fianna Fáil supporters.

The question of unification was brought to a head by the anticipated fourth periodic valuation of the approved societies, which was expected in late 1933. Because of the labyrinthine complexity of the financing of the

<hr />

94 *Dáil Debates*, vol. LXIV col. 433–42, 12 November 1936. 95 *Dáil Debates*, vol. LXV col. 1139, 3 March 1937.

individual societies, this was expected to show that, although the scheme in total was solvent, many individual societies would be in deficit. Indeed, the Department of Local Government was of the view that it would be necessary to make provision to meet deficiencies even before then. The Department had accordingly, in December 1931, asked the British government actuary, Sir Alfred Watson, to carry out an investigation. His report forecasted that while societies in surplus would have surpluses of £335,000, the poorer societies would have deficits of over £500,000. Allowing for the contingency funds of the societies in deficit and the central fund, this still left over £250,000 to be made good. And as the law stood, the funds of the societies in surplus could not be drawn on to meet this deficit.[96] Expenditure on national health insurance benefits had increased from £407,000 in 1923 to £742,000 by 1931 and showed no signs of abating. This issue was put before the approved society representatives on the National Health Insurance Advisory Committee in June 1932. They suggested a range of measures including a state grant or loan to meet deficiencies, an increase in contributions, the reduction of the age limit for old age pensions to 65 (which would effect savings in benefits as most insured persons of that age were in receipt of national health insurance benefits), contributions to be paid from the unemployment insurance fund during periods of unemployment, a committee of enquiry to be established, persons in sheltered employments (civil and public servants) to be insured, and the remuneration limit increased from £250 to £400 or £500 per annum. Thus the societies sought to increase the proportion of good lives, to increase general contributions and to transfer responsibility for societies with poor lives to the state and the unemployment insurance fund. The surpluses of 'good' societies would not be used for cross-subsidisation. In contrast, L.J. Duffy, chairman of the Association of Trade Union Approved Societies, proposed a comprehensive scheme of insurance. Neither option was attractive to Ó Ceallaigh or his Department.

In July 1932, Ó Ceallaigh brought proposals to government outlining this financial position and proposing a unification of societies which would mean that the resources of the better-off societies would be available to meet deficits.[97] He pointed out that there were 65 societies with a membership ranging from 60 to 90,000. The members varied from good lives with good conditions of employment to bad lives and high unemployment. Because of the structure of approved societies, there tended to be segregation of risks into different societies and under these circumstances some societies would

96 The societies in surplus were estimated to have additional contingency funds of £70,000, *Dáil Debates*, vol. XLVII, col. 1031, 17 May 1933. **97** Memorandum on National Health Insurance, 1 July 1932, NAI S. 3071.

always have a surplus while others would always have a deficit. This was both anomalous and illogical given that the scheme was one of *national* health insurance. Rejecting the proposals of the approved societies, he argued that it was not desirable, in the existing industrial and financial conditions, either to increase contributions or to place an extra burden on the State by reducing pension age. Instead a unified society offered twofold advantages: all insured people would be on equal terms and a more efficient and effective system of administration would be possible. Ó Ceallaigh anticipated opposition from the officials of societies who would lose their positions and from societies with surpluses whose members would object to losing their additional benefits. But, he argued, the greatest good of the greatest number of people should be kept in mind. MacEntee argued for a review of the underlying financial position of the scheme, i.e. that there was a need either to increase contributions or reduce benefits. However, Local Government resisted this as they felt that it was not immediately necessary and would make it much more difficult to get through the unification proposal.[98] Ultimately, MacEntee agreed not to press this and the cabinet approved the proposal in September 1932.[99]

In October Ó Ceallaigh and Ward met a delegation from the approved societies which, somewhat disingenuously, expressed surprise that the question of unification was being revived. The societies remained opposed but were prepared to accept that, if necessary, surpluses might be pooled to meet deficiencies. They advocated voluntary amalgamation. Ó Ceallaigh said that unless something dramatic was done the bottom would fall out of national health insurance so far as a large number of people were concerned. Ignoring the new willingness to pool surpluses, he regretted that the societies had no suggestions to meet this situation but assured them that full consideration would be given to their views.[100] However, his mind was clearly made up and ultimately the approved societies accepted this and did not oppose the measure.[101] The bill was discussed in the Dáil in April 1933. Ó Ceallaigh outlined the genesis of the proposal with the Committee of Inquiry and the fact that the current scheme instead of being a national one was composed of 'a number of separate units, differing widely from one another in their experience . . . of contribution income and sickness experience'.[102] He emphasised the serious deterioration in the financial position of societies and the need to take steps to advert the danger of 'financial breakdown'.[103] The bill proposed

---

98 NAI IA 85/53K; NAI IA 87/53D. 99 MacEntee to NHIC, 9 September 1932, ibid. 100 16 October 1932 NAI IA 87/53D. 101 See the evidence of M.P. O'Donnell, secretary of the Approved Societies Association to the Seanad Select Committee on the National Health Insurance bill, 1933, 20 June 1933. O'Donnell was to become Treasurer of the NHIS. 102 *Dáil Debates* vol. XXXXVII col. 103–4. 26 April 1933. 103 Ibid., col 105.

that all insured persons would be members of the same society. However, there was not to be a 'nationalisation' of health insurance. The National Health Insurance Society or Cumann an Arachais Náisiúnta ar Shláinte, as it was to be known, was to be clearly separate from the State and to be run by a committee of management consisting of 15 people: three trustees appointed by the Minister, nine people representing insured persons and three people representing employers. However, for the first three years, the Society would be run by a provisional committee appointed by the Minister. Cumann na nGaedheal opposed unification on the basis that it would work an injustice on the members of the societies in surplus and would move away from the principle of involving insured persons in the management of schemes.[104] However, Labour supported the proposal while expressing a preference for the co-ordination of all social legislation.[105] In practice, much of the debate of the bill focussed on compensation for redundant employees of insured societies and the bill passed largely as proposed in July 1933.[106]

It had been decided that the provisional committee of management to oversee the establishment of the NHIS should consist solely of civil servants and three Local Government civil servants were subsequently appointed. D.J. (Dan) O'Donovan, formerly Ó Ceallaigh's private secretary, and a man who was to play an important and colourful part in the establishment of the social welfare system, was to act as chair with P.J. Keady, fresh from his service as secretary to the Widows and Orphans' Pensions Committee, and W. Kavanagh as the other members. However, in August 1935, with the election of the permanent committee approaching in July 1936 the composition of that committee again came before government.[107] Local Government was concerned that the method of election provided for the insured persons' representatives was unworkable and that an alternative approach was necessary. The provisional committee took a more extreme view. O'Donovan proposed that the committee be reduced to three with a chair representing the State and one member each representing employers and insured persons. Ó Ceallaigh, however, felt that this was too sharp a change from the original approved societies and recommended instead that the insured persons' representatives be elected by delegates. The delegates in turn were to be elected: three on the nomination of the ITUC and five to be elected by local authorities. In addition, Ó Ceallaigh added the chairman as a separate government nomination. This meant that, of a committee of 15, government now controlled the nomination of three trustees and the chairman and, it might

104 Ibid., col. 110–12, Deputy Costello.   **105** Ibid., col. 115, Deputy Norton.   **106** The NHIC was dissolved and absorbed into the Department of Local Government.   **107** NAI S. 8227; *Dáil Debates*, vol. LX col. 621– 4, 13 February 1936.

be assumed, could have some influence over the election of five further members though the local authority delegates. These proposals were heavily criticised by the opposition parties in the Dáil as 'complicated and unworkable' and 'ineffective, unsatisfactory and undemocratic'.[108] However, given the Fianna Fáil majority the measure was adopted. Ó Ceallaigh appointed Bishop John Dignan of Clonfert as the first chairman. Dignan was one of the few Catholic bishops who had supported the anti-treaty side in the Civil War and was a long-time Fianna Fáil supporter.[109]

From its original establishment and despite, or because of, the fact that its original management committee was appointed by Ó Ceallaigh, the NHIS had always taken a broad view of its functions. In the first edition of its annual journal, *Sláinte*, it editorialised that the real value of unification was that it removed the obstacles 'to a progressive development of health insurance and the proper co-ordination and improvement of our social services'.[110] The Society quickly identified two key issues for advancement: firstly, the extension of health insurance to include medical benefit;[111] and secondly, the unification of social services.[112] The full committee of management, which met for the first time in July 1936, continued this approach. In 1937, it submitted a proposal to Ó Ceallaigh arguing that the NHIS was capable of radical change so as to provide better protection and greater advantage for insured persons.[113] It proposed the establishment of a committee of experts to inquire into the financial structure of national health insurance (e.g. whether it should be on an actuarial or assessment basis), rates of benefit, the income limit for insurance cover, the scope of insurance (whether it should be extended to exempted classes such as public servants), whether broader health services and pension at age 65 should be included, whether it should cover medical benefit, whether social services should be administered jointly, whether there should be a Ministry of Social Services, and whether workmen's compensation should be compulsory and form part of national health insurance. In October 1937, Ó Ceallaigh submitted these proposals to government together with his own views and those of his department. The

108 *Dáil Debates*, vol. LX col. 627, Deputy Morrissey (who had left Labour in 1933 to join Fine Gael); col. 640 Deputy Norton.   109 P. Murray, *Oracles of God: The Roman Catholic Church and Irish Politics, 1922–37* (UCD, Dublin, 2000); D. Keogh, *The Vatican, the Bishops and Irish Politics 1919–39* (Cambridge University Press, Cambridge, 1986).   110 *Sláinte 1935*, p. 8.   111 D. J. O'Donovan, speech at the opening of Arus Brugha, 30 June 1934 reported in *Sláinte 1935*, p. 16. Continuing the tradition of dubious historical interpretation, O'Donovan ascribed the fact that medical benefits had not applied to Ireland to the 'British framers of that British statute'.   112 Ibid., pp. 18–19. And see the anonymous article '"A State of 'Chassis'": Is Co-ordination Desirable?' pp. 64–66 which concluded that it was 'more than desirable, it has become an urgent necessity'.   113 NAI S.10254. And see *Sláinte 1937–8*, p. 9.

Department accepted that existing schemes were inadequate in many cases and produced illogical anomalies. Ideally a comprehensive scheme would cover the full range of contingencies. However, it felt that it was very unlikely that government would be prepared to agree to the introduction of all these changes simultaneously and that it was more likely that growth would be gradual. The Department felt that the requirements were sufficiently well known and, somewhat unctuously, that a committee of enquiry could not be more comprehensive than the Executive Council. It felt that any improvements should await the 1938 Actuarial review. However, the case for medical benefit was 'rather different' and there was a general demand for this. It argued that a separate Ministry of Social Services would be of some advantage and would help to co-ordinate the various services. It was however difficult to separate health services from the Department of Local Government and Public Health. Ó Ceallaigh was not in favour of appointing a committee. He recommended, however, that the cabinet should approve the introduction of medical benefit for persons insured under national health insurance. He argued that the need for a medical benefit had been recognised in other countries, there was strong demand for it, that expenditure on medical certification without treatment was wasteful and uneconomic, and that the introduction of medical benefit would help to reduce excessive expenditure of sickness and disablement benefit. In November, Ó Ceallaigh submitted a further memorandum on the cost of medical benefit. The cabinet authorised preparation of a scheme of medical benefit on the basis of a total cost to the Exchequer not exceeding £45,000 per year.

CONCLUSION

Thus the initial period of Fianna Fáil government saw a dramatic change in the approach to social services. If the initial foundations for the Irish welfare state were laid by the 1838 Poor Law and then by the Conservative and New Liberal reforms of the late nineteenth and early twentieth centuries, the policies introduced in the mid 1930s raised the building skywards. It would be tempting to see Fianna Fáil's approach as a proto-Keynesian policy of debt-financed expenditure to boost the economy – consistent with its approach of adopting protection and import substitution industrialisation.[114] Public sector debt increased in the period and, indeed, the approach may have had

114 Girvin, for example, suggest that the Lemass' unemployment assistance proposals were based on the belief that under-consumption was a major obstacle to growth, *Between Two Worlds*, pp. 93–4.

some effect in boosting consumer expenditure and encouraging indigenous economic growth.[115] However, there can be no question that any such economic policy actually existed in the minds either of the Fianna Fáil government or the civil service. Both unemployment assistance and public works were introduced to address the numbers of unemployed people who could not find work and were not planned to increase demand nor to help convert a largely agricultural workforce to a more industrialised model. Indeed, one of the uses to which UA was put was effectively to subsidise an agriculture population hard hit by the Economic War. MacEntee and Finance were adamant that the relief of unemployment should generally be funded from increased taxation and not from borrowing,[116] although some element of public employment funding was in fact borrowed.[117] Likewise, the other schemes introduced were to meet the needs of disadvantaged groups rather than to play any economic role.

Indeed, there was an absence of any coherent economic challenge to the fiscal orthodoxy best exemplified, in an Irish context, in the report of the Banking Commission published in 1938. Such a lack of any alternative was not confined to government circles. As Fanning has shown, the Irish economic community was both small and, with very limited exceptions, fundamentally conservative in its outlook.[118] It is perhaps unsurprising, therefore, that the Fianna Fáil government did not adopt a Keynesian approach despite its occasional leanings in the direction of fiscal heterodoxy. After all, the UK Labour party also rejected such a position in the 1930s.[119] And Weir and Skocpol have shown that the 'first' New Deal in the USA was also without any explicitly Keynesian underpinning and that it was only later in the 1930s that a more explicitly Keynesian approach was adopted in that country.[120] What is surprising, however, is not only that no such approach was adopted but that no coherent alternative economic viewpoint was even considered in the 1930s. The alternatives to fiscal liberalism put forward in the Banking Commission were not the more mainstream arguments of

115 Investment in public housing and hospital building clearly had this effect.   116 See, for example, MacEntee's comments at *Dáil Debates*, vol. XLI col. 1498, 11 May 1932; vol. LXXV, col 1973, 10 May 1939; M. Daly, *Buffer State*, p. 191.   117 *Dáil Debates*, vol. LXXV, col. 1991, 10 May 1939.   118 R. Fanning, 'Economists and governments: Ireland 1922–52' in A. Murphy (ed.), *Economists and the Irish Economy* (Irish Academic Press, Dublin, 1984). On this issue see generally P.A. Hall (ed.), *The Political Power of Economic Ideas: Keynesianism across Nations* (Princeton University Press, Princeton, 1989).   119 R. Skidelsky, *Politicians and the Slump: The Labour Government of 1929–1931* (Macmillan, London, 1967).   120 M. Weir and T. Skocpol, 'State Structures and the Possibilities for Keynesian Responses to the Great Depression in Sweden, Britain and the United States' in P. Evans et al. (eds.), *Bringing the State Back In* (Cambridge University Press, Cambridge, 1985), pp. 107–68.

Keynes and similar economists who were part of the UK debate but rather more 'heretic' views such as 'social credit' and that advocated by social catholicism.[121] No coherent Keynesian approach to Irish economic policy appears to have been published until 1945.[122] Fianna Fáil's policy mix of protectionism, industrial development, agricultural policy and welfare measures represented a political rather than a coherent economic logic.

The social policy measures introduced by Fianna Fáil did, however, represent a major redistribution of resources in the Ireland of the 1930s. Social expenditure on income maintenance schemes increased from under £5 million in 1931 to approaching £8 million by 1937–8. In the absence of income distribution data it is impossible to measure the precise effects of these changes. Nonetheless, there can be little doubt that the introduction of widows' pensions, unemployment assistance and the extension of old age pensions – all funded in whole or in part from general taxation – did benefit those who were less well off. And the reform of the national health insurance scheme again used the resources of the better off societies to subsidise those with more disadvantaged members. Nonetheless the extent of social solidarity was limited. There was, for example, no question that public servants or the higher paid would be brought into the national health insurance.

The Fianna Fáil social policy measures were, in some cases, highly gendered. The two major reforms of existing schemes: the unification of national health insurance and the changes in old age pensions did not have any explicit gender dimension. The improvements in the old age pension appeared to favour men slightly with the proportion of women pensioners declining from about 58% in 1932 to about 56% after the reforms, presumably as women were less likely to have additional means. The impact of the unification of national insurance would require further research. Insured women were somewhat concentrated in the larger approved societies making up 35% of the largest six societies as compared with only 30% of overall membership.[123] However, while total sickness and disablement benefit expenditure for men fell from 1931 to 1935, expenditure for women increased over the period so there is no indication that the amalgamation had any adverse impact on women.[124] However, the two new areas of unemployment assistance

---

121 F. O'Driscoll, 'Social Catholicism and the Social Question in Independent Ireland: The Challenge to the Fiscal System' in M. Cronin and J.M. Regan (eds.), *Ireland: The Politics of Independence, 1922–49* (Macmillan, London, 2000). 122 A. Marsh, *Full Employment in Ireland* (Browne & Nolan, Dublin, 1945). And even then a reviewer suggested that the author had no more than an intuitive and sometimes imprecise understanding of the theory, *Studies* (1946) 35, pp. 422–3. 123 The six largest societies (the AOH, Prudential, Liver, Sláinte, Irish National Foresters and Irish Amalgamated) made up 50% of total membership. See 'Table of Transferred Membership' in *Sláinte 1935*, pp. 36–8. 124 *Sláinte 1936*, pp. 27–28.

and widows' pensions were explicitly gendered. At first sight there appears to be a contradiction between the two because, on the one hand, women were largely excluded from unemployment assistance, while, on the other, women were treated quite generously in widows pensions. However, the logic of the Fianna Fáil approach meant that both approaches were perfectly consistent. Fianna Fáil policy saw women as part of a broader family unit and as economically dependent on men. Accordingly women should not, in general, be entitled to unemployment assistance as (a) they didn't need support which should be provided by the male head of household and (b) it would only encourage them into the labour force. Widows, on the other hand, no longer had a male head of household to depend on (and this through no fault of their own). Accordingly they were entitled to public support. In addition, key Fianna Fáil figures were strongly attached to providing support to widows on the basis of desert – such women were much more deserving of support than spinsters.

In terms of technology, we have seen that the New Liberal reforms employed an eclectic mix of means testing and social insurance. The Fianna Fáil approach was similarly flexible. The Fianna Fáil government was certainly not opposed to social insurance. Its reforms of national health insurance and workmen's compensation consolidated an insurance-based approach. And the original widows' and orphans' pensions scheme was a predominantly insurance based approach – despite the recommendation of a means tested approach by the majority of the Widows' Pension Committee. On the other hand, however, there was little strong commitment to expanding social insurance. There was, for example, no increase in the income thresholds of social insurance cover. Nor does there appear to have been any serious consideration given to introducing a contributory old age pension scheme (despite the precedent in the UK where the Conservative government introduced a contributory pension scheme in 1925). Perhaps of more importance was the fact that policy makers ran up against the difficulty of applying a social insurance approach in a country which was heavily agricultural – an issue which was to return again in the discussions on a unified social insurance scheme in the late 1940s. The widows' pension scheme was effectively remade into a dual insurance and assistance scheme in 1937.[125]

Having served four and a half years, de Valera called an election in June 1937 to coincide with the vote on the new Constitution. In its first general

---

125 A mean tested approach was also taken to unemployment relief but this probably had as much to do with the high level of unemployment and the perceived impossibility of sustaining a solvent unemployment insurance fund. The difficulties in the UK, where the Labour government fell in 1931 largely over a decision to cut unemployment insurance payments, would have been well known to Irish policy makers. See Skidelsky, *Politicians and the Slump*.

election, Fine Gael ran a perhaps surprisingly strong campaign, given the difficulties of its birth.[126] It emphasised the maintenance and co-ordination of social services and the increase in the cost-of-living. In a sure sign of the opposition's success, MacEntee and Ryan furiously attacked Fine Gael proposals accusing them of fighting on a Fianna Fáil policy.[127] Labour called for a range of social measures including family allowances payable to the fathers of children under 16, old age pensions at 65 and increases in payments. Fianna Fáil emphasised its achievements in improving social services and housing and argued that unemployment was its chief concern.[128] The *Irish Times* for the first time did not call explicitly for a vote against Fianna Fáil, but its advocacy of a vote 'for the Commonwealth' can hardly have misled many readers. The electorate proved unimpressed with Fianna Fáil's record. Its vote dropped by 5% and it scraped back into government with the support of Labour. Labour promised support in improving social conditions but strong resistance to any attempt to worsen social legislation.

As we have seen, Fianna Fáil did little enough on either score in the next year with the exception of some relatively minor increases in unemployment assistance. The *Irish Times* had predicted another election soon and de Valera did not disappoint. He secured the Anglo-Irish Trade Agreement which came into force in May 1938 and, as Daly has emphasised 'reflected a new alliance of conservative forces in Irish society: owner-occupier farmers, protected manufacturers, and equally protected industrial workers'.[129] Having subsequently adopted an 'as-you-were' Budget in the same month, Dev was defeated in the Dáil on a relatively unimportant motion to establish an Arbitration Board for civil servants. He immediately decided to call an election for June. Emphasising the need for national unity, Fianna Fáil announced that much of the programme on which it had been elected in 1932 had now been achieved. Now was the time for five years of reconstruction and development. Fianna Fáil promised to establish 200 new factories employing 25,000 extra workers, to intensify the housing programme and extend the social services.[130] Also, Partition was identified as the one major constitutional issue remaining.[131] But the 1938 campaign marked one important turning point. In contrast to previous elections, the relationship with Labour deteriorated drastically. Labour was highly critical of the snap

126 It did not, however, profit in votes as its vote was less than that of its constituent parts in 1933.   127 *Irish Press*, 18, 22 June 1937.   128 *Irish Press*, 22, 23, 24, 26 June, 1 July 1937.   129 M.E. Daly, *Industrial Development and Irish National Identity, 1922–1939* (Syracuse University Press, Syracuse, 1992), p. 175 – although it is perhaps debatable whether industrial workers were 'equally' protected.   130 *Irish Press*, 2 June 1938.   131 *Irish Times*, 30 May 1938.

dissolution and of the continuing level of unemployment. Labour called for improvements in the social services as in its 1937 campaign but this time called for a vote against the government.[132] The *Irish Times* while arguing that there was 'no earthly reason for a General Election' conceded that Dev's personal popularity never stood higher. The *Times* felt there was 'hardly anything to choose between the two big parties in respect of high policy' and that the choice for the voters was a question of personalities. For the first time, its editorial made no recommendation as to which way readers should vote.[133] Fianna Fáil swept back to power with its largest ever share of the vote and a clear majority. Despite only a small drop in votes both Fine Gael and Labour dropped a number of seats.

132 *Irish Press*, 7 June 1938.   133 *Irish Times*, 27 May, 13, 16 June 1938.

4

In the shadow of the Emergency, 1938–42

'[A] radical and fundamental change is needed in National Health Insurance and . . . a comprehensive review of medical and indeed all social services in Ireland is required with a view to their co-ordination'.[1]

'Stringent and straitened as our position, I believe that we can endure it so long as peace is maintained. If a widespread war comes, however, our difficulties will be intensified beyond measure . . . [W]ith a much diminished real income, we shall be called upon to shoulder vastly increased public burdens'.[2]

As we have seen, Fianna Fáil was elected with an overall majority in the election of 1938. De Valera was at the height of his powers. Five years of reconstruction and development had been promised. But, while the tenth Dáil was to last for a full five years, the period is generally seen as one when Fianna Fáil ran out of steam and, to a considerable extent, reflecting its supporting 'conservative alliance,' lost the radicalism which it had in its earlier years. As we will see, this analysis is to some extent borne out in a study of developments in the income maintenance area in the late 1930s and early 1940s. In September 1939, the outbreak of war led to the creation of two new government departments: the Department of Supplies and the Department of the Co-ordination of Defence Measures. This allowed de Valera to reshuffle his ministers and to move MacEntee, who had, not for the first time, considered resignation earlier in the year from Finance. Lemass moved from Industry and Commerce to Supplies with MacEntee replacing him. Seán T. Ó Ceallaigh moved from Local Government to Finance with his place being

---

1 Most Rev. J. Dignan DD, Bishop of Clonfert, 'His Lordship the Chairman's Address to the Committee of Management', 20 July 1938, *Sláinte 1937–8*, p. 9. 2 Seán MacEntee, Budget speech 1939, *Dáil Debates*, vol. LXXV col. 1999, 10 May 1939.

taken by P.J. Ruttledge. Ruttledge was quite ill for much of his term of office and he eventually resigned in August 1941. This led to a further reshuffle with Lemass moving back to Industry and Commerce (while retaining his Ministry of Supplies) and MacEntee moving to Local Government and Public Health. This chapter looks at developments from 1938 through to the early years of the War. As will be seen, employment growth plateaued after 1938 and the impending European war led to an increase in the Live Register in 1939. MacEntee was strongly opposed to any further expansion in public expenditure and wished to cut back rather than expand services. By the time he was replaced as Minister for Finance in September 1939, Fianna Fáil Ministers were very concerned about the potential implications of the war for the Irish economy. As we will see, in contrast to the period to 1937, there were very few social policy developments in the late 1930s. To some extent, of course, this reflects the major developments in the earlier years: Lemass could not introduce unemployment assistance twice. But there were a number of areas, in particular the further development of national health insurance, the improvement of old age pensions and the co-ordination of schemes, where developments might have been, but were not, made. However, the early 1940s did see one dramatic exception to this trend: the introduction of a major scheme of children's allowances. The introduction of children's allowances is examined in chapter 5 together with the measures to address the rise in the cost-of-living. The issue of the co-ordination of social services, which was close to, if not on, the agenda for most of this period is discussed in more detail in chapter 6.

UNEMPLOYMENT

In 1937 the Live Register had fallen to its lowest yearly average since the introduction of UA (82,000). This rose in 1938 and 1939 due to a fall-off in employment, a reduction in the numbers on public works and the ending of net migration to the UK in 1939.[3] In response, the government relied on a range of almost wholly negative measures to keep the Live Register down. The numbers on public works were allowed to decline from almost 20,000 in 1938 to only 8,000 by 1942. Instead, policy was to keep people off the Register either by excluding them under EPOs or through a new policy of a

3 In March 1938, given the development of a surplus in the Unemployment Insurance Fund, the ITUC had proposed that this be used to increase benefits. Fine Gael wanted it used to reduce contributions. Labour put down a Dáil motion seeking an inquiry on the issue in 1938 but, given the worsening employment situation, Industry and Commerce were opposed to any improvement in benefits. In any event the motion was not debated until 1941. NAI EB 222247.

'labour corps'. These two measures focused respectively on rural and urban unemployment. In September 1939, reflecting government concerns about the impact of World War on the Irish economy which led to a Supplementary Budget in November, an Economy Committee was established to recommend cuts in public spending. This included the area of unemployment assistance and will be discussed in more detail below.

The Construction Corps

In October 1938, inspired by the US Civilian Construction Corps, Hugo Flinn and de Valera spoke about the possibility of establishing 'labour battalions'. Flinn immediately set in train a preliminary investigation of the issue including the practice in other countries.[4] De Valera was clearly pushing the idea as in early November he spoke to Lemass about the desirability of operating a similar scheme here.[5] In response, Lemass prepared a short memorandum. Lemass stated that it would be desirable that the Corps be employed on work which would not be undertaken in the ordinary course and that it should include training which would improve participants' prospects of obtaining regular employment. He argued that the scheme should be voluntary but, somewhat disingenuously, that the voluntary element would be assisted by withholding the dole from applicants of a certain age who had never had employment and who had no hope of work. As discipline would be necessary, he argued that control should be entrusted to persons with military training. In December, Flinn submitted a preliminary report to de Valera suggesting an experiment with three camps of 180 men each. T.A. Smiddy, de Valera's economic adviser, was also involved in the discussions. But he advised that the approach was 'inapplicable to this country except in its general principle and its inspiration'.[6] However, it appears that Dev was distracted by other events and did not come to an immediate decision on the issue.[7] Lemass pushed the issue forward resubmitting his proposals for the establishment of Labour Corps in March 1939. He sought a decision as to whether the idea was approved in principle and, if so, which department should be responsible. In response, MacEntee argued that the cost of such a Corps would be high compared to existing rotational public works. He referred to the problem of finding suitable work and of placing workers after discharge from the Corps. However, as he sympathised with the objects aimed at, MacEntee was prepared to agree to an experiment of one camp

---

4 Flinn to de Valera 13 October 1938, NAI S. 10927.   5 Lemass to de Valera 17 November 1938 ibid. De Valera had also made inquiries in his Department of External Affairs on the Civilian Construction Corps, ibid.   6 Smiddy to de Valera 16 December 1938, ibid.   7 File note 16 February 1939, ibid.

with 180 youths. MacEntee suggested that discipline should be sympathetic and not entirely of the kind imposed from above in military organisation but that it should be partly based on self-government. However, he did not believe that recruitment should be entirely voluntary and power should be taken to disqualify for UA. Arising from this discussion, government decided that Flinn should prepare a scheme for establishing Labour Corps on a voluntary basis similar to those of the American Civilian Construction Corps. In April, Flinn told the Dáil that it might be necessary to introduce large labour camps due to the exhaustion of schemes with a large labour content.[8]

In May a detailed survey was carried out on young men aged 18 to 25 on the Live Register.[9] It found that 95% were single and without dependants. The survey found a very low level of industrial and commercial skills amongst the unemployed. Only 10% were skilled manual workers while half were farmers, assisting relatives or road workers and a further quarter were classified as 'other labourers'. Thirteen per cent had no employment in the previous 12 months while, reflecting worsening employment conditions, three quarters had had no employment in the last six months. The experiment was carried out in Clonsast bog in County Offaly. There had already been significant difficulties in recruiting workers for this location and it was hardly the most propitious place to start.[10] As might have been expected, young men from Dublin showed little enthusiasm for a trip to the bog. The OPW submitted a memorandum in June 1940 outlining the experience in Clonsast. The results to date had been disappointing. Of 200 names submitted, 174 had been considered eligible; 106 had failed to attend or declined employment; 57 had actually travelled to Clonsast but 30 left of their own accord in the first week so that, at the time of writing, only 9 of the original 200 remained. And of a second batch of 200, only 23 had even travelled to Clonsast. However, the government was not deterred by this failure and in July the cabinet decided that the Minister for Defence should examine the question of establishing an Army Labour Corps. De Valera recognised that any proposals would have to be discussed with representatives of labour.[11] In August de Valera spoke to Norton who 'reacted fairly well' and to Jim Larkin who 'did not react unfavourably'.[12] Having secured neutrality, if not support, from key Labour figures the proposals were agreed in principle by government and de Valera subsequently met with Norton and Senators Campbell, Lynch and William O'Brien. Following correspondence between the Secretary to the Government, Maurice Moynihan and the ITUC, O'Brien spoke to de Valera by phone in October and confirmed that the

8 *Dáil Debates*, vol. LXXV col. 786, 20 April 1939. 9 NAI EB 232993. 10 NAI S 101/2/40. 11 File note 18 July 1940, NAI S. 11994. 12 File note 12 August 1940, ibid.

ITUC were taking a 'non-committal attitude' and that this was the best that could be done.[13]

In the planning stage a key issue had arisen in Industry and Commerce as to whether people who refused to join the Corps could be disallowed UA. In August 1940, Defence had enquired whether this was possible.[14] Industry and Commerce officials felt that the question would have to be decided on a case-by-case basis. However, a difficulty arose in that an Umpire (an independent statutory adjudicator) had previously indicated that service in the Army was not employment within the meaning of the Act although there was no formal decision to that effect. Nonetheless, Industry and Commerce felt that it was never intended that the existing legislation should be used to pressurise people to join the Defence Forces. Ferguson, the secretary of the Department, also felt that the law as it stood would not debar people from UA and Defence were advised accordingly. However, it would appear that Lemass was of the view that people refusing to participate should be denied UA so that when recruitment began, Keane instructed the manager of the local exchange to suspend payment to anybody refusing work. Following internal discussion, it was agreed to refer cases to the Court of Referees for decision. The initiative was publicly announced in early October.[15] Lemass was immediately concerned about the low level of response and the fact that the majority of initial recruits were not on UA.[16] He argued that recruitment should be confined to those on UA and proposed that young men who refused to join the Corps should be disqualified for UA. He reported that in the five test cases referred to the Dublin Court of Referees, the Court had decided in all cases that UA should be disallowed. Finance remained unconvinced on its merits arguing in March 1941 that the Construction Corps was 'a very expensive method of providing for the unemployed'. Nonetheless government authorised an additional battalion to be established. In April, the ITUC wrote to Moynihan complaining that UA had been refused to claimants who did not joining the Corps. The ITUC could not agree to this approach and sought a meeting with de Valera. Industry and Commerce informed Moynihan that of 3,000 offers of places in the Construction Corps, only 700 had been accepted and 1,900 of the balance had been disallowed UA. Unsurprisingly Moynihan recommended against a meeting. In 1941, recruitment for the Corps was extended to all towns with a population of over 1,000. The Construction Corps continued throughout the War and was eventually disbanded in 1948. There is little indication that it was successful in

13 File note 2 October 1940, ibid. See generally K. Allen, *Fianna Fáil and Irish Labour* (Pluto, London, 1997, pp. 67–9). 14 NAI EB 245645. 15 *Irish Press*, 3 October 1940. 16 NAI S. 12158; EB 246964.

achieving its more positive objectives of carrying out constructive works and improving employment opportunities. Over the period of its operation, 17,000 young men were invited to join but only 2,400 were willing to do so. However, the Corps played a much more significant role in reducing the numbers on the Live Register with no less than 7,500 being disallowed.[17]

Employment Period Orders

In early January 1939, Industry and Commerce proposed that the EPOs for 1939 be on the same basis as in the previous year.[18] The cabinet agreed the first EPO (covering occupiers of land) but the second EPO (referring to single men) was withdrawn for consultation with the Minister for Agriculture. Agriculture proposed that this be extended to married men and other men with children – a proposal which Industry and Commerce felt 'could be described as drastic'. The Department outlined the results of a survey of the employment experience of 19,000 people affected by the EPO in 1939. Almost a third had got no work, 40% had got between one day and 4 weeks work, 20% between 4 and 12 weeks, 8% from 12 to 30 weeks and only 93 had got more than 30 weeks work. Industry and Commerce argued that the figures showed that it was neither necessary nor desirable to extend the scope of the EPO. The cabinet initially agreed. However, faced with a continued rise in unemployment and net immigration, in September 1939, Industry and Commerce brought forward proposals to make a third EPO in beet growing areas from November to early January (i.e. the beet processing season). This was agreed by cabinet but only for the month of November.

In September 1939, an Economy Committee was appointed to review existing service and to report on possible discontinuance or curtailment.[19] However, the Committee was told not to unduly restrict services for the unemployed in urban areas. The Committee reported on, inter alia, unemployment assistance in November. It recommended that the second EPO be extended to cover the period from March to October at an estimated saving of £212,000 in a full year. It also recommended that expenditure of Employment Schemes be reduced by £200,000 and be limited to £835,000 in 1940–41. However, the Committee did recognise the extreme difficulties faced by the unemployed in the so-called 'Back Areas' (the Congested Districts along the western seaboard) and the need to concentrate rural relief in those areas. In early 1940, MacEntee, now Minister for Industry and Commerce, sought to extend the EPOs so that both occupiers and single men were excluded from March to October. This was in line with the recommen-

17 *Trends in Employment and Unemployment for the Years 1947 and 1948*, p. 10.   18 NAI S. 9537A.   19 NAI. S. 101/7/39. See Fanning, *Finance*, pp. 317–27.

dations of the Economy Committee.[20] It was anticipated that the policy of compulsory tillage should increase the employment of the land. This was agreed in February 1940 and in March MacEntee brought forward further proposals to exclude all men with dependants in rural areas (i.e. those currently not affected by EPOs) from April to October. Jim Ryan, while supporting this approach, felt that it should not apply in the Congested Districts and MacEntee put this to the cabinet for decision. Following discussions, MacEntee proposed in April that all persons be debarred from UA (except married men with dependants who were occupiers of land of under £2 rateable valuation in the Congested Districts) from June to October. It was estimated that this would affect about 20,000 people. Government agreed this subject to an increase in the rateable valuation to £4 and the broadening of the Congested Districts to include contiguous areas where similar conditions prevailed. In September L.J. Duffy of the Labour party wrote to de Valera objecting, amongst other things, to the third EPO.[21] Industry and Commerce acknowledged that it had received complaints from various parts of the country but argued that evidence of 'grave or widespread hardship' had not been adduced.

It was estimated that over 50,000 were excluded from UA as a result of the EPOs in 1940. In February 1941, MacEntee proposed to exclude (a) every person in rural areas except married men and widowers with dependants in the Congested Districts (with no land or land of up to £2 rateable valuation) and men discharged from the Defence Forces; and (b) all unmarried men or widowers under 25 without dependants in an *urban* area (again with the exception of those discharged from the Defence Forces). MacEntee accepted that there had been 350 complaints to his Department concerning the previous years EPOs. However, in language not normally to be found in government memoranda, he argued that 'in a country surrounded by sea and abounding in rivers, many districts of which are overrun by rabbits, an excellent food to be had for the taking, a man with a holding of land and sufficient industry to till it should be able to make ample provision against want'. MacEntee argued that the proposed extension to urban areas arose from the 'pressing need for economy in the present emergency'. His colleagues either did not see the need as so pressing or were not prepared to endure the political repercussions, as while the rural proposals were agreed, the extension to urban areas was withdrawn. The result was that the number of people debarred was greater in 1940 from March to June but less from June to

---

20 It appears that this was one of the relatively few recommendations to be accepted by government. See Ó Ceallaigh's comments at *Seanad Debates*, vol. XXIV col. 1003, 14 March 1940. **21** L.J. Duffy to de Valera, 17 September 1940, NAI S. 9537A.

October. In total the EPOs disbarred a further 40,000 people in 1941. In March 1941, three Fianna Fáil Senators wrote to de Valera objecting to the exclusion of married men. Clearly there were other concerns about the impact the EPOs were having as, in March, cabinet decided to make a contribution of 50% of the additional expenditure incurred by any local authority on home assistance as a result of the exclusion of married men under the EPO. In 1942, the return of Lemass saw a slight relaxation of the EPOs which, given the fall in the Live Register, now affected only 21,400 people. However, in April 1942, Lemass proved that he could be just as draconian as MacEntee when the mood took him. He proposed that any person who refused or failed to seek suitable employment in agriculture or in the turf industry or who left such employment without good cause or lost it through misconduct should be disqualified for UA for the remainder of the year.[22] His colleagues agreed and this measure was brought in by Emergency Powers Order in May. In total 8,500 people were disqualified under the Order, mainly in relation to refusal to accept work at the government turf camps in Kildare although most of the effect was only in the months of November and December.[23] The EPOs were continued in a similar form to 1948 but the draconian Emergency Powers Order was not repeated.

An unemployment crisis?

By 1940, the government was becoming seriously concerned about the potential impact of the War and the resultant shortage of supplies on unemployment.[24] In January 1940, MacEntee met with the ITUC and was prepared to consider their proposal of a Commission on Unemployment.[25] In June 1940, MacEntee established an inter-departmental committee to consider the issues which reported in July and predicted that an additional 260,000 people could find themselves unemployed at an early date. And later that year, government agreed to accept a Labour party motion calling for the establishment of a Commission on Unemployment.[26] In February 1941, MacEntee reported to his colleagues that there were serious shortages of supplies and that it was not possible to substitute native raw materials except to a very limited extent. There was also a limited possibility of switching industrial machinery to new tasks (citing the closure of the Ford works in Cork). MacEntee took 'the gloomiest view as to the extent to which unemployment, particularly on

22 NAI S. 12809. This was part of a coercive policy to ensure sufficient workers for turf production, see Allen, *Fianna Fáil and Irish Labour*, pp. 76–7. 23 *Trend of Employment and Unemployment in the Years 1941 and 1942*, p. 10. 24 NAI S. 12296. 25 NAI S. 11644. 26 Ibid. In fact, in October 1941, Lemass, now back in Industry and Commerce recommended against proceeding with the Commission and de Valera ultimately decided to take no action.

industrial production, will develop'.[27] He was now of the view that the estimate of an additional 260,000 unemployed might 'fall far short of the mark' and that unemployment could reach 'almost 400,000'. He recommended the establishment of a committee to be chaired by Flinn to report on the possibility of providing employment for male workers in public works. Government approved a range of measures including an investigation by Flinn. However, by March Flinn was able to report that the position was 'very much better that we might have feared'.[28] By July MacEntee felt that migration was likely to mop up any unemployment. And so it was to prove. While the level of insured employment fell slightly during the war years, migration increased massively with 46,000 people emigrating in 1942. In addition, employment in the Defence Forces and on agricultural and turf works meant that the Live Register continued to fall to a yearly average of 60,000 by 1944.

OLD AGE PENSIONS

The only remarkable thing in relation to old age pensions in the period is that nothing happened. The cost-of-living index had increased by almost two thirds from 1932 to 1942 while the maximum pension remained at 10s. The Department of Finance received a significant number of proposals from the ITUC and from local authorities in the late 1930s in relation to pensions.[29] These ranged from increasing the rates, to removing the means test, and reducing the age limit to 60 or 65. However, there was surprisingly little debate in the Oireachtas on the issue in contrast to the considerable pressures which arose in the UK in the same period.[30] MacEntee, however, far from looking at possible improvements, was thinking about how savings could be made. In late 1938, he raised a particular case which had come to his attention with the Revenue Commissioners.[31] A man with four farms had qualified for a pension but the Revenue explained that he had handed over the land to his son-in-law on marriage and therefore qualified for a pension. MacEntee was concerned that the provisions allowing the disposal of property were too

---

27 Memorandum 22 February 1941 NAI S. 12296. Fanning, *Finance*, pp. 343–7.   28 Flinn to MacEntee 25 March 1941 ibid. MacEntee, at this time, was still unconvinced that things were turning for the better and was considering radical reform of unemployment insurance and assistance. He proposed to broaden UI so that regular workers did not fall onto UA. It might also be necessary to adjust UA to prevent claimants falling onto home assistance. MacEntee even envisaged bringing unemployed widows and spinsters onto UA.   29 See, for example, NAI S. 11036A; NAI S. 88/1/38 – 3/38; S. 88/5/38; S. 88/2/39 – 88/7/39; S. 88/3/40.   30 J. Macnicol, *Politics of Retirement*.   31 NAI S. 88/1/39.

wide and suggested that there should be a limit on the amount which could
be disposed of without affecting the pension. The Revenue Commissioners,
however, pointed out that over 90% of the property transfers accepted as
legitimate were marriage settlements. They felt there were good reasons for
this and that pensioners should not be penalised because of such a transfer.

Learning from their predecessors, pensions did not feature heavily in the
work of the 1939 Economy Committee and it was not until 1943 and 1944
that the issue became a matter of serious debate in the Dáil.

PUBLIC ASSISTANCE

Fianna Fáil introduced an extensive bill on reform of the home assistance
legislation in 1939 but this represented delayed action rather than any
renewed vigour. Firstly, the legislation was to consolidate the existing position rather than to bring forward new provisions. Secondly, the legislation
had been drafted in the late 1920s and its appearance in the late 1930s was
simply due to a delay in finalising the proposals. As early as May 1934 Local
Government had notified the cabinet that Ó Ceallaigh proposed to introduce
comprehensive legislation to deal with the law relating to the relief of the
poor.[32] This was to involve 'nothing new in principle' but was to consolidate
the existing law, make permanent the county schemes and bring Dublin into
line with the rest of the country. The Minister for Finance had given his
approval and heads had been drafted. However, various relatively minor
matters delayed the bill and in March 1936 the Attorney General was asked
to give it drafting priority. Legislation allowing public authorities to support
certain voluntary societies intervened,[33] and it was not until 1939 that the
legislation finally appeared. It followed closely the 1934 heads. Despite the
passage of time, as published, it still did not apply to Dublin city or county
but Conn Ward amended the legislation during its passage through the
House to apply to Dublin.[34] The legislation largely codified the existing position although the public assistance bodies now became the local county
council rather than a committee of the council. This change formed part of
the overall reform of local government.[35] The legislation did mark the last

---

32 NAI S. 2957. Unusually the government secretariat appears to have misfiled the papers on
this file. What became the 1939 Act starts out on S. 2957 but in 1939 this material switches to
S. 9322. S. 9322 was originally opened in October 1936 to deal with a separate and shorter piece
of legislation which became the Public Assistance Act 1937 but this material switches to S. 2957
in 1937. 33 NAI S. 9322. 34 *Dáil Debates*, vol. LXXVI col. 571–2. 6 June 1939; col. 1773
et seq. 4 July 1939. 35 *Dáil Debates*, vol. LXXVI col. 519–20 6 June 1939. See generally M.
Daly, *The Buffer State*, Chapter 7.

step in the change from direct 'democratic' control of assistance payments to its replacement with bureaucratic decision making. As we have seen, decisions in relation to entitlement under the Poor Law were to be made by the (at least partially) elected board of guardians following investigation by relieving officers.[36] The County Board of Health (Assistance) Order, 1924, provided that the superintendent assistance officers were to 'receive, examine and investigate' all applications which were then to be submitted to the public assistance authority for decision. However, this decision now became the function of the county manager.[37] Thus in a period of just over 40 years, the administration of poor relief underwent a fundamental shift from being purely a matter for the elected guardians to a position, following the coming into effect of the County Management Act 1940, whereby elected members of the Boards of Assistance were excluded from the decision making process on individual claims for home assistance.

NATIONAL HEALTH INSURANCE

As we saw in the previous chapter, the cabinet had in late 1937 authorised the preparation of a scheme of medical benefit. However, for reasons which are unclear, this was not publicly announced and no scheme appears to have been prepared. It may be that the practical difficulties of combining a system of medical benefits with the existing health services, which had caused some of the difficulties in 1911, had again deterred the planners. In April 1938, O Ceallaigh, seemingly having had a change of heart in the intervening period, told the Dáil that the government had, during the last year, taken up the question of medical benefits.[38] However, this was a 'very thorny and difficult problem' and one could not devise any quick method of putting medical benefit into operation as long as the existing poor law medical system was in operation. Very long and detailed examination was required and was in progress. But Ó Ceallaigh now said that he was interested in seeing if a variety of other benefits should be made a part of national health insurance. In December 1938, McCarron, controller of national heath insurance,

36 That this function was not simply nominal or one which could be delegated had been shown in the High Court case of *R (O'Mahony) v. Ellis* [1898] 2 IR 57 in which the Fermoy guardians were surcharged by the Poor Law auditor because of their practice of only approving the first weekly payment of relief and of then simply retrospectively sanctioning payments already made by the relieving officer. The High Court held that the guardians must grant authority in each case *before* payment was made. 37 County Management Act, 1940 and Public Assistance (General Regulations) Order, 1942. 38 *Dáil Debates*, vol. LXX col. 1659–60 7 April 1938.

reported to Ó Ceallaigh that the UK actuary, Sir George Epps, was carrying out an examination of sickness experience under national health insurance while the Department was also looking at fundamental changes in the financial structure of the NHIS to set free money for additional benefits.[39] By January 1939 Ó Ceallaigh appeared to have reversed his original position. Now, instead of supporting medical benefit and opposing an enquiry, he proposed to government to establish an interdepartmental committee to examine the broader issue of the development or extension of arrangements concerning the full range of contingencies, the extension of the contributory principle and a possible extension of insurance to include workmen's compensation.[40] Government did decide to establish a committee to examine and report on the desirability of establishing a department of social services but, as discussed in chapter 6, this was not proceeded with. It would appear that the departmental officials at least saw their main priority as being to restructure the NHIS finances. McCarron wrote to Epps in January 1939 stating that there was a 'strong feeling' as to whether the continued accumulation of resources in the national health insurance fund was 'any longer justifiable'.[41] Although Bishop Dignan was thinking along the same lines, there is no sign of any close co-operation between the two organisations.[42] In April 1939, Ó Ceallaigh again told the Dáil that the question of medical benefits was a 'very difficult and thorny problem', one which required co-ordination with the dispensary medical services. While he hoped that the issue would be tackled soon, his overall caution gave little sign that he was actively working to see this happen.[43]

In May 1939 a draft of the UK government actuary's report was received. This showed that the level of sickness claims was about normal but that disablement (i.e. long term) claims were two to three times higher than standard. McCarron recognised that the report required urgent consideration and that it meant that contributions would have to be increased or benefits reduced, at least for women who constituted the main part of the extra claims. In July 1939 the NHIS was given a copy of the final report. Henderson, secretary to the NHIS, accepted that disablement benefit claims were, in effect, changing into permanent invalidity pensions. In August the key departmental officials met to consider their response. McCarron argued that the funding basis needed to be altered and that capitalisation should be replaced by assessment, i.e. providing for current benefits out of current

39 NAI IA 91/53.   40 NAI S. 10254.   41 McCarron to Epps 24 January 1939, ibid.   42 His Lordship the Chairman's Address to the Committee of Management of Cumann an Arachais Naisiunta ar Shlainte, 20 July 1938, in *Sláinte 1937–8*, pp. 4– 11.   43 *Dáil Debates*, vol. LXXV col. 971, 21 April 1939.

funding. Keady was more dubious about this approach suggesting that the NHIS was not doing all that was possible to reduce expenditure. In terms of expansion, McCarron and his colleagues Duffy and Keady all took the view at this point that medical benefit should be first priority for expansion of the service. Later that month McCarron met James Hurson[44] the secretary of the Department concerning the slow progress on the proposals concerning medical benefit. Hurson attributed the delay to Finance but pointed out that action on the actuarial report was a separate problem irrespective of any question as to issues of co-ordination and the setting up of a Ministry of Social Services. McCarron proposed the adoption of assessment, i.e. providing for current benefits out of current funding and limiting the reserve fund to the amount necessary to provide a margin of safety for epidemic disease and disablement benefit, which might provide additional benefits such as medical and dental benefit. McCarron felt he needed some direction as to what was favoured. He pointed out that medical benefit would require an increase in contributions. In September 1939, Local Government submitted proposals to Finance on the reform of the financial basis of NHI. It proposed a switch to funding on an assessment basis. In October, the department decided to ask the UK actuary for advice on abandoning capitalisation. In November 1940, Epps wrote to McCarron hoping that he would be able to restrain his Minister from 'saying anything which might suggest the possibility of substantial increases in benefits under the Scheme'. Epps reported that there would be some resources available but that these would only go a short distance in providing new or increased benefits. It was not until December 1940 that draft legislation providing for a restructuring of national health insurance finances and the provision of additional benefits was submitted to and approved by the Minister. While the benefits were not specified in the legislation, the accompanying memo indicated that these were to be dental, hospital and optical benefit. These were immediately submitted to Finance.

Predictably, in March 1941, McElligott responded that Finance could not agree to any additional burden being placed on the State. In the same month the actuary's report was received. While expressing concerns about the high sickness experience, inadequate medical certification and the low level of contributions paid, this agreed that funding could now be released for additional benefits.[45] On this basis, Local Government wrote again to Finance

44 Hurson became secretary after Edward McCarron's dismissal in 1936 and served until his retirement in 1946 on grounds of ill health. 45 *Actuarial Report on the Financial Position of the National Health Insurance System*, March 1941. The report pointed out that, on average men made only 38 contributions per annum and women 42. In addition, only 42% of the total

arguing that, as the law stood, the forthcoming valuation would show a defi-
ciency requiring an increase in contributions or a reduction in benefits. The
Minister was not prepared to agree to either so a reform of the funding basis
was essential. However, at this stage Dignan took matters into his own hands
and raised the matter personally with de Valera. De Valera wrote to him later
the same day stating that he had arranged for the relevant departments to
carry out an investigation in consultation with the NHIS into the possibility
of providing, without assistance from the Exchequer, for the extension of
medical benefits out of the moneys available in the NHI Fund. However, he
added that the Minister for Finance was prepared, if necessary, to make an
Exchequer contribution such as the present Emergency would allow.[46]
Immediately afterwards Finance (including Arthur Codling and Leon
Ó'Broin) and Local Government officials (McCarron and Duffy) met with
Bishop Dignan and Henderson to sort out the details.[47] Dignan produced the
letter from the Taoiseach. Codling indicated the Finance objections but
Dignan questioned whether Finance was competent to criticise the scheme.
In his view the sole purpose of the meeting was to examine whether and how
money could be found and not to discuss the scheme which had been
approved in principle by the Taoiseach and Tánaiste. Following somewhat
acrimonious exchanges, Codling said he would report to his Minister and
Dignan pressed for an early decision. The following day, Codling reported
the gist of the discussion to Ó Ceallaigh and, after some consideration, Ó
Ceallaigh wrote to Dignan stating that he had now 'decided to accept the
principle of making additional benefits available' if justified by the actuary
and to make a State contribution to the cost.[48]

In June Local Government submitted proposals to government outlining
the need for reform of the financial basis of national health insurance.[49] The
current capitalised basis was designed to meet the needs of a multiplicity of
societies. With only one society, there was no need for such a complicated
funding arrangement or for any further accumulation of funds. It was
proposed to discontinue the existing system and to provide that the difference between income and expenditure over a five year period be used to
provide additional benefits (dental, optical and hospital) in the subsequent
five year period. In August, the government formally agreed to the drafting
of the bill which would stabilise the accumulated funds at the existing level
and use additional income on additional benefits. This would result in an

male population of working age (16–70) were insured compared to 81% of the UK population
(16–65). **46** De Valera to Dignan, 3 June 1941, NAI S. 12457. **47** Note of Conference in
Department of Finance, 5 June 1941, NAI IA 91/53A. **48** Ó Ceallaigh to Dignan 10 June
1941, ibid. **49** NAI S. 12457.

annual sum of £175,000 being made available involving an Exchequer cost of £40,000. While small in terms of overall social spending, this represented a relatively significant sum to the national insurance scheme in the context of total NHIS expenditure of about £750,000 in 1941. In January 1942, MacEntee, who had been appointed Minister in August 1941, noted to the secretary that he had read the actuary's report and wanted steps taken to eradicate the 'claim habit'. He was 'very doubtful of the wisdom of the deci-sion . . . to proceed with this scheme for additional benefits' but recognised that government might by now be too 'deeply committed to it to go back'.[50] MacEntee submitted a summary of the actuary's report to government.[51] The legislation was introduced in the Dáil by Conn Ward in early 1942 and became law in late March.

CONCLUSION

In contrast to the preceding five years, the late 1930s and early 1940s thus saw little movement in social policy. On unemployment, the two main policies involved the exclusion of young men in urban areas who refused to enlist in the Construction Corps and the exclusion of men in rural areas through the Employment Period Orders. The Construction Corps could, in many ways, be seen as a variation on the public works theme. Given the perceived lack of success of public works, key figures including de Valera and Flinn advocated the idea of 'Labour Corps'. While the idea obviously had potential benefits for participants, ministers were always aware that young men were likely to be struck off UA and, in the end, this turned out to be perhaps the main function of the Corps. The National Health Insurance Society was the dynamic organisation in this period calling for co-ordination of all services and the introduction of medical benefit. As we have seen, Local Government originally did not support the idea of a study on co-ordination and argued for the introduction of medical benefit. However, having won a decision in prin-ciple in favour of this approach, Ó Ceallaigh and the Department seemed to lose interest and ended up proposing a broader study. Ultimately the Department and the NHIS saw the reorganisation of the finances of national health insurance as the first priority and this, relatively minor, issue occupied all concerned up to 1942. In view of the breakdown in relationships between

50 MacEntee to Hurson 13 January 1942. In a response to the note Keady explained that a separate report was being prepared on sickness claims. As to whether things had gone too far to turn back, Keady simply attached a copy of Ó Ceallaigh's letter to Dignan.   51 His own officials received a copy of this from his private secretary, NAI IA 91/53F.

MacEntee and Dignan, which will be discussed in chapter 6, it is worth noting that while there is little sign of a very close working relationship between the NHIS and the Department, nonetheless relationships were cordial and both frequently had broadly similar interests. Overall, the period does support the 'loss of radicalism' thesis. However, one set of proposals – on support for families – which emerged in the late 30s was to become the focus of the most significant developments in social policy in the early 1940s. This is discussed in the next chapter.

5

Children's allowances and a 'cheap ration', 1939–44.[1]

> Our ability to provide social security services depends on our productivity. Our only source of wealth is what we produce by the application of human effort to natural resources. . . . The development of social services must, therefore, proceed side by side with the development of plans for economic development. We are, by setting up this service, proposing to divert purchasing power from one section of the community to another, and we think we are justified in doing so because of the need of the section which will benefit. That is all we are doing.[2]

The introduction of a system of children's allowances in Ireland was a very important social policy measure, particularly given the fact that it took place during the Second World War. Children's allowances represented an entirely new form of welfare payment costing no less than £2,250,000 per annum and representing an increase of over one-quarter in the then expenditure on 'social welfare' payments. As such, this represents a major innovation in social policy and is also the more surprising given that the Fianna Fáil government of the 1940s is rarely represented as one given to major innovations. To date, the introduction of children's allowances has received only limited consideration by historians and social policy writers.[3] This chapter aims to look in detail at the proposals which were put forward and debated in the period from 1939 to 1944. It also looks at another key policy issue of the Emergency years: measures to compensate for the increased cost-of-living, in particular as these relate to income maintenance payments.

1 Chapter V of Keynes' *How to Win the War* was entitled 'A Plan for Deferred Pay, Family Allowances and a Cheap Ration' and recommended both the introduction on family allowances and that 'a minimum ration of consumption goods be made available at a low fixed price'. 2 Seán Lemass, Minister for Industry and Commerce, *Seánad Debates*, vol. XXVIII, col. 522, 14 January 1944. 3 See, in particular, J.J. Lee, *Ireland 1912–1985: Politics and Society* (Cambridge University Press, Cambridge, 1989), pp. 277–85; F. Powell, *The Politics of Irish Social Policy* (Edwin Mellen, Lewiston, 1992), pp. 213–15.

As we have seen, by 1939 Fianna Fáil had been in power for seven years having won no less than four successive general elections. The 1938 election was one of the most successful ever, with Fianna Fáil achieving 52% of total first preference votes and 55% of seats. Nonetheless, in the following years Fianna Fáil was under political pressure from a resurgent Labour party and from the newly formed Clann na Talmhan (founded in 1938). The latter party threatened Fianna Fáil in its own heartland of the West and sought support from core Fianna Fáil voters: small farmers and their families. At the same time, the perceived radicalism of Fianna Fáil in the 1930s and the success of its early policies was beginning to wear off. The growth in industrial employment, generated by Fianna Fáil's protectionist policies in the 1930s, slowed down after 1937.[4]

In 1939, there was no state system of child support as such, although higher rates were payable in relation to some – but not all – the general social welfare schemes where the claimant had dependent children and, as we have seen, widows' pensions had been introduced in 1935. However, these addressed child poverty in certain families only, and poverty in families in low paid employment or self-employment remained outside the scope of state support. Family allowances were introduced in various forms in a number of continental European countries in the 1920s and 1930s.[5] In the UK, there was considerable debate about the need for a general system of children's or family allowances.[6] In its first Budget Fianna Fáil had provided funding for free milk for children and mothers. Tax allowances for children had been introduced by the Lloyd George government in 1919 and in its first Budget and again in 1936 Fianna Fáil had significantly increased these allowances. However, unlike the United Kingdom, there had not been any sustained debate about children's allowances in Ireland in the 1920s and early 1930s.

Although the Irish Labour party had raised the issue in the 1937 and 1938 elections, it was not until 1939 that the issue was seriously considered. One of the first important references came from James Dillon TD.[7] He argued that in order to combat the problems faced by large families, family

---

4 B. Girvin, *Between Two Worlds: Politics and Economy in Independent Ireland* (Gill & Macmillan, Dublin, 1989), pp. 107–8; C. Ó Grada, *Ireland: A New Economic History 1780–1939* (Oxford University Press, Oxford, 1994), p. 400.   5 S. Pedersen, *Family, Dependence and the Origins of the Welfare State* (Cambridge University Press, Cambridge, 1993); I. Wennemo *Sharing the Costs of Children: Studies on the Development of Family Support in OECD Countries* (Swedish Institute for Social Research, Stockholm, 1994).   6 H. Land, 'The Introduction of Family Allowances: an Act of Historic Justice?' in P. Hall, H. Land, R. Parker and A. Webb, *Change, Choice and Conflict in Social Policy* (Heinemann, London, 1975); J. Macnicol, *The Movement for Family Allowances, 1918–1945* (Heinemann, London, 1980); S. Pedersen, op. cit.   7 *Dáil Debates*, vol. LXXV, col. 403–11, 30 March 1939.

allowances should be introduced for all children after the fourth for persons with an income less than £2 per week. He estimated that this would reach 30,000 children at a total cost of about £500,000. Seán T. Ó Ceallaigh, the Minister for Local Government and Public Health, replied that he would be deeply interested in the question of family allowances, but gave no commitment to do anything.[8] The issue of population was one which received considerable debate in the late 1930s.[9] The 1936 census of population had revealed a decline in the population since the earlier census in 1926. The second volume of the 1936 census was published in March 1939 and provided detailed information in relation to the population decline.[10] This was a matter of concern to several members of government, in particular, Lemass and de Valera, and, in June 1939, Lemass, in his capacity as Minister for Industry and Commerce, submitted a memorandum to government summarising the findings of the census.[11] Whether or not it was related to the population issue, de Valera was discussing the introduction of a system of children's allowances with his associates by May 1939. In a conversation with his private economic advisor, Professor Smiddy, de Valera proposed a system of family allowances to families with weekly wages under £3 10s. per week or, in the case of farmers, an income of £38 per annum.[12] In mid-1939, the Minister for Defence, Frank Aiken, submitted a memorandum to government on family allowances proposing that payments should be made to agricultural workers and small farmers. At a meeting in July 1939, the cabinet decided to request the Department of Local Government and Public Health to investigate the matter despite the opposition of the Minister for Finance, Seán MacEntee.[13]

CABINET COMMITTEE ON FAMILY ALLOWANCES

In November 1939, following the government reshuffle, Local Government reported back to the cabinet.[14] Arising from this, a cabinet committee was

---

8 *Dáil Debates*, vol. LXXV, col. 580, 31 March 1939. 9 See, for example, M.E. Daly, *The Spirit of Earnest Inquiry* (Statistical and Social Inquiry Society of Ireland, Dublin, 1997), pp. 116–20; and the discussions in *Journal of the Statistical and Social Inquiry Society of Ireland* (1937–8) xvi, p. 112 *et seq.* and *Ireland Today* (1936) p. 6 *et seq.* 10 Although published second, this was in fact *Census of Population, Vol. V Part 1: Ages, Orphanhood and Conjugal Conditions* (Stationery Office, Dublin, 1939). 11 Department of Industry and Commerce, 'Some Observations on the Population Problem of this Country', June 1939, NAI S. 12117A. 12 T.A. Smiddy to E. de Valera 26 May 1939, NAI S 11265B. 13 NAI S. 11265A. This file was not available in the National Archives at the time of my research. For Aiken's proposal see NAI EB 237766 and UCDA P104/676. 14 NAI IA 129/53E.

established whose membership clearly favoured the idea of children's allowances. It consisted of the Ministers for Local Government and Public Health (P.J. Ruttledge), Supplies (Lemass), Agriculture (James Ryan), Coordination of Defence Measures (Frank Aiken) and Lands (Tom Derrig). Significantly, both the Minister for Finance and the Minister for Industry and Commerce were not included. The Minister for Local Government and Public Health was to act as chair. However, as Lee points out, his private secretary, one Brian O'Nolan (better known as Myles na gCopaleen or Flann O'Brien), had other interests at the time and, despite repeated reminders from the Taoiseach, the committee did not meet until April 1940.[15] By that time it appears that Lemass was extremely frustrated with the lack of progress and he immediately submitted a four-page memorandum to Maurice Moynihan, the secretary to the government, for circulation.[16] Lemass stated that the memorandum had been prepared by him as a result of discussions at the cabinet committee on family allowances. He claimed that it 'is in a sense the report of that Committee' and went on to state that, while it had not been prepared by the committee, they were recommending its consideration by government particularly the proposal for the establishment of an inter-departmental committee to draw up a detailed scheme of family allowances.

The memorandum set out the first detailed proposals in relation to children's allowances. Lemass proposed payment to all children in families under the age of fourteen (excluding children already provided for under the widows' and orphans' pension scheme, children whose parents' means exceed stated limits and children in institutions). He estimated that 700,000 children would be covered: half of these being the children of wage earners and half the children of self-employed persons. He proposed that wage earners should pay a substantial contribution to the cost of the scheme and receive allowances which would be double those received by non contributors (2s. per week with 1s. for the children of non contributors). He estimated the cost of the scheme at £3 million per annum with £2 million coming from contributions and the balance being made up by cuts in other welfare payments and increased taxation. Lemass' memorandum was not particularly well thought out and it was criticised on a number of grounds, both of principle and of detail, by the Departments of Local Government and Public Health, Finance and Industry and Commerce. It was pointed out, for example, that the memorandum did not specify why a scheme of family allowances was required in the first place. The Department of Finance argued that, assuming the

15 Lee, *Ireland* p. 278. See NAI S 12117A.   16 'Outline of Proposals for the Payment of Family Allowances to Children under 14 Years', 8 April 1940, S 12117A.

purpose of the scheme was to increase the population, there was already a natural increase in the population if emigration could be checked; that no need for a higher rate of natural increase had been proved; and that in any case there was no proof that family allowances would have the effect of increasing the population. However, perhaps sensing defeat, both Industry and Commerce and Finance proposed that a commission of enquiry should be set up to investigate the matter further before making any decision in favour of family allowances, although the Department of Local Government and Public Health questioned whether there was any point in establishing such a body unless the finance was available to provide for such a system.

INTERDEPARTMENTAL COMMITTEE ON FAMILY ALLOWANCES

Despite the fact that the Lemass memorandum was not a particularly impressive document and despite the opposition of the three main departments concerned, the cabinet, on 4 October 1940, decided that the question of family allowances should be referred to an inter-departmental committee representing the Departments of Local Government and Public Health, Education, Industry and Commerce and Finance.[17] The Minister for Finance was to be responsible for providing the chair for the committee but, indicating the interest which de Valera took in the matter, the Department of the Taoiseach prepared draft terms of reference. On 22 October the government approved the final terms of reference which required the committee to examine whether, having regard to social, economic and financial considerations, it would be practicable to establish a system of family or children's allowances having for its object the making of due provision for family needs; if such a scheme was to be introduced, to make recommendations as to a scheme of family allowances; and to report on the probable social, economic and industrial consequences of the scheme.[18] On 22 November 1940, Ó Ceallaigh appointed a committee, chaired by O.J. Redmond, principal officer of that department (and future secretary), including representatives from Education, Industry and Commercial and Local Government and Public Health (P.J. Keady) and with T.K. Whitaker acting as secretary. The Department of Finance was concerned that the final terms of reference excluded, in particular, the question of the desirability of the scheme.[19] Following discussions between the secretary, J.J. McElligott, and Ó Ceallaigh,

17 4 October 1940, NAI S 12117B. 18 22 October 1940, NAI S. 12117B. 19 NAI S 101/12/40.

it was decided to convey orally to the chair of the committee that this issue could, in fact, be considered by it.

The committee took almost two years to produce its report. The Taoiseach's continued interest in the topic is apparent from a number of reminders to the Department of Finance in relation to the committee.[20] The committee's minutes indicate that it had effectively decided in favour of the desirability of children's allowances by its third meeting in January 1941 and the remainder of the time was spent in constructing a coherent scheme.[21] By 10 July 1942, Redmond was able to inform Maurice Moynihan that conclusions had been reached and that proposals would be made in relation to a scheme of children's allowances. Seán T. Ó Ceallaigh was also obviously aware that proposals would be made and on 11 July 1942 he wrote to the Taoiseach stating that the committee had drafted a scheme but that further consideration was required.[22] Ó Ceallaigh suggested that the Taoiseach should not volunteer any statement on the subject of children's allowances until departments had been able to comment on proposals and a formal government decision made.

THE DEBATE ON THE COST-OF-LIVING

In the intervening period the cost-of-living had accelerated rapidly and a lively debate developed about how best to address this issue. Having remained at about 170 from 1937 to 1939, the cost-of-living index increased dramatically to 206 in 1940 and to 228 in 1941. In January 1941, the Irish Trade Union Congress wrote to de Valera calling for control of prices.[23] In February, the Cabinet Committee on Emergency Problems asked McEntee for the cost of doubling UA in respect of children.[24] In March Lemass submitted tentative proposals for food subsidies. He argued that when prices began to fall, subsidies could be reduced whereas if wages and unemployment payments were increased to provide compensation, it would not be possible to reduce them at a later date. Finance opposed the proposal but without providing an alternative option. Early in April 1941, Professor Felix Hackett of UCD wrote to Moynihan enclosing details of targeted food subsidies (Food Stamps) in the USA.[25] De Valera immediately asked Local

20 NAI S 12117B. In the intervening period two motions on the topic were introduced in the Senate, in April and October 1942: *Seánad Debates* vol. XVI, cols. 1001 *et seq.* 24 April 1942; 2569 *et seq.* 14 October 1942. 21 Copies of the minutes of the committee's meetings are on NAI IA 129/53H. 22 S. T. Ó Ceallaigh to É. de Valera, 11 July 1942, NAI S. 12117B. 23 NAI S. 12331. 24 NAI S. 12296. 25 F. Hackett to M. Moynihan 2 April 1941, NAI. S. 13144A. On food stamps, see K. Finegold, 'Agriculture and the Politics of U.S. Social

Government and Industry and Commerce to consider this option. Later in April, Industry and Commerce submitted detailed proposals arguing that bread, meat, milk, butter, sugar, tea and potatoes constituted 86% of the expenditure of a sample of poor families. Subsidisation of these goods, funded from taxation, would transfer resources to the poorer classes. However, general food subsidies were 'more calculated to be effective as a means of preventing increased wages . . . rather than as a means of assisting the unemployed and poor through a difficult period'.[26] The proposal discussed the possibility of food vouchers for these disadvantaged groups. At the end of April, without any formal proposals to this effect, government agreed in principle that free food be made available to UA recipients with dependants, old age pensioners in towns and to other classes to be determined. This was to involve half a pint of milk per day, a quarter pound of butter and two pounds of bread per week per person.[27]

Industry and Commerce and Local Government submitted detailed proposals in May. Industry and Commerce broadly supported the approach which would encourage home consumption (especially of butter which was then being exported at an uneconomic price) and provide support to those in need. Finance argued that one department should take responsibility for operating a scheme and, in view of the administrative difficulties involved in a voucher system, it took the view that vouchers should be restricted to milk (which was universally available) and that a cash allowance be substituted for the other items. Government agreed to assign responsibility to Industry and Commerce but remained committed to delivering benefits-in-kind. Following proposals from that department, the food voucher scheme came into effect in September 1941 for persons in urban areas on home assistance, unemployment assistance, national health insurance, widow's and orphan's pensions, and old age and blind pension. Lemass made it clear to the Dáil that this approach had been adopted as an alternative to increasing the general rates of payment.[28] This was just one of the measures taken to compensate people for inflation. In May 1941, government made £200,000 available to local authorities for the relief of home assistance recipients due to the Emergency.[29] And in June, government, recognising the difficulties faced by families, agreed to increase the rates of unemployment insurance payable in respect of a dependant adult and child from 5s. and 1s. respectively to 7s. 6d.

Provision: Social Insurance and Food Stamps' in M. Weir et al. (eds.), *The Politics of Social Policy in the United States* (Princeton University Press, Princeton, 1988) pp. 218–20. **26** Industry and Commerce memorandum, 9 April 1941, NAI S. 12331.   **27** 29 April 1941, NAI S. 13144A.   **28** *Dáil Debates*, vol. LXXXVI col.1769, 7 May 1942.   **29** NAI S. 13140. **30** *Dáil Debates*, vol. LXXXVIII col. 1282, 15 October 1942; NAI S. 13142.

and 2*s*. 6*d*. [30] More generally, in October 1941, following the establishment of
a Wage Standstill Order, food subsidies were introduced to offset a prospec-
tive increase in flour and bread prices. In 1942, the retail price of butter was
also subsidised. In October 1942, with the cost-of-living index increasing to
250, Lemass, now back in Industry and Commerce, sought approval to
increase the dependant payments to people on UA in rural areas (who did not
qualify for food vouchers).[31] MacEntee opposed this proposal as, he argued,
UA had already reduced the incentive to find or retain employment and as
people in rural areas were in a better position to produce their own food or
purchase it direct. Finance also opposed any increase in view of the possible
knock-on effects to pensioners and others. However, the government agreed
the proposal which came into effect in November 1942.

THE REPORT OF THE FAMILY ALLOWANCES COMMITTEE

The report of the inter-departmental committee[32] in October 1942 provided
a detailed examination of the rationale for children's allowances and the
methods by which it might be delivered. The committee understood the term
'family or children's allowance' as involving 'payments, other than ordinary
remuneration for work or services, related to the number of dependent children in a family'.[33] The committee suggested that the principal argument in
favour of children's allowances was that the then system of remuneration for
work was inequitable in disregarding family circumstances. It looked at the
evidence of the link between large families and poverty, drawing on a number
of surveys in the United Kingdom. It took the view that there was general
acceptance of the principle that the national income should be distributed so
that no one would be without 'the bare necessaries of life'. The committee
also looked at the population argument for children's allowances but
remained unconvinced by this approach. It argued that 'the evidence available
from countries where family allowances have been adopted or extended with
pro-natalist aims is not conclusive of their efficacy in bringing about an
increase in the birth rate'.[34] The committee was equally unconvinced by
feminist and socialist arguments, such as the arguments of Eleanor Rathbone
that family allowances should be introduced as a payment to mothers. It
claimed that such an arrangement 'would run counter to generally accepted
principles concerning the responsibility of parents for the rearing and educa-

31 NAI S. 12975. 32 Inter-Departmental Committee on Family Allowances, *Report*, 14
October 1942, Copies at NAI S. 12117B; NAI S 101/12/40 and NAI IA 129/53E. 33 Ibid.,
p. 3. 34 Ibid., p. 13.

tion of their children and the father's position as head of the family'.[35] The committee discussed the implications of these general arguments for the situation in Ireland. It suggested that much of the public interest in family allowances seemed to have derived from concerns about the declining population demonstrated by the 1936 Census. However, the committee concluded that 'family allowances are not required for the purposes of increasing the population since . . . the existing birth and marriage rates are high enough to ensure its continued natural increase'.[36] It found that the primary problem in relation to population was emigration and that there was considerable doubt, in any case, as to the efficacy of family allowances as a corrective of population trends.

The committee discussed in some detail the evidence relating to poverty in Ireland. It was evident that considerable poverty existed in large families. It found that 'the present economic system does not contemplate payment of a wage which would take account of varying family needs'. It considered 'therefore, that, for the purpose of mitigating distress in large families with low incomes, some form of assistance to the heads of such families in socially desirable.' While 'the extension of existing social services would not meet the problem satisfactorily . . . [a] system of family allowances would afford at once a practicable and sustainable solution'.[37] The committee considered the ways by which family allowances might be provided. In view of the limited extent of industrialisation in Ireland and the small size of many employers, it considered that an insurance based system would only provide a partial solution and that some form of non-contributory scheme would have to be established for those who were not wage earners. Accordingly, the committee recommended a means tested scheme.[38] The committee recommended payments at a rate of 2s. 6d. per week in large urban areas declining to 1s. 6d. for rural areas. It estimated that this would provide support to about 100,000 children at an annual cost of the order of £520,000 (including administrative costs). The committee concluded that the father should be the person to receive the payment as the head of the family. It also suggested that the Department of Industry and Commerce should be the appropriate department to administer the scheme since it was basically wage related. On the finance of the scheme, the committee thought that it would be inequitable to offset the cost by cutting other social services. Accordingly, it proposed to fund the payment by an increase in income tax 'on the principle of transferring income from persons with higher incomes and the least family responsibilities' to those with lower incomes and the most family responsibilities.[39]

---

35 Ibid., p. 16.   36 Ibid., p. 22.   37 Ibid., p. 28.   38 Payable to persons with weekly income below 50 shillings in boroughs, 40 shillings in other towns and 33 shillings in the rest of the country.   39 Ibid., p. 55.

Thus the committee provided a detailed examination of and rationale for a system of children's allowances in Ireland. It would seem that the report of the committee effectively ensured that some form of children's allowance was going to be introduced. Although, as we will see, the precise form of children's allowance recommended by the committee was not, in fact, introduced, the rationale it proposed – that of the relief of poverty in large families – was adopted by the government, although its real rationale for the scheme was arguably broader.

WORKING OUT THE DETAILS

The Department of Finance predictably opposed the recommendations of the report.[40] It argued that 'the principle has not been generally accepted that the State has responsibility for the relief of poverty in all its degrees'. The state's responsibility lay only in relation to 'the relief of destitution, i.e. extreme cases where employment and the minimum necessities of existence are lacking'. A system of family allowances would introduce a further degree of state interference in the domestic affairs of families and strengthen the tendency towards bureaucratic control. However, in December 1942, the government decided that the Minister for Industry and Commerce should submit the principles of a children's allowance scheme by compulsory, contributory insurance.[41] Only four days later, Lemass circulated a memo to government proposing that he should prepare legislation for a scheme of children's allowances for all children after the first, both contributory and non-contributory, very similar to his original outline.[42] It was estimated that the cost would be of the order of £5.5 million with an income from contributions of about £3 million leaving over £2 million to be provided by the state. These proposals were approved by government. It is noteworthy that, despite the fact that the files do not disclose any memo to government on the issue, the government decided to opt for a contributory system of children's allowance contrary to the recommendations of the inter-departmental committee. In addition, Lemass was able to produce a memo on this issue within only four days of the original government decision. Some informal consultation between Lemass and de Valera on the topic seems very likely. However, MacEntee – dissatisfied with the decision to allocate responsibility

---

40 2 November 1942, NAI S 12117B. **41** NAI S 12117B. **42** The contributory scheme would provide payment of 5s. per week for all children under sixteen after the first. Contributions would be set at about 1s. 8d. per week. The non-contributory scheme would cover all children under sixteen subject to a means test (of £250 per annum). This would provide a payment of 2s. 6d. for all children after the first.

to Industry and Commerce and with the shape of Lemass' proposals – instructed his civil servants to prepare proposals for a wholly contributory scheme of children's allowances.[43]

In February 1943, Lemass circulated the heads of a bill to establish a system of children's allowances. On his specific instruction, other departments were not notified of the proposal but, despite this breach of procedures, the Taoiseach directed that the item be accepted on the government agenda on condition that the decision would be in principle only. The heads of the bill also proposed a contributory and non-contributory scheme. However, there was a very significant difference from Lemass' earlier proposal. This time, the non-contributory scheme was not to be means tested. Accordingly, every person was to receive 2s. 6d. per week for each child after the first and, in addition, persons covered by the contributory scheme were to receive an additional payment of 2s. 6d. with the cost to be shared by contributions from employers and employees. Lemass argued that public objections to the means test and the considerable administrative difficulties and expense offset the attraction of the savings resulting from having a means test. The non-contributory scheme would cost an estimated £3.55 million gross per annum reduced by savings and cuts in existing services to £2.8 million with the contributory scheme being fully supported by contributions from employers and employees. Although this is not specifically identified in the proposal, the change meant that, for the first time, a system of general support for families was being proposed as opposed to one focused on children in poor families. However, in order to offset part of the cost, the proposal did suggest that income tax allowances in respect of children should be reduced and that part of the agricultural grant to larger farmers should be withdrawn. Lemass' new proposal produced a plethora of memoranda to government from the Minister for Local Government and Public Health, the Taoiseach himself, and the Department of Finance. However, Lemass felt sufficiently confident that the principle of children's allowances had been accepted that, on 4 February 1943, in response to a question from James Dillon as to whether he intended to introduce legislation to establish family allowances in Ireland, he was able to respond that a scheme was in preparation.[44]

In February 1943, Seán MacEntee submitted a memorandum to government on the topic. He argued that the Lemass proposal was objectionable as it was likely to be criticised by Catholic sociologists. He suggested that, if a scheme was to be established, it should be the responsibility of his department. He felt that a contributory and non-contributory scheme would create anomalies and additional expense and that a non-contributory scheme was

43 NAI IA 129/53F.   44 *Dáil Debates*, vol. LXXXIX, col. 493, 4 February, 1943.

contrary to Catholic principles. On 20 February, he submitted alternative proposals for a wholly contributory scheme with a compulsory and voluntary branch. The scheme was to be compulsory for wage earners, allowances would be paid directly by employers and the allowance would be inversely related to earnings.[45] On 23 February the Taoiseach circulated a memorandum summarising the key points of the two different schemes proposed by Industry and Commerce and Local Government and subsequently set out a number of key questions of principle for decision by the government. On 1 March, the Taoiseach set out a number of suggested responses to his own key questions. In particular, it was suggested that the scheme should be entirely non-contributory and the cost should be met by the exchequer. Secondly, consideration should be given to paying children's allowance to all irrespective of means. Thirdly, it should apply to children under sixteen. Fourthly, the question was raised as to whether school attendance should be a requirement for payment. Fifthly, children's allowance should not be paid to the first and, possibly, the second child. Sixthly, only half the standard rate should be payable to the first eligible child. Seventhly, income tax relief and the agricultural grant should not be cut and, finally, the allowance should be paid by the state and not directly by the employer. It is clear that de Valera himself was taking a particular interest in the question of children's allowance and was primarily concerned with whether a contributory scheme might be seen as more favourable towards wage earners vis-à-vis self employed persons.

On 5 March 1943 the government came to tentative conclusions in relation to children's allowance subject to further discussion. These were that there should be non-contributory and contributory schemes (despite de Valera's reservations), that there should be no means test, and that the age limit should be sixteen. Thus, this 'tentative' decision broadly endorsed Lemass' February 1943 proposal. Both MacEntee and McElligott continued to oppose but to little effect.[46] McEntee submitted a memorandum entitled 'Childrens' Allowance, "Beveridgism" and the Catholic Church' in which he argued that the Beveridge approach, which he clearly saw encapsulated in

---

45 A further memorandum was promised to set out the details of the voluntary scheme. It does not appear that any such memorandum was ever submitted. This is unsurprising since a voluntary scheme would be entirely unworkable. Persons intending to have a large number of children would contribute and persons intending not to have any children would not with consequent unfavourable financial implications for such a scheme. This point was made to MacEntee by his own officials. For the background to this proposal see N.A. I. IA 129/53F.
46 At this time, James Dillon and Alfie Byrne proposed a Dáil motion to the effect that family allowances should be introduced forthwith. *Dáil Debates*, vol. LXXXIX, col. 1461 *et seq.* 24 March 1943. Dillon proposed payment without a means test and the abolition of the income tax relief for children, ibid. col. 1469.

Lemass' proposals, was inconsistent with the approach set out in *Quadragesimo Anno*. More importantly for the progress of the proposal, on 26 March, the Taoiseach submitted observations on the principle of a contributory scheme. De Valera submitted that the main objection to a contributory scheme is that 'a glaring disparity is involved in the treatment of persons employed for wages and those who are self-employed or are themselves employers in a small way'. He suggested that 'the only possible object of the contributory system is to conceal the cost of the children's allowance. The concealment of a burden does not, however, reduce its economic effects on the community'. On 13 April, the government gave authority for the drafting of a bill to provide for children's allowances on the basis that allowances were to be payable irrespective of means, with the cost to be borne entirely out of state funds. Decisions as to the number of children in respect of whom allowances would be paid and the rates of allowance were deferred. It was agreed that income tax relief would be reduced on the introduction of the allowance.

At about the same time government agreed to Industry and Commerce's proposal to extend further the food voucher scheme.[47] However, the opposition parties continued to press for further increases to meet the increased cost-of-living.[48] In addition to the general food subsidies costing £2.3 million and food vouchers which cost over £500,000 per annum by 1943–44, a range of other measures had been introduced to assist with increased prices include assistance in kind for those on home assistance (£170,000), additional UA for agricultural and turf workers in October 1942 (£104,000), assistance with the cost of fuel in the winter of 1942 (£120,000), the increase in UA in cases where the fuel voucher was not payable (£140,000) and the increase in unemployment insurance for dependants (£75,000).[49]

LEGISLATING FOR CHILDREN'S ALLOWANCES

The 1938 Dáil ran its full term, which meant that elections had to be held in the summer of 1943. This led to a long run-in to the election. Early in 1943, Lemass made a number of public speeches referring to the future development of social security under Fianna Fáil and, in particular, the introduction of children's allowances.[50] However, in April, in a seeming change of electoral

47 NAI S. 13144A.   **48** *Dáil Debates*, vol. LXXXIX col. 905 *et seq.*, 3 March 1943. **49** Department of the Taoiseach memorandum 13 January 1944, NAI S. 13384. Costs relate to the financial year 1943–44. In addition compensation under the workmens compensation legislation was increased by 25% by Emergency Powers Order.   **50** *Irish Press*, 13 February, 2 March, 8 March 1943.

strategy, Lemass announced that the approach of the election had made sensible consideration of public issues impossible. In particular, he announced that the government did not propose to introduce legislation on children's allowances until the election was over. Fianna Fáil would not attempt to outbid the opposition.[51] Fianna Fáil's electoral strategy followed this approach and was long on responsibility and short on social benefits. In fact, it was Fine Gael which attempted to make children's allowances an election issue with W.T. Cosgrave giving a commitment to spend £2.5 million to introduce a scheme.[52] Only in response to this did Lemass make a major speech on children's allowances, announcing that the scheme would soon be ready to introduce in the Dáil.[53] The election, held in June 1943, resulted in the return of a minority Fianna Fáil government. The Fianna Fáil vote dropped by 10% to 42% and seats dropped to 48%. Labour seats rose dramatically from 7% to 12% and Clann na Talmhan, which had not existed at the time of the 1938 election, achieved no less than 10% of total seats.

Following Lemass' return as Minister for Industry and Commerce, he sought clarification from government as to the number of children to be entitled to the allowance and as to the rate of payment. He put forward a range of different options varying from payment after the first child at a rate of up to 2s. 6d. per week to payment after the third child at a rate of 1s. 6d. per week. The total cost ranged from £850,000 for the least costly option up to £3,300,000. On 24 September the government opted for payment to be made to children after the second at a rate of 2s. 6d. per week. The bill was approved by the government on 26 October 1943. Despite this, the Department of Finance submitted a further memorandum on 9 November complaining about the possible impact of children's allowances and claiming that it would 'accentuate inflationary tendencies'. The bill was quickly introduced in the Dáil by Lemass and the second stage was begun on 23 November 1943.[54] Despite the fact that the purpose of the scheme had effectively changed from the relief of large families to a system of general family support (albeit initially focussed on large families), Lemass argued in the Dáil that the basis of the argument for children's allowance was that in an economic system where wages were related to productivity or determined by supply and demand, the amount of wages was frequently inadequate to provide for a large family. He argued that 'the basis of the whole case for the establishment of a children's allowance is the need of large families'. He went

---

51 *Irish Press*, 17 April 1943. See also *Irish Press*, 29 April 1943. The 1943 Budget made no provision for children's allowances in the financial year, *Dáil Debates*, vol. LXXXIX col. 2284, 5 May 1943. 52 *Irish Times, Irish Press*, 5 June 1943. 53 *Irish Press*, 18 June 1943. 54 *Dáil Debates*, vol. XCII, col. 23 *et seq*. 23 November 1943.

on to specify that 'it is not contemplated that the enactment of this measure and the establishment of children's allowances will influence either the birth rate or the marriage rate'. He stated that it was his personal opinion that it would have no effect on either.[55]

The scheme was generally welcomed both in the Dáil and subsequently in the Seanad.[56] However, Lemass was opposed on a key issue of payment of the children's allowance to the father. Several deputies argued that payment should be made instead to the mother as the prime carer. Lemass was adamant in his rejection of these proposals. He argued that 'we should regard the father as the head of the family and responsible for the proper utilisation of the family income'.[57] In contrast to the situation in the United Kingdom, where the government originally proposed payment to the father but where a free vote in parliament reversed this, Lemass refused to accept a proposal that payment should be made to the mother and this was defeated on a vote in the Dáil.[58] Lemass referred to the 'rather revolutionary' views of some deputies who regarded payment of children's allowances to the mother as a first step towards economic independence for married women.[59] The bill finally became law on 23 February 1944. Lemass had made it quite clear on the passage of the Children's Allowance Bill through the Dáil and the Seanad that cuts in the income tax relief for children would be entailed in the subsequent Finance bill. These were, indeed, introduced although they were estimated to save only about £90–100,000 per annum and, at report stage, the Minister for Finance accepted a revised amendment from Fine Gael to reduce the scale of the cuts in order to ensure that no taxpayer would lose out as a result of the change.[60]

Meanwhile, however, the cost-of-living index had continued to rise to 284 in 1943. In October 1943, government decided to establish an interdepartmental committee to examine the cost-of-living including whether its increase was causing undue hardship to any section of the community. And de Valera sought Smiddy's advice on possible measures. In October 1943, Smiddy argued for the subsidisation of the price of necessaries and in December he submitted a memo on the effect on prices of increased monetary relief to 'the poor and indigent'. Smiddy argued that any increase would only have a limited effect on the cost-of-living index but that once increased

55 *Dáil Debates*, vol. XCII, col. 27–8, 23 November 1943.   56 Clann na Talmhan in particular argued that it was a 'Godsend in rural areas' and that small landholders and small property owners would derive greater benefit that any other sector of the community. *Dáil Debates*, vol. XCII, cols. 59, 87–8, 23 November 1943.   57 Ibid., col. 224, 24 November 1943. On this point see C. Clear, *Women of the House: Women's household work in Ireland 1926–61* (Irish Academic Press, Dublin, 2000), pp. 51–6.   58 Ibid., col. 576 *et seq.* 2 December 1943.   59 Ibid., col. 636.   60 *Dáil Debates*, vol. XCIV col. 1099, 27 June 1944.

it would be difficult ever to reduce payments. In early 1944, Fianna Fáil provided additional allowances of 2s. 6d. per week and 1s. 6d. for dependants for certain persons on old age and blind pensions, disablement benefit and widows' and orphans' pensions (1s. 6d. for widows and their dependants) where the food voucher scheme was not in operation.[61] The interdepartmental committee on the cost-of-living reported in June 1944. It discussed possible measures to compensate wage earners for the rise in the cost-of-living (notably without mentioning children's allowances) but concluded that the scope for subsidies was 'distinctly limited'.[62] The majority of the committee felt that the measures already taken to address the rise in the cost-of-living meant that 'no undue hardship need be experienced'. However, the Local Government members signed the report with the reservation that they felt the increase in costs was causing undue hardship and recommended a further widening of the classes covered by food vouchers. Largely as a result of extensive food subsidisation, the cost-of-living broadly stabilised after 1943.

It took some months to bring the children's allowance legislation into force. In the surprise 1944 election campaign, in contrast to the 1943 campaign, Fianna Fáil heavily emphasised social policy measures Hardly had the election been called than Lemass announced that the next major development after children's allowances was to be pension schemes for industrial workers.[63] Through the campaign, Lemass emphasised that Fianna Fáil was 'the worker's party' while even MacEntee lauded the 'great social reforms,' including children's allowances, achieved by Fianna Fáil.[64] Fianna Fáil returned to power – aided by the spilt in the Labour party – with a much improved performance: 49% of votes and 55% of seats. Children's allowances finally went into payment in August 1944.

WHY WERE CHILDREN'S ALLOWANCES ESTABLISHED?

There can be no doubt but that children's allowances represented a major development in Irish social policy at a time when such major developments might have been entirely unexpected. Various rationales have been put forward for the introduction of children's allowances at that time. Powell argues that 'demographic considerations were of crucial importance in the Fianna Fáil government's decision to introduce children's allowances in the

61 NAI S. 13140.   62 Interdepartmental committee on the cost-of-living, *Report*, NAI S. 12331.   63 *Irish Press*, 13 May 1944. See below p. 135.   64 *Irish Press*, 14, 26, 27 June 1944.

1940s'.[65] However, while there is no doubt that demographic considerations played a major part in raising interest in the issue at an early stage, it seems clear that the demographic arguments were challenged, and eventually buried by the report of the inter-departmental committee. As we have seen, Lemass specifically disclaimed any hopes that children's allowances would have an effect of increasing the number of births or marriages. Lee, in contrast, sees the debate about children's allowances as involving a struggle between the forces of modernisation (represented by Lemass) and the 'forces of resistance' represented by McElligott, MacEntee and Ó Ceallaigh. He describes this episode as 'one of the few battles that the forces of resistance lost'.[66] Yet, his account gives little indication as to why Lemass won this battle when, during the period in question, many of his other 'radical proposals' (such as his policy on full employment) were rejected by the Fianna Fáil government.[67] In addition, Lee's account appears to give insufficient weight to that unlikely moderniser, Eamon de Valera himself. Our analysis suggests that de Valera's contribution was crucial not only in raising the issue and in supporting Lemass's proposals but in shaping the final outcome of the scheme itself.

In order to identify why children's allowances were introduced, we must first attempt to analyse the different schemes that were put forward. Even looking only at the more detailed proposals, we can identify no less than six different approaches. The first was that of the Department of Finance itself which, drawing on the principles of fiscal liberalism, wished to limit the extent of state expenditure to the greatest degree possible and suggested that the state should only have responsibility in relation to the alleviation of poverty in situations of absolute deprivation. However, the submissions from the Department of Finance tended to be negative and simply to criticise other proposals. Any positive suggestions were of a tactical nature designed to counteract or delay whatever proposal they happened to be combating. Thus, in its arguments on the children's allowance scheme, the Department did not display any very coherent ideology and this is perhaps one of the reasons why it lost this battle. The second approach, exemplified in the recommendations of the inter-departmental committee, was a more 'modern' variation of the first. While the committee would have preferred that the labour market would provide a solution to the problem of inadequate income, it did accept that the state had a somewhat wider role in relation to the alleviation of poverty by ensuring that the national income was distributed so that no one would be without the bare necessaries of life. The committee

65 F. Powell, *Politics of Irish Social Policy*, p. 213. **66** Lee, *Ireland*, p. 277. **67** See Lee, *Ireland*, pp. 230–2; Girvin, *Between Two Worlds*, pp. 151–8.

put forward a coherent approach in relation to a means tested system of children's allowance. Thirdly, we have the approach recommended by Lemass both in his original outline and in his December 1942 memorandum for a contributory and non-contributory (means tested) scheme. The purpose of this scheme remained essentially the alleviation of poverty in large families although it went beyond the inter-departmental committee approach by envisaging a much more extensive redistribution of income.

Fourthly, and this marks a crucial shift from the earlier proposals, we have Lemass' proposal of a contributory and non-contributory (non–means tested) scheme in the heads of the bill proposed in February 1943.[68] Here the purpose of the scheme had shifted from alleviation of poverty in large families to a system of general family support, albeit one focused on larger families. The system involved some element of progressive income redistribution in that the lower income categories tended to have more children and that the proposal envisaged limited income tax cuts on higher earners. The proposal envisaged a much greater state role in the redistribution of resources than did earlier approaches. Fifthly, we have the eventual outcome: a universal scheme for all, albeit that the scheme initially applied only to families of three or more children. The force behind the shift away from Lemass' original proposal was de Valera who was concerned that a contributory system would be seen as benefiting wage earners. While this approach envisaged an extended role for the state in terms of income redistribution, at the same time it saw the family as an area within which the state should not interfere. Payment was to be made to the father and the state was not to interfere in how the payment was made.[69] Finally, and, in this case, unsuccessfully, we have quite a different proposal from Seán MacEntee in his position as Minister for Local Government and Public Health. This proposal was for a contributory scheme, payable through the employer. It envisaged a system much more in line with the Catholic corporatist system of social insurance prevalent in much of mainland Europe. It is noteworthy that while MacEntee was consistently opposed to Lemass' proposals for children's allowance and to what he described as, 'Beveridgism', he was not opposed to the development of social security systems.[70] Rather, he saw that social security should be developed,

---

68 Unfortunately, I have not been able to locate Industry and Commerce files for this period which might throw some light on the reasons for this shift.   69 In the Senate Lemass did not agree with a proposal that the state should take positive measures to ensure that allowances were used for the benefit of children. He stated that 'we are proposing to increase the income of the family. What happens the income is the concern of the family. I do not think that we should interfere so as to ensure that this particular proportion of the family income should be used for the benefit of the children any more than we should interfere with any other portion of the family income'. *Seánad Debates*, vol. XXVIII, col. 527, 14 January 1944.   70 One interesting

insofar as possible, by those directly involved, i.e. employees and employers. This approach was broadly consistent with the response of a number of Catholic thinkers to the proposals of the Beveridge Report.[71]

What then are the reasons for the establishment of children's allowances at this time? Lemass gave the alleviation of *poverty* in large families as a key rationale. Clearly this was one of the primary reasons. While the inter-departmental committee found limited survey information in relation to poverty in large families, it had no doubt that such poverty existed and subsequent studies confirmed its findings.[72] Poverty in large families was not, however, a new phenomenon. Why did it lead to action in the 1940s? Firstly, the domains of life for which the state was perceived as having some responsibility were expanding in the 1930s and 1940s. Despite the reservations of the Department of Finance, the Fianna Fáil government did see itself as having responsibility for the relief of poverty in, at least, many of its aspects. Secondly, the option of combating family poverty by increasing the employment of wives and children were inconsistent with other policy goals. Fianna Fáil policy was, effectively, to discourage married women from working outside the home while school attendance and employment legislation limited the possibility of children working.[73] Therefore, once poverty in large families was seen as a problem of public policy, some system of children's allowances was the only effective way of addressing the issue. While it is surprisingly rarely articulated, clearly one of the key purposes of the children's allowance scheme was to provide support for *families*. De Valera's commitment to the family was emphasised in the 1937 constitution which described the family, based on marriage, as 'the natural primary and fundamental unit group of Society, and as a moral institution possessing inalienable and imprescriptible rights, antecedent and superior to all positive law'. In the constitution, the state guaranteed 'to protect the Family in its Constitution and Authority, as the necessary basis of social order and as indispensable to the welfare of the Nation and the State'. By its establishment

issue in relation to MacEntee's position is the apparent contradiction between his opposition to Beveridge and his (MacEntee's) support for centralising and interventionist measures sponsored by his own Department (such as the Public Health bill, 1945). **71** Rev. P. McKevitt, 'The Beveridge Plan Reviewed' *Irish Ecclesiastical Record* (1943) LXI, p.145; Rev. C. Lucey, 'The Beveridge Report and Éire' *Studies* (1943) XXXII, p. 36: Bishop J. Dignan, *Social security: Outlines of a Scheme of National Health Insurance* (Sligo, 1945). Ironically, of course, the contradictions in MacEntee's thinking were to contribute to a furious disagreement with Bishop Dignan. **72** C. Clancy-Gore 'Nutritional Standards of Some Working Class Families in Dublin, 1943', *Journal of the Statistical and Social Inquiry Society of Ireland* (1943–4), 241. **73** School Attendance Act, 1926; Employment of Women, Young Persons and Children Act, 1920, Conditions of Employment Acts, 1936 and 1944; Shops (Conditions of Employment) Acts, 1938 and 1942.

of a system of children's allowances, the state gave some tangible effect to that guarantee.

Politically also, the establishment of a system of children's allowances was obviously attractive. As we have seen, Fianna Fáil had lost much of its radical lustre by the early 1940s. A system of children's allowances payable universally to all larger families (including farmers) would be of benefit to those voters specifically targeted by Fianna Fáil, i.e. farmers and the working class. The 1946 census indicates that farmers were the most fertile category of family followed by general labourers and semi-skilled workers. Thus a universal payment of children's allowances funded in part by specific (albeit limited) withdrawals of income tax relief from higher earners would be likely to provide benefits to those voters targeted by Fianna Fáil (and whose vote was currently being sought by the Labour party and Clann na Talmhan) while at the same time directing some of the cost of the allowances towards better-off Fine Gael voters who were not going to vote for Fianna Fáil in any case.

It has been argued that the introduction of children's allowances in other countries, including the United Kingdom,[74] Canada and Australia,[75] was largely dependent on the fact that the respective governments identified children's allowances as a potential means of dealing with wartime inflation of the cost-of-living without having to concede on wage demands. On the face of it, a quite similar analysis applies in Ireland. Wage standstills were imposed in Ireland in 1941 and these were modified and extended in 1942. As a result, particularly from 1940 on, the cost-of-living rose at a much faster rate than did wages generally. Looking at the outside evidence one might have anticipated that the potential wage control effect of children's allowances would have played an important part in Ireland as well. However, there is simply no reference to this issue at all either in the public or private considerations of government. Perhaps the only clear hint of it is in the inter-departmental family allowances committee report which devotes one paragraph to a brief outline of the Keynesian argument that children's allowances could contribute to meeting the needs of large families at a time of rapid inflation without any knock-on effect on overall wages. However, the committee itself made no comment on the relevance or otherwise of this argument to Irish conditions and, in fact, appeared quite open to the idea that the introduction of children's allowances would be deferred until after the War. In fact, food subsidies

74 See Macnicol, op. cit. p. 201 and Land, op. cit. Macnicol has also suggested that the UK government saw family allowances as a solution to the benefit wage overlap as an alternative to significant wage increases. Again there is no evidence that this factor was influential in an Irish context. 75 R. Watts, 'Family allowances in Canada and Australia 1940–1945: a comparative critical case study', *Journal of Social Policy* 16 (1987), 19–48.

fulfilled this counter-inflationary role in the Irish context. By 1943–4, subsidisation was costing £2.3 million per annum. However, while the items subsidised did make up a significant proportion of the expenditure of the poorer classes, general food subsidisation was clearly a means of relieving wage pressures rather than one of supporting the poor. Food vouchers, on the other hand, combined with limited increases for dependants, were a cheaper alternative to increasing overall payments and also had the beneficial effect of directly encouraging consumption of agricultural products. A general increase in payments to compensate for the increase in the cost-of-living between 1939 and 1943 would have cost of the order of £4 million as opposed to the additional £1.1 million being spent by 1943 on food vouchers and miscellaneous increases. However, the existence of rapid wartime inflation did contribute to the poverty affecting large families which, as we have suggested above, was a key feature in the introduction of the legislation.[76]

Faced by the issues of supporting families (particularly poorer large families) and garnering electoral support, the government was presented with a new form of technology which promised to provide a solution to its problems: children's allowances. Systems of children's allowances were extremely popular in the 1930s and 1940s. In total, eleven European countries introduced family allowances in the period between 1921 and 1945, as did a number of other countries including Canada and Australia. In particular, there had been extensive debate about the rationale for and potential systems of children's allowance in the United Kingdom.[77] Pope Pius XI had considered a system of family allowances in the encyclical *Quadragesimo Anno*. He had argued that

> Every effort must . . . be made that fathers of families receive a wage sufficient to meet adequately ordinary domestic needs. If in the present state of society this is not always feasible, social justice demands that reforms be introduced without delay which will guarantee every adult working man just such a wage. In this connection We might utter a word of praise for various systems . . . by which an increased wage is paid in view of increased family burdens, and a special provision is made for special needs.[78]

76 For example, Clancy Gore, 'Nutritional Standards of Some Working Class Families in Dublin, 1943' p. 253 in a study of nutritional standards of working class families suggests that while, in normal circumstances families might be able to get by, 'it is "absolutely impossible"for the larger families to provide adequately for themselves, at present' i.e. in 1943.   77 See, in particular, E. Rathbone, *The Disinherited Family* (Bristol, 1986, originally published 1924).
78 Pius XI, *On Social Reconstruction*, p. 36. It would seem likely that the Pope had in mind here

Children's allowances supplemented rather than superseded the family wage – in accordance with Catholic social thought.[79] Thus, in its introduction of universal children's allowances payable to the father of the family, Fianna Fáil introduced a system of children's allowances which responded to Irish needs, drawing on a combination of those aspects of British and Catholic social thinking which it perceived to be most relevant to Irish conditions. It is noteworthy that, while the political advantages of the introduction of such a system were clearly envisaged, there was little if any input from organised pressure groups or employer or trade union organisations in the formulation of children's allowance proposals.[80] At least in this instance, the state was acting with a high degree of autonomy in its development of social policy. In contrast to several other countries where civil service advisers were seen to have a key role in developing children's allowances, in Ireland the key initiative in introducing the allowances and in shaping the type of system appears to have come from politicians, in particular Lemass and de Valera.[81]

CONCLUSION

In summary, we suggest that the reasons behind the introduction of children's allowances related to Fianna Fáil policy on the alleviation of poverty in large families, general support for the family (as evidenced in the Constitution) and the fact that it was politically attractive to introduce a system of children's allowances that would primarily benefit those groups of people who were (or who were potentially) supporters of Fianna Fáil. Faced

the system of equalisation funds operating in many Continental countries. However, despite MacEntee's protestations, there is little indication that Catholic social thinking in Ireland was opposed to universal children's allowances. Several publications which received episcopal imprimatur referred in favourable terms to the Irish approach: A. O'Rahilly, *Social Principles* (Cork University Press, Cork, 1948), p. 22; J. Kavanagh, *Manual of Social Ethics* (Gill, Dublin, 1954), pp. 158–9. And see Rev. Cornelius Lucey's support for children's allowances cited in Kelly 'Social Security in Independent Ireland' p. 195.   79 A. O'Rahilly, op. cit.   80 In 1942, the ITUC established a sub-committee to examine family allowances, arising from a resolution proposed by the Irish Women Workers' Union. One year later, the committee had only established that the issue 'was neither as simple as many advocates seem to believe nor as easy of solution as most would desire'. The committee did finally come to the general conclusion that in all the circumstances the available evidence indicated the desirability of universal, tax-funded, cash allowances. However, the fact that Lemass had published the children's allowances bill before the committee reported raises the question as to who was influencing who? See ITUC, *Annual Reports, 1941–2*, p. 153; *1942–3*, p. 38; *1943–4*, p. 28.   81 Seán T. Ó Ceallaigh stated that there were four members of the cabinet enthusiastic on children's allowances (he not being one). See *Dáil Debates*, vol. XCIV, col. 240, 13 June 1944.

by a number of what it identified as problems of public policy – including initially population decline – the Fianna Fáil government turned to a new form of welfare: children's allowances. Although, children's allowances of various types appeared in many Western countries in the 1930s and 1940s, the particular shape they took varied greatly to reflect local conditions. Thus the Irish system was very different to that in, for example, France and, despite surface similarities, to that in the UK. Although the development of children's allowances in Ireland was clearly influenced by policy debates in the UK, it is interesting to note that the Irish government decided to introduce a system of children's allowances *before* the UK and for very different reasons. This chapter suggests that, despite some wavering, Fianna Fáil in the early 1940s still realised the importance of social policy development to its overall electoral success and that the party still had the potential for quite radical social policy measures.

6

Beveridge, Dignan and the establishment of the Department of Social Welfare, 1943–47

'Social security in its wide sense . . . is not to protect people from the problems and difficulties of life, it is to enable them to meet those difficulties on a footing of approximate equality. It is not a slavish dependence on government or state but a recognition that, in modern conditions, only state action can to a large extent be effective enough to shape, modify and adapt those conditions to the varying needs of the different sectors of the community'.[1]

'By all means let us strive to improve our social services . . . . But we must be prudent and we must be careful lest by wild improvidence and thriftless spending we not only damage our national economy, but do something much worse, rot the moral fibre of our people.'[2]

This chapter looks at the first major step in the birth of a unified social welfare scheme: the establishment of a new Department of Social Welfare. As we have seen, in 1940, the social welfare system as we know it today simply did not exist. Rather, there were a range of different payments catering for different categories of the population and administered by different public bodies. However, by the time of the enactment of the Social Welfare Act, 1952, the various schemes had been brought together and amalgamated under the control and planning of one department: the Department of Social Welfare. A first step in the amalgamation of the various different organisations into one unified social welfare system had taken place place in 1935 with the establishment of the unified National Health Insurance Society. As outlined in chapter 3, in 1937, the National Health Insurance Society requested the Minister for Local Government to investigate the system of

1 P.J. Keady, memorandum to MacEntee 3 February 1945, UCDA P67/261. 2 Seán MacEntee speaking at Rathmines in the 1943 General Election, 17 June 1943, UCDA P67/364.

national health insurance with a view to providing improved services. This investigation was to include the question as to whether all social and health services should be coordinated under the supervision of a Minister for Social Services. However, both the Minister, Seán T. Ó Ceallaigh and his department had shown little support for this proposal although the department had expressed the view that a new ministry would be of advantage as it would help to coordinate schemes, allowing social services to be considered as a whole and difficulties to be more readily overcome.[3]

Subsequently, in January 1939, Ó Ceallaigh recommended that an interdepartmental committee should carry out an examination of this issue. And on 31 January 1939, government decided to set up an inter-departmental committee consisting of representatives of the Departments of Finance, Local Government and Public Health, and Industry and Commerce to examine and report on the desirability of establishing a new Department of Social Services and to make recommendations as to the services to be assigned to such a new department in the event of government deciding in favour of its establishment. The Department of the Taoiseach prepared, but did not circulate, a memorandum on the creation of new Departments of State. Finance was somewhat unenthusiastic about the proposed committee and, after some 'toing and froing' in relation to the proposed terms of reference and membership of the committee, the Department noted on 5 May 1939, that no further action need be taken as it appeared that the Taoiseach was no longer interested in the proposal.[4] A further memo in July of that year noted that Maurice Moynihan, secretary to the government, 'agree[d] as to the undesirability of the inquiry'. It appears that interest resumed early in the new year and on 9 February 1940, the government considered appointing Dr Conn Ward, the Parliamentary Secretary at the Department of Local Government and Public Health, to chair the committee. However, in March it was decided that the question of the Department of Social Services was to be included in the terms of reference of a committee being set up under the Minister for the Coordination of Defensive Measures, Frank Aiken, to investigate the organisation and staffing of government departments. Again, however, this committee did not proceed.[5] Later in 1940 consideration was given to including examination on establishing a 'unified scheme of social services' in the terms of reference of the family allowances committee (discussed in chapter 5) but this idea was also eventually dropped. Thus an opportunity to have preempted the Beveridge Report was lost.

Nothing further appears to have happened in relation to this issue until February 1942 when William Norton TD, leader of the Labour party, put

3 Department of the Taoiseach memorandum 'Creation of Departments of State', 4 February 1939, NAI S11109. 4 NAI S101/2/39. 5 Fanning, *Finance*, pp. 325–7.

down a parliamentary question to the Taoiseach asking if he would consider
the establishment of a Department of Social Welfare. In reply, de Valera said
that this would be attended by many difficulties and that it was not clear that
it would result in any economy or increased efficiency.[6] The proposed
wording of the Taoiseach's reply to Norton was circulated to the Ministers
of relevant departments all of whom agreed with this approach. Also in
February, the national executive of the ITUC had met Conn Ward to discuss
national health insurance and had sought 'a comprehensive, all-inclusive
scheme of social services, probably under a Minister of Social Services'.[7]

THE PUBLICATION OF THE BEVERIDGE REPORT

The Beveridge Report on social security was published in the UK in
December 1942.[8] It provided a blueprint for the establishment of a unified
system of social security in that country in the post war period.[9] The
Beveridge Report recommended the establishment of a unified scheme of
social security, amalgamating all the various different social insurance and
social assistance schemes then operating in the United Kingdom. In relation
to the administration, Beveridge recommended the establishment of a
ministry of social security on the basis that this would provide for immensely
improved efficiency. Unification of administrative responsibility was seen as
a 'fundamental principle' in the interests of economy and efficiency. It
received extensive, and favourable, comment in the Irish newspapers immediately on publication.[10] On 10 December 1942, a Fine Gael motion was put
down in the Dáil to the effect that the Beveridge Report should receive the
earnest consideration of government and requesting that a White Paper on
future social security policy be prepared. On 14 December, copies of the
Beveridge Report were circulated to all Ministers and on 16 December, at a
meeting of the Cabinet Committee on Economic Planning, Seán Lemass
stated that arrangements would be made in his department for an examina-

6 *Dáil Debates* vol. LXXV col. 1818 et seq., 18 February 1942.   7 ITUC, *Annual Report
1941–2*, p. 38–9.   8 *Social Assistance and Allied Services*, HMSO, 1942.   9 See generally J.
Hills, J. Ditch and H. Glennerster, *Beveridge and Social Security* (Oxford University Press,
Oxford,1994); J. Harris, *William Beveridge: A Biography* (Oxford University Press, Oxford,
1977); P. Baldwin, *The Politics of Social Solidarity* (Cambridge University Press, Cambridge,
1990), pp. 116–27.   10 See, for example, *Irish Times*, 21 & 22 December 1942. On the Irish
response see generally Bew and Patterson *Seán Lemass and the Making of Modern Ireland* (Gill
and Macmillan, Dublin, 1982), pp. 29–34, S. Ó Cinnéide 'The 1949 White Paper and the
Foundations of Social Welfare' in A. Lavan (ed.), *50 Years of Social Welfare Policy* (Department
of Social, Community and Family Affairs, 2000).

tion of the Beveridge Report as soon as time could be spared from the Family Allowance bill.[11] Hugo Flinn immediately wrote to de Valera pointing out that the publication of the report and the promise of the 'Six County' government to implement it if adopted at Westminster was a 'god send' to Labour and 'properly worked worth quite a few seats'.[12] It is clear that the Beveridge Report did have a significant impact on Irish thinking, both among the general public and in political circles. Speaking in March 1943, Lemass accepted that the report had created a high conception of social security standards and had made Irish provisions appear inadequate, almost parsimonious.[13]

As we saw in the last chapter, faced with an election in June 1943, Fianna Fáil adopted an electoral campaign based on responsible government and refused to be "out-bid" by the opposition in the run up to the election campaign. Fianna Fáil performed comparatively poorly in that election and were returned to power only as a minority government. It appears that the importance of the social policy measures to the electorate may have been re-emphasised in the mind of the government by this experience. In any case, on 21 September, the government decided to establish a Cabinet Committee consisting of Ó Ceallaigh, Lemass, Seán MacEntee and James Ryan, Minister for Agriculture, to examine and report on a new Department of Social Services.[14] Again, however, it does not appear that this Cabinet Committee ever functioned. However, on 1 December 1943, the Taoiseach's office wrote to the Revenue Commissioners and the Departments of Industry and Commerce and Local Government referring to recent criticisms in the press and elsewhere in relation to overlapping and duplication in the administration of social services. All departments denied these allegations.[15] The Department of the Taoiseach reviewed these responses and the assistant secretary to the government, Patrick Kennedy, came to the conclusion that there was 'no avoidable overlapping and duplication and that no material economy would be effected by the transfer or amalgamation of any of the existing services'. He went on to state that 'the general conclusion, therefore, appears to be that the present system of administration of social services by

---

11 NAI S. 13053A.   12 Flinn to de Valera 13 December 1942, NAI S. 13053A.   13 *Irish Press*, 2 March 1943. It should be noted that Lemass went on to defend the performance of the Irish government in this regard and to refer to the next stage in the development of social policy as being the establishment of a system of childrens' allowances. As we have seen in the previous chapter, MacEntee in contrast strongly opposed 'Beveridgism'.   14 NAI S. 11036A.   15 See submissions from the Department of Local Government, 8 December 1943, Revenue Commissioners, 13 December 1943 and Department of Industry and Commerce, 24 December 1943, NAI S11109.

government departments is economical and that nothing is to be gained by moving them around or by re-arrangement . . .'. This conclusion was agreed to by Maurice Moynihan.[16]

However, the pressure for reform of social services was continuing and in January 1944, James Ryan, sent a memorandum to the Taoiseach on the re-organisation of departments suggesting that there was a case for at least three new units or departments in the areas of social services, public health and labour. In February William Norton TD again put down a parliamentary question to the Taoiseach asking him to give early attention to the question of the establishment of a special department for the administration of all social services. The Taoiseach's reply was, however, still in the negative. De Valera stated that the matter had been further investigated in some detail and that the general conclusion would seem to be that the existing system of administration was efficient and economical. He stated that while the government had taken no decision adverse to the establishment of a Department of Social Services, it was of the opinion that there was no urgent need for any closer investigation.[17]

As we have seen, in the surprise June 1944 election, Fianna Fáil put much more emphasis on social policy measures.[18] Shortly afterwards, in September 1944, the UK Government White Paper on Social Insurance was published.[19] This document accepted many of the recommendations of the Beveridge Report and, whereas in the past it had been possible to argue that the Beveridge Report was simply the recommendation of a committee and not official government policy, this explanation was no longer available. The White Paper received extensive newspaper coverage in the Irish papers.[20] Irish public opinion sought social services on a par with those available in Northern Ireland.[21] However, much worse was to happen for the Fianna Fáil government with the publication by Dr Dignan, the chairman of the National Health Insurance Society, of proposals for reform of social security.

16 Department of the Taoiseach, internal memo, 13 December 1943, S11109.   17 *Dáil Debates*, vol. XCII col.1237 *et seq.*, 17 February 1944.   18 See, for example, *Irish Press*, 13 May, 14, 26, 27 June, 1944.   19 *Social Insurance*, HMSO, 1944.   20 See *Irish Times*, 26 & 27 September 1944; *Irish Press*, 27 September 1944; *Irish Independent*, 27 September 1944. 21 See, for example, Norton *Dáil Debates* vol. CIII col. 1161, 20 January 1946 and an ITUC resolution calling for a social security scheme 'as comprehensive and all-embracing' as that enjoyed in the Six Counties (sic), *Annual Report 1950–1*, p. 89. And Unionists were not above making an issue of this comparison; see the Ulster Unionist Council pamphlet comparing social services in Ulster and Eire (*sic*), *A Warning to the Ulster People*, UUC, Belfast,1949 ILHA Norton papers 116.

THE DIGNAN PLAN

As we have seen the NHIS had long seen the co-ordination of services as essential to the future development of social services. While its initial proposals in this area in 1937 had not been supported by the Department or the Minister for Local Government, both had come around to tentative support for this idea by 1939. While there is little evidence of close co-oper-ation between the department and the NHIS, both were able to work in tandem on issues such as the change in the basis of national health insurance funding. However, crucially for the development of events, the relationship between the NHIS and, in particular, Dignan and MacEntee and his depart-ment had deteriorated in 1943. The precise event over which difficulties arose was relatively minor and it is unclear whether it was a cause or merely a symptom of the differences between MacEntee and Dignan, both of whom were well aware of the dignity of their respective offices. The Society had, without seeking the permission of the Minister or department, sanctioned bonus payments in respect of its staff, a matter which was the more contentious due to the wartime control on wages.[22] In May 1943 Keady, on behalf of the Minister, had argued that the NHIS was, in effect, subject to the general direction of the Minister in its actions. Subsequently, Duffy, now controller, and Keady met Dignan and Henderson to discuss the issue.[23] Apparently Dignan had originally intended to seek a meeting with MacEntee but had been persuaded to meet officials first. Dignan stated that he was 'agitated' by MacEntee's intervention against the bonus which he regarded as suggesting that the committee of management could not be trusted to look after the interests of insured people and by the claims of ministerial control which Keady had advanced. While accepting that no effort to interfere with the Society had been made, Dignan said he was concerned that a new depar-ture was being initiated. He pointed out that if the Minister was not satisfied with the actions of his nominees, he could refuse to re-appoint them. However, after considerable discussion, Duffy was able to satisfy Dignan that no new departure was intended. Duffy tellingly noted that it was 'not neces-sary' to show his note of the meeting to MacEntee.

Perhaps spurred on by the publication of the Beveridge Report in the UK, in the latter half of 1943 the committee of management of the NHIS consid-ered the issue of the future development of social security services. In August

22 UCDA P67/257. It would also appear that there was tension between the department and the society over the operation of the additional benefits scheme. See Department of Local Government memo 28 September 1942, NAI S. 11036A. 23 File note by J. Duffy 13 May 1943, NAI IA 92/53.

1943, Dignan discussed with the committee of management the need to plan ahead and Henderson agreed to consider and prepare proposals.[24] In early 1944, preliminary work in this regard was done both by Dignan and Henderson. This was mentioned by Dr Dignan to Dr Ward in April 1944.[25] By June 1944, Henderson had prepared a paper on the topic[26] and at the subsequent meeting of the committee in July, Dignan stated that he would redraft it. Later that month Henderson wrote to Ward giving him a very brief synopsis of the proposals. At the committee meetings in August and September, Dignan discussed the proposals. At the September meeting, Dignan agreed that the proposals would be redrafted and circulated before the next meeting so that members could consult with their constituencies. He emphasised the strictly confidential nature of the proposals and stated that when the document was finalised it would be put in final form for publication and presentation to the Minister. However, on 11 October 1944, Dr Dignan told the committee that while he had rewritten the paper, he had not had time to circulate the final document. He announced that he was taking full and personal responsibility for the proposals: the committee would not be asked to adopt it and the question of consulting the respective interests would not arise. Dignan then read the paper at a meeting of the committee of management and subsequently released it to the papers. At the same time, he sent copies to both Seán MacEntee and Dr Ward. On 18 October 1944 the Dignan Plan, as it became known, received extensive and favourable coverage in the Irish radio and print media.[27] However, Seán MacEntee took extreme exception to the fact that the bishop had published his proposals rather than presenting them to himself and his department in the first case.[28] He immediately notified the newspapers that no social service plan had been submitted to him.[29]

The Dignan Plan proposed major reforms of both the existing health and social security services. It was highly critical of existing services describing these as still tainted with pauperism and destitution. It proposed a model based on coverage for the full range of recognised risks, including health care, through social insurance. Following the approach of the recent report of the Commission on Vocational Organisation, it recommended that services be

24 Henderson to Hurson 2 November 1944, NAI IA 92/53.   25 Ward had been formally given delegated responsibility for the NHIS in January 1944.   26 Henderson 'Replanning National Health Insurance' UCDA P67/257.   27 *Irish Press, Irish Times* and *Irish Independent*, 18 October 1944. See NAI S. 13570.   28 D. O'Leary, *Vocationalism and Social Catholicism in Twentieth-Century Ireland* (Irish Academic Press, Dublin, 2000), p. 111. On the dispute, see H. Riordan, '"A Political Blackthorn": Seán MacEntee, the Dignan Plan & the Principle of Ministerial Responsibility', *Ir. Econ. Soc. Hist.* XXVII (2000), pp. 44-62.   29 *Irish Press, Irish Times* and *Irish Independent*, 19 October 1944.

administered by an independent and vocational organisation reporting to a Minister of Social Services.[30] Benefits and contributions were to be be related to earnings. Dignan's approach was along the line of that advocated by other prominent clerics of the time including Fr Cornelius Lucey and Fr Peter McKevitt.[31] Dignan's plan did have some shortcomings. It did not deal adequately with how the self-employed were to be included in such a social insurance system. Not was any effort made to cost the proposals. Nonetheless it was a sincere attempt to set out a new approach to the provision of social services in Ireland. The Dignan Plan received very widespread support from a broad range of political parties, trade unions and other organisations.[32] However, MacEntee, buttressed by the contemporaneous rejection of the proposals of the Commission on Vocational Organisation, remained implacably opposed. In response to a parliamentary question from William Norton, he stated that the bishop's proposals were entirely impracticable.[33] In February 1945 MacEntee submitted documents to government in relation to the Dignan Plan including a summary of events and criticisms of the proposals. Given that MacEntee felt that his position of authority in relation to the NHIS was somewhat unclear, he proposed to government that he be given 'clear and unequivocal control' over the Society.[34]

Matters deteriorated further when on 12 March 1945, Dr Dignan, speaking in Loughrea, replied to MacEntee's criticisms of his proposals. This was followed by a public response from MacEntee on the following day.[35]

---

30 Myles na gCopaleen (whose alter ego, Brian O'Nolan was a civil servant in the Department of Local Government and Public Health) published a hardly impartial rebuttal of the scheme, *Irish Times* 26,27,28 October 1944. Myles envisaged the 'neofacist' proposals as leading to 'a new tri-partitioned Ireland full of "members" bemused with drugs and nursing, jack-booted secret police from Cork ranging the country in "travelling motor clinics", and the whole thing vocationally organised!' For an analysis placing this in the broader context of Myles' views on social policy, see S. Curran '"Could Paddy leave off copying just for five minutes": Brian O'Nolan & Eire's Beveridge Plan' *Irish University Review* 31 (2001). 31 Rev. P. McKevitt, 'The Beveridge Plan Reviewed' *Irish Ecclesiastical Record* (1943) LXI, p. 145; Rev. C. Lucey 'The Beveridge Report and Éire' *Studies*, (1943) XXXII, p. 36. And see Rev. C. Lucey, 'The Dignan Plan', *The Leader*, 15 December 1945. 32 See NAI S. 13570; UCDA P67/257. 33 *Dáil Debates*, vol. XCV col.1488-9, 24 January 1945. 34 NAI S. 13570. And see NAI IA 92/53; UCDA P67/257. The department's legal advice suggested that the Minister did not have any general power of control over the NHIS other than the specific powers granted in the 1933 legislation. MacEntee proposed to amend the legislation to clarify his powers and to alter the composition of the committee of management but this proposal was overtaken by the broader realignment of responsibilities discussed below. 35 13 March 1945, UCDA P67/270. The response to Dignan was hastily added to a previously prepared criticism of Beveridge's proposals for full employment which described them as 'neo-totalitarian' and argued that in Ireland social security was based on ownership of property. See also MacEntee's May 1945 speech to the UCD Commerce Society on full employment in which he again criticised

There followed an exchange of letters between the two but despite an attempt by Seán T. Ó Ceallaigh in the Senate on 20 March to conciliate and a conciliatory letter from MacEntee to the bishop of 20 March, the bishop published his proposals in pamphlet form in March and wrote to the press defending himself.[36] Although the Dignan Plan continued to attract favourable comment in the media, it is clear that MacEntee's vehement opposition meant that the proposals were dead in the water. In response to a request from Local Government for observations on the plan, J.J. McElligott did not even bother to submit detailed opposition on the basis that both departments were in agreement as to the 'complete unsuitability of the scheme for adoption in any form'.[37] In contrast, Industry and Commerce's evaluation of the Dignan Plan, although also critical, was much more balanced. William Maguire wrote that the Plan was 'very far indeed from being a full Plan'. It was 'rather an expression, and that in very general terms in some respects, of what benefits should be provided without any real attempt at estimating the cost or whether the country can afford it'.[38] Subsequently, when Dignan's term of office expired in August 1945, MacEntee effectively sacked him by not renewing his appointment and appointing D.J. O'Donovan in his place. All other members of the committee of management were asked to serve again as, MacEntee argued, they had not, unlike the bishop, publicly committed themselves.[39] However, the three trustees were required to give assurances that there would be no further public disputation. Only Keady was prepared to do so and the other trustees were replaced.[39a]

While MacEntee's response to the Dignan Plan was autocratic in the extreme, Dignan himself was, at best, disingenuous in relation to MacEntee and Ward in the lead up to the publication of the proposals.[40] Despite

Beveridge both for his theoretical approach and for his 'formidable apparatus of coercion and regimentation'. UCDA P67/570. See T. Feeny 'The Road to Serfdom: Seán MacEntee, "Beveridgism" and the Development of Irish Social Policy' *History Review* XII (2001), pp. 63–72. 36 *Seanad Debates*, vol. XXIX col. 1909–10, 20 March 1945; *Irish Press, Irish Independent*, 27 March 1945. 37 McElligott to Hurson, 31 May 1945, NAI S. 72/12/44. 38 NAI. EB 286160; EB 281862 . See UCDA P67/257 for the (predictably) negative Local Government response. 39 UCDA P67/257. In November 1944, MacEntee had replaced a deceased trustee (Dr Rowlette) with a civil servant. Duffy, the first name proposed, had objected that his position (and the fact that his son was employed by the NHIS) created a potential conflict of interest. Keady, to whom the chalice then passed, also wished to have 'on the record' his view that similar considerations applied to him. MacEntee, showing his nastier side, objected to this attitude and, noting Keady's desire to have his objections on the record, directed that they be filed for reference when the vacancy of controller arose. Keady apologised and, subsequently, got the job. Duffy, close to retirement, provided a more muted apology. UCDA P67/259. **39a** *Dáil Debates*, vol. XCIX col. 2295-8, 13 March 1946. See H. Riordan, 'Political Blackthorn' p. 59. **40** Writing to Dr Bob Collis on 23 October 1944, Dignan adopted a very

Dignan's subsequent indignation, a negative response from MacEntee was highly predictable. While responsibility for national health insurance had been delegated to Ward in early 1944, MacEntee was still responsible to cabinet for this area and was likely to take his responsibilities personally. In any case, the information the NHIS had provided to Ward was scanty in the extreme and gave little indication of what was to occur. Dignan clearly intended to keep the proposals away from MacEntee and Ward and to ensure maximum publicity for them. Of course, whether a more conciliatory approach would have succeeded must be open to question and Dignan was clearly motivated by his desire to improve social services. Whether or not there was any justification for MacEntee's response, more importantly for a senior Minister, his blunt rejection of popular proposals was undeniably impolitic.[41] The government's, and in particular MacEntee's, response to the Dignan Plan effectively meant that any proposals for a non-departmental body responsible for the administration of social security were very unlikely to be successful. However, the public relations fiasco arising from MacEntee's handling of the bishop's proposals must have increased the pressure on the government to produce some alternative response.

OLD AGE PENSION PRESSURES

A further area of increased pressure on the government was in relation to reform of old age pensions. As we saw in chapter 4, there was, perhaps surprisingly, little parliamentary pressure for reform until 1943. After that date, however, given the rising cost-of-living an increasing number of motions were put down for the Dáil and Seanad calling for reform of the means test, payment of pension at a reduced age (generally 65), and an increase in pension rate.[42] And the ITUC also regularly passed resolutions

different tone to that in his later letters to MacEntee and the press. He felt that his scheme had 'got too good a press' and that 'the reaction [would] set in shortly'. However, what did this matter as the publicity and interest the plan had received would 'compel the Government to make some move in the matter'. Somebody, perhaps Dr Shanley to whom Collis sent a copy of the letter, helpfully passed this on to MacEntee, UCDA P67/258. **41** Lest MacEntee simply be seen as opposed to reform, it is important to recall that he supported his department's proposal for radical health reform and strongly advocated the establishment of a separate Department of Health. **42** Motions were debated in the Dáil and Seanad on various pension issues, see *Dáil Debates*, 94, col. 1317, 27 June 1944, vol. 94 col. 2005, 26 September 1944; *Dáil Debates*, 99, cols. 2054, 2251, 6 March 1946; *Seanad Debates*, XXXII, cols. 820, 1109, 17 July 1946, 1 August 1946, *Dáil Debates*, vol. CIV, col. 2569, 20 March 1947, vol. CVIII col. 809, 22 October 1947. Motions in respect of these debates were generally put down some considerable time before the debate took place and a number were not debated, NAI S.11036.

calling for improved pensions.[43] Following his commitment to pension schemes for industrial workers, in November 1944, Lemass had circulated options on establishing a retirement pension at age 65.[44] He set out the options of voluntary action by employers facilitated by legislation, legislation to require employers to establish a pension fund, and a state scheme. Local Government favoured a state scheme with contributory old age pensions added to the widows' pension scheme. The Departments of Defence, Agriculture and Posts and Telegraphs also favoured a state scheme but several departments suggested the need for detailed examination of such a proposal. Finance, of course, felt bound to raise objections to the scheme. However, in March 1945, Finance undertook to further examine the proposal for a state scheme. Unsurprisingly, progress was slow and no real advances had been made by 1947.

THE INTER-DEPARTMENTAL COMMITTEE
ON A DEPARTMENT OF SOCIAL SERVICES

Political pressure had continued to mount on the government in relation to general social security reform. In October 1944 Deputies Everett and Pattison, of the National Labour party, had put down a motion in relation to the establishment of a Department of Social Services and a unified scheme of social security. This motion was put on the agenda of the government, being adjourned no less than twelve times in October, November and December 1944. On 29 November 1944, the Taoiseach responded to a parliamentary question on the impact of the social security White Paper in the UK and the introduction of a comprehensive social security system in Ireland. De Valera argued that any expansion in social services here would be dependent on an increase in actual wealth.[45] In response to the National Labour motion, MacEntee requested the personal views of his senior civil servants on the issue.[46] The responses were mainly negative. Keady, however, took a more positive view arguing that while 'social security' was not limited to social insurance, social insurance was a desirable method of redistribution.

In February 1945 the government decided to establish an inter-departmental committee consisting of Finance, Industry and Commerce and Local

---

43 See the annual reports of the ITUC for the period. However, as Jim Larkin jnr. was later to point out Congress seemed 'to have the very happy knack of passing resolutions . . . and forgetting all about them' ITUC, *Annual Report 1950–1*, p. 92–3. 44 NAI S. 13616. 45 *Dáil Debates*, vol. XCV col. 1021, 29 November 1944. 46 UCDA P67/261. The departmental file includes submissions from Keady, James Deeny and a number of other officials.

Government to report on the desirability and practicality of assigning social services (such as old age pensions, widows' and orphans' pensions, unemployment assistance, unemployment insurance, national health insurance, childrens' allowances, etc.) to a single ministry and to advise on the practical steps necessary if this was decided on by government.[47] On 26 February 1945, MacEntee submitted a memorandum arguing that the decision to establish an inter-departmental committee was at variance with the Taoiseach's response to the parliamentary question in February 1944. As nothing further had transpired in relation to the administration of social services, he argued that the decision to establish an inter-departmental committee was not appropriate. If such a committee was to proceed, MacEntee further argued that Local Government should have two members. However, the government refused to revise its decision to establish a committee. On 27 February it decided that the Department of Post & Telegraphs was to be included in the committee but conceded that each department would be entitled to one or two representatives as it saw fit. The Department of Local Government submitted further memoranda arguing that proposals in relation to the reform of health services should be submitted to the committee and subsequently, having withdrawn the first memorandum, that health insurance should be excluded from the remit of the committee as the service should be associated with health services. This memorandum was also subsequently withdrawn.

In what may be interpreted as a preemptive strike, in his Budget speech in May 1945, Ó Ceallaigh dismissed the possibility of introducing a scheme of social security along the lines of the Beveridge Report as both impracticable and unsuited to Irish conditions.[48] However, on 15 May 1945 the committee was appointed by the Minister for Finance. It was chaired by L.M. Fitzgerald, principal officer in Finance, and included representatives from Finance, Industry and Commerce (including William Maguire), Local Government (Deeny and Garvin) and Posts and Telegraphs. The committee produced a report extremely quickly in July of 1945 after only eight meetings.[49] After prolonged discussion, the committee decided that its terms of reference restricted it to income maintenance services defrayed from voted money or statutory funds to which the Exchequer contributed.[50] On that

47 NAI S. 11109. 48 *Dáil Debates*, vol. XCVII, col. 39–41, 2 May 1945. See the Industry and Commerce memo costing the Beveridge proposals at £38.8 million p.a. compared to existing expenditure of £9.5 million, 19 April 1945 UCDA P67/261. See also B.F. Shields 'Some Considerations Regarding the Cost of Social Welfare in Ireland' which gave a cost for implementing Beveridge of £34 million (excluding health services) *JSSISI*, xvii (1942–3) p. 134. 49 Minutes of the meetings and draft reports are on files NAI S. 101/2/45 and NAI EB 285665. 50 The minutes indicate that the chair was instructed by Maurice Moynihan that the

basis, public health, home assistance and all other services administered wholly or substantially by local authorities were treated as being outside the committee's scope. The rationale for amalgamating income maintenance responsibilities centred on two main arguments: economies arising from rationalisation, and the need for centralised planning. The committee looked in detail at the administration of services within the different public bodies. It felt certain that some economy of staff would necessarily result from the amalgamation under one department but could not provide any estimate as to the likely scope of savings. The minutes of the committee indicate that the chairman argued for the establishment of a new department because of the advantages from the point of view of planning the development of income maintenance services. The Local Government representatives argued against a new income maintenance department incorporating health insurance and suggested that a Department of Public Health should be established to which the National Health Insurance Society would be attached. The committee considered transferring all income maintenance services to Local Government but felt that this would create an unmanageable burden on the Department. It also considered setting up a Department of Public Health and Social Services but this was opposed on the grounds that the separation of public health matters from Local Government would be a 'dramatic departure'.[51]

In the end, the majority of the committee strongly recommended that 'if the future developments of social services are to be adequately supervised, planned and coordinated, the Government should have at its disposal the specialist advice of a Minister and a Department established for that purpose'. The committee felt that it might safely be assumed that the State was entering an era of increased demand for social services and government should have 'a centre of informed opinion, abreast of modern trends and capable of formulating a policy which will maintain a satisfactory balance between modern developments and our domestic problems, needs and resources'.[52] A minority report signed by the representatives of the Department of Local Government argued that national health insurance should not be separated from public health matters. It argued that social services extended far beyond income maintenance and that a Department of Income Maintenance Services would not result in a proper basis for a constructive and comprehensive social policy.

In July 1945, the Department of Finance responded to the report of the

terms of reference were to be interpreted as applying to services of an income maintenance character only. **51** Minutes of meeting 11 June 1945, NAI S. 101/2/45. In the event, of course, this is precisely what was to occur. **52** *Report*, p. 10.

inter-departmental committee. The Department was disposed to agree that coordinated control of income maintenance services would be desirable and lead to some economy in what it saw as the existing high cost of administration. However, the Department was satisfied that the administration of services did not justify the establishment of a new department and recommended that all should be brought together under the Department of Local Government and Public Health with the establishment of a sub-department for such services. The Department of Industry and Commerce agreed with the majority report subject to the co-ordination of the employment and payment functions of employment exchanges. In October 1945, the relevant documents were circulated by the government secretariat for the government meeting to take place on 23 October. De Valera wished to discuss the attitude to be adopted in relation to the Dáil motion which had been put forward the previous year by Deputies Everett and Pattison and which would shortly be debated. Local Government argued that social services were defined too narrowly and must include health. It argued that the bringing together of services would be regarded as the time for laying the basis for a real social service structure including health care and opposed the establishment of the proposed new Department of Social Services. However, on 13 November 1945 the government adopted the majority report in principle.[53] The Dáil motion on the Department of Social Services was debated in November 1945 and was concluded in January 1946. Replying to the motion, the Taoiseach did not agree that the new Department of Social Services would result in greater coordination or savings. Echoing the committe's conclusions, he stated that the 'real basis for the decision . . . is that if future developments of social services . . . are to be envisaged and adequately planned, supervised and coordinated the Government should have at its disposal the specialist advice of a Minister and a Department established for that purpose'.[54] However, de Valera went on to say that he would not like it to be taken that the government considered it as a matter of course that a considerable expansion of services was practicable. He argued that 'no further considerable expansion of the social services will be possible without an appreciable expansion of our actual wealth'.[55]

Interestingly, also in November 1945, the new chair of the NHIS, the ubiquitous D.J. O'Donovan had submitted proposals for reform to Ward.[56] Recalling the shortcomings of the existing scheme, including the inadequacy of benefits and the limited scope of insurance, O'Donovan proposed urgent legislation to remedy the more obvious defects, possibly followed by a general

53 NAI S.11109.　54 *Dáil Debates*, vol. XCIX col.171, 30 January 1946.　55 Ibid., col. 172.
56 O'Donovan to Ward 9 November 1945, UCDA P67/261.

review. Indicating his awareness of the correct protocol (from a government perspective) O'Donovan said that he had not yet discussed these proposals with the committee of management and, before doing so, would like to feel that they were within acceptable limits. He proposed to extend insurance up to earnings of £450 p.a.; to include civil and public servants; to introduce wage related payments and contributions;[57] to increase maternity and marriage benefit; to provide a hospital benefit; and to introduce uniform contributions for men and women. Again learning from the Dignan Plan, he included estimated costings. Around this time, Conn Ward was also examining the issue of extending social insurance to the rural community.[58] Ward felt that despite the difficulties involved, there was a case for extending social insurance in this way as it would be undesirable to make major developments which did not include this group and as there was an overwhelming argument in favour of abandoning pensions paid solely on the basis of a means test. He felt that there was a need to establish a committee or commission to consider the issue.

It was not until 16 May 1946 that Maurice Moynihan wrote to the Department of Finance requesting it to prepare the heads of legislation for the establishment of a new Department of Social Services and a new Department of Health. On the 5 October, the Taoiseach requested that special consideration be given to the title of the new department. Later that month the heads of a bill – the Ministers and Secretaries (Amendment) Bill, 1946 – were circulated. This provided that the Department of Social Services, as it was called in the proposal, was to be responsible for old age pensions, blind pensions, widows' and orphans' pensions, national health insurance, unemployment assistance and insurance, children's allowance and other services for the relief of necessitous persons.[59] After the delays in early 1946, it is clear that the matter was now being regarded by government as a matter of great urgency.[60] On 1 November, the government, having informally discussed the issue, decided that the title of the new department should be changed to the Department of Social Welfare. Seán MacEntee subsequently explained this decision on the basis that the term 'social welfare' was adopted as being more accurately descriptive of the functions of the new department which would be only one of several departments concerned with social services in the wider meaning of that term.[61] On 5 November the

57 This had been a long-standing policy of O'Donovan's. See *Sláinte 1935*.   58 Undated memo to MacEntee based of the preliminary research of the Parliamentary Secretary, UCDA P67/261.   59 NAI E 259/46.   60 Letter from the Department of Finance to Industry and Commerce, 24 October, 1946, NAI E 259/46.   61 *Dáil Debates*, vol. CIII col.1031, 15 November 1946.

government gave authorisation for the introduction of the bill. The explanatory memorandum published with the bill explained that the Minister for Social Welfare was to have responsibility for the coordination, control and development of all those services designed to provide against the consequences of inadequate or loss or partial loss of family or individual income arising from constitutional incapacity, infirmity, sickness, unemployment, old age or death of the wage earner or against lack of means to support large families, orphans or deserted children. The relevant legislation was passed in both houses by November 1946 and the departments were formally established on 21 January 1947.

James Ryan was appointed as the Minister for both departments and D.J. O'Donovan was appointed as the secretary of the Department of Social Welfare. As of January 1947, the functions of the other departments in relation to old age pensions, national health insurance, widow's and orphan's pensions, childrens allowance, unemployment insurance and assistance, wet time insurance and food allowances were immediately transferred to the Department of Social Welfare. Following some discussion between the departments as to the details of the transfer, a number of remaining services, in particular, home assistance, were subsequently transferred from Local Government to the new Department in October 1947. The National Health Insurance Society was subsequently abolished in 1950 which meant that the administration and/or control of almost all income maintenance payments came, for the first time, under the new Department of Social Welfare.

WHY A DEPARTMENT OF SOCIAL WELFARE?

There are two key issues arising from the establishment of the new Department of Social Welfare. Firstly, to what extent was the establishment of a new department part of the overall birth of the social welfare system as opposed to a simple administrative re-organisation of responsibilities? Secondly, why did the department take the particular shape it did as opposed to some possible alternatives? In both Ireland and the UK, as income maintenance systems were established, they were attached on a more or less pragmatic basis to whatever appeared to be the most appropriate agency at the time. This led to the wide diversity of agencies involved in the administration of income maintenance. As the system of income maintenance payments grew in size – particularly after the establishment in the 1930s and 1940s of unemployment assistance, widows' and orphans' pensions and children's allowance – the administrative logic for bringing all these services together in one department grew apace. However, there was certainly no administrative *necessity* to bring them together at the end of the Second World War. As we have seen, the investigation into the administrative efficiency of services carried out in late 1943 and early 1944 found that there was relatively little overlapping between the different agencies and the inter-departmental committee report was unable to estimate the extent of savings which might be achieved through bringing all the services together. Rather, it is clear that the key reason for the establishment of the Department of Social Welfare was in the anticipation of a further development in social welfare services in the post war period. Despite de Valera's warnings that growth in social welfare could not be taken for granted, developments along these lines were clearly envisaged or there would have been no need for 'the specialist advice' of a dedicated department. The particular timing of the establishment of the Department of Social Welfare was clearly influenced by successive developments in the United Kingdom, in particular the publication of the Beveridge Report in 1942, the White Paper on Social Insurance in 1944 and the National Insurance Act in 1946. Fianna Fáil had learned in the 1943 and 1944 elections that an emphasis on social benefits was likely to be much more popular with the electorate than an emphasis on responsible government. However, the government had arrogantly dismissed the one significant proposal which had been made in the Irish context – the Dignan Plan. In order to respond to these pressures, the government needed to produce some tangible indication of social welfare developments itself and the Department of Social Welfare filled this need, with the possibility of a future white paper on social welfare.

The second issue which arises is the particular form which the department took. One possibility, canvassed by the Department of Finance, would have been for one of the existing departments to have taken over responsibility for all social welfare services. However, none of the departments showed much enthusiasm for this option and, even if they had, it is difficult to believe that departments would have agreed amongst each other as to which was to be responsible. In the Department of Local Government and Public Health, it was already perceived that the local government functions were being affected by the pressure of work arising from the public health commitments and the inter-departmental committee felt that a transfer would be 'unworkable'.[62] A second possibility, one which occurs in several European countries, would be to combine social welfare and labour affairs under one ministry. After all, one of the main purposes of the social welfare system is to compensate for income lost because of lack of work. However, one problem in the Irish context was that there was no ministry of labour. Indeed, there was no labour policy in any real sense of the word. While labour policy fell within the

62 NAI S. 101/2/45.

remit of Seán Lemass in his capacity as Minister for Industry and Commerce, his attempts to develop a broader labour policy were largely unsuccessful.[63] In July 1942 Lemass had proposed the establishment of a Ministry of Labour to be responsible for labour policy. This department would take over the functions of Industry and Commerce in relation to all aspects of labour policy including the administration of unemployment insurance and unemployment assistance. Lemass also envisaged that 'the idea of amalgamating the social services in one Ministry might be implemented after the Emergency though the Ministry of Labour'. However, this, like his later proposal on full employment, received little support from his cabinet colleagues and no Ministry of Labour was established. Perhaps reflecting this general subordination of labour policy to other policy measures, it also appears that the administration of existing income maintenance services was not closely related on a day-to-day basis to labour market policy. For example, the interdepartmental committee report found that the labour placement aspect of employment exchanges occupied a much smaller proportion of time than did the administration of unemployment payments – a trend already seen in the 1930s. Accordingly, the report recommended that the new Department of Social Services should take over the administration of employment exchanges acting on an agency basis for Industry and Commerce in relation to labour placement activities.[64]

A further, and perhaps more realistic option, would have been to amalgamate health and social welfare services in one department. Such an option was considered by some members of the inter-departmental committee.[65] After all, the National Health Insurance Society was then responsible for some health services. In addition, the Departmental Committee on Health Services which reported in 1945 envisaged the continuation of a contributory system in relation to health services. As we have seen, the Department of Local Government and Public Health did not wish to lose responsibility for the National Health Insurance Society and one might have expected that this department would have pushed strongly for a unified Department of Health and Social Welfare. However, a number of factors argued against this result.

63 NAI S 12882A; NAI S 13101. See B. Girvin, *Between Two Worlds*, pp. 136–40, 151–8.
64 In the UK, Beveridge had proposed that the employment service of the then Ministry of Labour should either be transferred to his proposed Ministry of Social Security or, if retained in the Ministry of Labour, that the service should be conducted at local social security offices. However, the subsequent White Paper on Social Insurance did not accept this. It took the view that there must be a close link between paying unemployment payments and placement in work but that to make the organisation of the latter dependent on the former would be the wrong emphasis. It recommended that the employment service should remain in employment exchanges and under the Ministry of Labour. 65 NAI S. 101/2/45.

Firstly, the initial failure to include medical benefits under the national insurance scheme in Ireland in 1911 meant that the link between health insurance and health services *per se* was much weaker than otherwise would have been the case.[66] Secondly, although both operated under the same department, we have seen that there was an element of tension between the NHIS and Local Government and Public Health civil servants even prior to the publication of the Dignan Plan. Indeed, within the department, it seems clear that Deeny, the chief medical officer who was primarily concerned with health services, and Keady, controller of national health insurance and primarily concerned with income maintenance, had different perspectives on the issue. Thirdly, the proposed contributory element of the health services reform was largely a method of raising finance and the Departmental Committee on Health Services saw the self-employed nature of many Irish workers as being a barrier to any real social insurance based health service. In addition, there was a reluctance on the part of those who favoured a new income maintenance department to separate public health matters from local government. Overall it seems likely that the key civil servants in the public health section who were responsible for pushing the notion of a unified health service had enough on their plate with this development without trying to run an additional battle to bring in social welfare services as well. Conversely, those civil servants who supported the establishment of a department responsible for income maintenance showed little interest in incorporating health issues.

Thus, we have seen the development of the first part of the birth of social welfare – the establishment of a new department. I have argued that this should not be seen as simply an administrative bringing together of existing services but rather that it must be seen as an intrinsic part of the overall establishment of a reformed and unified system of social welfare. While the timing of, and rationale for, the establishment of the new department was a political response to pressures for improved social rights, the particular shape which the department took was very much influenced by the existing administrative structures and by the views of key civil servants. In contrast to the development of children's allowances which was largely an initiative of the politicians themselves, there is little sign of direct input from the politicians into the shape which the new department was to take.

Writing in October 1940, a perceptive civil servant in the Department of Finance, commenting on a proposal to include the establishment of a unified

---

66 In fact, at about the same time as the Local Government representatives on the interdepartmental committee were arguing that the NHIS and Public Health were closely interlined, civil servants in the same Department were arguing – in the context of a review of the Dignan Plan – that the NHIS had little to do with health services.

scheme of social security in the terms of reference of the inter-departmental committee on family allowances, argued that 'unified schemes of the kind suggested, even when they function, have an unpleasant habit of being very much more expensive than an aggregate of separate and distinct schemes'.[67] The initial steps towards establishing a 'much more expensive' scheme could be seen even before the establishment of the Department of Social Welfare itself, when the Department of Local Government and Public Health circulated a memorandum on 'Income Maintenance Services'.[68] This memorandum, discussed in the next chapter, set out a number of options for the development of social welfare services which were to come to fruition with the publication in 1949 of the White Paper on Social Security.

67 File note initialled LMF[itzgerald], 7 October 1940, S 101/12/40. 68 S11109; UCDA P67/280.

7

The failure of politics: from the establishment of the Department to the Social Welfare Act, 1947–52

> I claim nothing for this Bill except that it represents a genuine effort to produce the best, the most satisfactory, the most comprehensive scheme possible having regard to the pattern of life in Ireland, the resources of the nation and the ability of the workers and employers to pay. We may hear it said in a smug, complacent way that this scheme aims at the welfare State. This scheme provides benefit for a sick man and his wife and children, unemployment benefit for the man who is out of work, a pension for widows and orphans, death benefits if death stalks through the home, and a retirement pension for men and women who have served the nation though the spring, summer and autumn of their lives. If doing these things represents a step towards the welfare State, then I, for one, proudly plead guilty to the charge. The provision of these benefits represents the fulfilment of its natural duty by a Christian State and it would be unworthy of us if we were to shirk the responsibility which high concepts of human values demand.[1]

In this chapter, we look at developments from the establishment of the Department of Social Welfare in 1947, through the publication of a White Paper entitled *Social Security* in 1949, to the final enactment of a comprehensive social welfare scheme in the Social Welfare Act, 1952. This legislation was implemented in 1952 and 1953. The period saw two changes of government. Firstly, before the Fianna Fáil government had produced a White Paper, that government fell in early 1948 and an Inter-Party government took office with the Labour party leader, William Norton, as Tánaiste and Minister for Social Welfare. This government produced both the White Paper and legislation to give effect to those proposals. This legislation passed second stage in the Dáil but the government fell in 1951 before the legislation

1 William Norton TD, *Dáil Debates*, vol. 124 col. 1092, 2 March 1951.

could be enacted. James Ryan was again appointed Minister for Social Welfare on Fianna Fáil's return to office and he was responsible for steering the legislation which became the Social Welfare Act, 1952 through the Oireachtas.

INITIAL DEVELOPMENTS (1946–48)

As we saw in chapter 6, even before the Department was established, work was being carried out as to the possible future development of income maintenance services. A memorandum on this issue was brought to government 'for information' by Seán MacEntee in November 1946.[2] This defined income maintenance' as 'any scheme operated by the State or a public authority in which periodical payments are made to persons of families to mitigate loss of income due to the ill-health, unemployment, old age or death of the wage earner'. The memorandum identified three types of scheme (i) means tested public assistance; (ii) non-contributory social assistance; and (iii) compulsory social insurance. It identified a general trend in international literature, including that of the ILO, from public assistance to social assistance and thence to social insurance – initially with benefits falling short of subsistence level leaving room for voluntary effort and personal thrift – and ultimately to an integrated social security scheme for all risks set at subsistence level. The memorandum identified the broad choices in the Irish context as being between social insurance and social assistance and suggested strongly that the general trend was towards an insurance-based approach. It outlined a number of defects in the existing system including anomalies as to the scope of the three insurance schemes; anomalies as to qualification conditions and rates of benefits; the absence of a contributory old age pension and the high pension age (then 70); and the non-inclusion in social insurance of independent workers including small holders.[3]

The memorandum identified four possible options:

i) To accept the existing position with social insurance applying to employees only; extend the scope of the existing insurance scheme to include agricultural labourers and domestic servants and to raise the remuneration limit for non-manual workers to £500 p.a.; rationalise benefit rates making provision for dependants and increase the level of

2 'Income Maintenance Services', Memorandum of Department of Local Government and Public Health, 11 November 1946 S.11109. 3 A number of difficulties were identified with the inclusion of independent workers, including the collection of contributions (which was seen as 'insuperable' in the case of smallholders) and the supervisions of claims.

benefits to one more consistent with existing price levels; and unify existing measures into one scheme. Person not covered by insurance would fall under a unified social assistance scheme (including home assistance).

ii)   In addition, to include old age pensions and workmen's compensation under the unified social insurance scheme.

iii) To decide that social insurance could be applied to independent workers subject to the provision that self-employed persons, at least in the lower grades, would require assistance in paying contributions and that this be provided by the state. All gainfully employed people (up to the £500 p.a. threshold) would be covered by a comprehensive social insurance scheme (although the self-employed would not be covered for unemployment or short-term sickness).

iv)   Finally, to provide comprehensive insurance for all along the lines of the British national insurance system.[4]

This memo, which appears to have been drafted by P.J. Keady,[5] soon to become assistant secretary in the new Department, is interesting for the insight in gives into the issues and options seen as key by senior civil servants. It appears to have been decided at an early stage that a White Paper on social insurance should be produced. It is not clear when or how this decision was made but there appears to have been an assumption from the establishment of the Department that a White Paper on a co-ordinated scheme was to be published. Indeed, given that White Papers were being produced in a range of 'social' areas at this time (TB, Health and Housing) and given the scale of the reforms involved, it would have been surprising if a White Paper was not envisaged. While the UK Conservative government had committed itself to implementing proposals along the lines of the Beveridge Report in 1944 and these proposals had broadly been implemented by the succeeding Labour government in 1946, the Irish 'welfare plan' came significantly later in the post-war period. By this stage, Irish governments were greatly concerned with industrial unrest and the upward pressure on wages after the war and were forced to introduce a supplementary budget and significant food subsidies in late 1947 in an effort to restrain wage demands.[6]

---

4 Interestingly, this option is not discussed at all and would appear not to be considered as a realistic option. 5 As we have seen, Keady had served as secretary of the Widows Pensions Commission, was a member of the Inter-departmental Committee on Family Allowances and the Departmental Committee on Health Services, a member of the provisional management committee of the National Health Insurance Society (1933–36) and was to become chair of the Society (1947–50) and subsequently secretary of the Department in 1954. On the attribution, see NAI. IA 123/53. 6 'Control of Prices and Earnings – Statement by the Taoiseach', *Dáil*

The drafting of the White Paper began in early 1947 with an actuary, William Honohan,[7] being transferred to the Department in March and initial papers being prepared in April and May 1947.[8] No doubt the Department also had its work cut out in amalgamating sections from several different departments into one unit. Minster Ryan himself, who was also appointed Minister for Health, appears to have had relatively little input into the planning process in 1947 and he may have been occupied by the Health Act 1947 and the publication of the White Paper on Improvement of the Health Services (which appeared in late 1947). In the Department of Social Welfare, Ryan's first main initiative in 1947 was to convert miscellaneous cash and in-kind payments (which had been introduced during the Emergency) into cash supplements.[9] He also increased the income thresholds for national health insurance and widow's and orphan's pensions to £500 p.a. in line with earnings increases during the war years.[10] By the end of 1947, the Department had prepared drafts of parts I and II of a proposed White Paper and copious memoranda and notes on specific aspects of a scheme.[11] The draft parts I and II set out in some detail the historical development of social security, the existing schemes in Ireland and, drawing on Keady's memo of November 1946, identified a number of issues on future policies. These parts correspond broadly in substance to the parts I and II of the subsequent White Paper, although there is little textual correspondence between the two. By February 1948 the Department had prepared an outline ('Outline of a Scheme of Social Insurance') of the type of scheme which might be introduced (see appendix for a summary of key points).[12] The Outline was strongly focused on a social insurance scheme with a range of new insurance benefits (old age, death, maternity and marriage) and with workmen's compensation integrated into the social insurance scheme (broadly similar to option ii) above). However, the Outline simply set out the benefits, scope and contributions payable under the proposed scheme[13] and it seems that the publication of a White Paper would have been several months off when de

Debates, vol. CVIII col. 384 *et seq.*, 15 October 1947. 7 Honohan had been private secretary to MacEntee in the 1930s and had gone on to work in the UK government actuary's office. He also was later to become secretary of the Department of Social Welfare. 8 See the chronology set out in Ryan's second stage speech on the 1951 bill, *Dáil Debates*, vol. 130 col. 621–3, 27 March 1952 and on ILHA Norton Papers 116. And see NAI Plan 3/51. 9 Department of Social Welfare memorandum, 5 March 1947, NAI S. 13384. 10 National Health Insurance Act, 1947. 11 NAI IA 123/53 and Plan 3/51; ILHA Norton Papers 116. 12 See ILHA Norton Papers 108 and *Dáil Debates*, vol. 130 col. 625, 27 March 1952. 13 Substantially similar in layout to Part IV of the final White Paper. In effect, it appears that the Outline was never intended to be read on its own but was a Part III to the already drafted Parts I and II which set the proposals in context.

Valera called an election in early 1948 in response to by-election losses. The decision to call an early election (the government could have continued for a further year or more) has been interpreted as a pre-emptive strike against the growing electoral popularity of Clann na Poblachta.[14]

Perhaps learning from the lessons of the 1943 and 44 elections that a social policy emphasis was likely to win votes, Fianna Fáil campaigned strongly on these issues in 1948. It emphasised the range of policy measures which it had or intended to introduce including a comprehensive social security scheme (which appears to have been broadly based on the approach set out in the 'Outline' document).[15] However, Fianna Fáil had been in office for 16 years and was vulnerable to attack by the opposition parties who ran a highly diverse campaign seeking votes from different sections of the community.[16] Both the Labour party and the Clann emphasised the failure of the government to achieve more in the social area.[17] Ultimately Fianna Fáil lost votes and after considerable speculation as to whether Fianna Fáil could return as a minority government with the support of National Labour or independents, an Inter-Party government involving Fine Gael (with John Costello as Taoiseach), Labour, Clann na Poblachta, National Labour, Clann na Talmhan and independents, took up office.

THE INTER-PARTY GOVERNMENT TAKES OFFICE (1948)

The new government took up office on the basis of a 'Ten Point Plan'[18] which included the 'introduction of a comprehensive social security plan to provide insurance against old age, illness, blindness, widowhood, unemployment, etc.' and the modification of the means test applied to old age, widows' and blind pensions.[19] William Norton, leader of the Labour party, was appointed

---

14 E. MacDermott, *Clann na Poblachta* (Cork University Press, Cork, 1998).   15 See *Irish Times* 10 January ('Fianna Fáil Plans for Social Security Outlined' by Lemass), 17 January ('A Plan for Security'), 22 January (Launch of Housing White Paper), 27 January (Launch of Health Scheme by Ryan); 31 January ('Fianna Fáil has a Plan') 1948; *Irish Press*, 5 January, 6 January, 10 January (Fianna Fáil is a Workers' Party – Lemass) 15 January, 17 January, 22 January, 31 January 1948. De Valera himself focused more on the need for strong government and the impending 'doom' of coalition.   16 Conversely, the fact which allowed them to draw votes from different quarters would also make it difficult for them to keep a coherent government together.   17 See *Irish Press*, 16 January (the Clann's Ten Point Plan including an 'adequate Social Security Plan'), *Irish Times* 30 January, 2 February 1948 and the famous Clann film *Our Country*.   18 *Irish Independent*, 18 February 1948; *Irish Times*, 17 February 1948.   19 Clann na Poblachta had expressed its support for the Dignan Plan while Labour had prepared its own social welfare proposals, see E. MacDermott, *Clann na Poblachta*, pp. 60–1; D. McCullagh, *A Makeshift Majority* (Institute of Public Administration, Dublin, 1998), p. 11;

as Tánaiste and Minister for Social Welfare. Norton subsequently claimed that, against the advice of his Department which wanted to proceed with comprehensive reform, he turned first to reform of the old age and other pensions.[20] This had been an issue raised by the opposition on a number of occasions in the previous Dáil and indeed had been a subject of ongoing political controversy throughout the whole period in question.[21] Norton introduced the Social Welfare Act, 1948, an omnibus measure including a range of proposals some of which dated back to the previous government.[22] The core of the legislation, however, involved significant improvements in old age and widow's pensions including a weekly increase of between 2s. 6d. and 5s. (benefiting over 170,000 people) and modification of the means test in line with the Ten Point Plan at a cost of £2.5 million. The bill made the cash supplements, introduced the previous year by Ryan, an integral part of the general payment but, in doing so, shifted the cost of supplements payable to those entitled to social insurance payments from the Exchequer to the relevant insurance fund. The latter aspect was heavily criticised by Fianna Fáil.[23] Norton also provided for an increase in the compensation payable under the Workmen's Compensation Acts and increased the scope of the scheme to workmen earning up to £500 p.a.[24] In June 1948, Norton brought a memorandum to government on the future of the National Health Insurance Society.[25] He proposed that the NHIS be merged into the Department. Despite opposition from Patrick McGilligan, the new Minister for Finance who argued that the Society had done its work satisfactorily and efficiently, this was approved by the government on 12 July 1948.[26]

ILHA Norton papers 106. In contrast Fine Gael leaders were initially poorly disposed to social spending and the 'Servile State'. **20** *Dáil Debates*, vol. 130 col. 650–1, 27 March 1952. Certainly a slackening off of the pace appears in a chronology set out by the Department entitled 'Progress on the Comprehensive Scheme', 27 September 1948, ILHA Norton papers 116. **21** See NAI S. 11036 and chapter 6 above. **22** See NAI S. 14367; *Dáil Debates*, vol. CXII col. 1626 *et seq.*, 28 July 1948. The Act provided for an increase in the unemployment insurance threshold to £500 p.a. and further reduced the age threshold to qualify for widow's pension to 48 (for widows without dependant children). **23** *Dáil Debates*, vol. CXII col. 1679–80, 28 July 1948. **24** Workmen's Compensation Act 1948, see *Dáil Debates*, vol. CXIII col. 1185 *et seq.*, 9 December 1948. **25** NAI S. 13384. **26** Reversing the previous Finance approach, McGilligan in a memorandum circulated at the government meeting of 12 July 1948, quoted the Vocational Commission in favour of retaining the NHIS and suggested that 'it might be argued that from the points of view of efficiency and economy some of Social Service work could profitably be transferred from the Department to the Society' as was suggested by Dr Dignan.

DRAFTING THE WHITE PAPER (1948–49)

The 1948 legislation out of the way, the Department returned to the task of preparing a White Paper. A rough draft of the White Paper appears to have been completed in late 1948.[27] This built on the initial parts I and II and the February 1948 'Outline'. It envisaged the inclusion of all employees (including higher earners and civil servants). In addition, it envisaged the inclusion over time not only of the self-employed but also of assisting relatives and persons on home duties (other than married women). These were to be included for all benefits other than unemployment and short-term sickness. Married women on home duties (who were 'already adequately covered if married to an insured man') would be the only large group to be excluded. Further internal discussion led to a final draft which was circulated to other Departments on 8 April 1949. The April draft consisted of five parts: an overview of the development of social security in Ireland; a section on general principles and modern thought; an identification of the problems in Ireland; details of the scheme proposed; and a concluding section on statistics and finance. The April draft very much reflects the final version and relatively few changes were made other than the addition of a final concluding section which took some of the material from the draft part V. The April draft, like the 1948 Outline, was a strongly social insurance oriented document (see appendix for details). It envisaged social insurance being extended to all employees (including higher earners and public servants) but – in contrast to the earlier draft – concluded that it was not practicable to include the self-employed. It rationalised the three existing insurance schemes into one and aligned benefit rates and qualification conditions. Benefits were to be significantly increased in most cases. It also proposed the introduction of new benefits for old age (at age 65 for men and 60 for women), marriage, maternity and death. To fund this it proposed significant increases in contributions for both employers and employees. A new two-tier system was proposed with lower paid employees (it appears that this was primarily intended to cover low paid agricultural workers) paying lower contributions and receiving reduced benefit in some cases. The White Paper provided for an assessment-based system of funding and the actuarial, pre-funded approach was entirely dropped.

In June 1949, the Department submitted a memorandum to government outlining the observations from other Departments.[28] Finance predictably opposed the scope of the proposals with J.J. McElligott arguing that 'redistribution of incomes [had] already gone far in this country'.[29] He objected to

27 See Norton's undated copy, ILHA Norton papers 120. 28 NAI S. 13384. 29 7 June

the inclusion of civil servants and the higher paid as 'a form of discriminatory taxation' and objected to equal benefits for men and women in view of the potential implications of equalisation of pay. James Dillon, Minister for Agriculture, strongly objected to the proposals on the basis that they were prepared with special reference to the needs of an industrialised population rather than those of a largely agricultural community.[30] He argued that taxpaying farmers would subsidise a scheme from which they could not benefit. In response, Norton noted that the only way that farmers could benefit would be to be insured under the scheme but that Dillon was not proposing that farmers should be included in insurance. The Department of Industry and Commerce argued that the proposed benefit rates were high and would diminish the incentive to seek work. It also considered that the proposed contributions were too high and argued that private social security schemes should be encouraged by 'opt-out' provisions. The Department expressed its concern about the impact of the proposed death grant on private insurance business. Several other Departments including Justice, Education, Posts and Telegraphs and Defence objected to or queried the extension of insurance to public servants within their remit (e.g. Gardaí).[31] Norton replied that he was strongly committed to the principle of comprehensive insurance and to the abolition of 'historical privileges'.

On 15 June, the government decided to hold a special meeting to discuss the proposals but this was not held due to the Tanaiste's absence.[32] And on 27 July, it was decided to refer the draft proposals to a Cabinet Committee comprising the Taoiseach, Tánaiste and the Ministers for Agriculture, Finance, Defence, Industry and Commerce and Health. In September, Seán McBride, Minister for External Affairs, somewhat belatedly added his name to the list of objectors arguing that the scheme excluded half the population

1949, NAI S. 13384. There is little indication that McGilligan played a strong personal role although his files do show that he sought advice on the draft White Paper from Fr E. J. Coyne – the advice being strongly negative, UCDA P35d/45 & 46.   **30** 'Observations on Draft White Paper on Social Security' 29 June 1949, NAI S. 13384. Dillon argued that the effect of the proposals was that about £16 million p.a. would be paid to about 700,000 employees of which over half of the cost would be provided by 600,000 'non trade unionists' mainly small farmers. He predicted that 'these proposals would never be accepted by the Oireachtas and that no Party could carry them'. Predicting 'insuperable opposition amongst farmers' Dillon argued that the Land Rehabilitation Project was 'the best social service that has ever been introduced into this country'. See also his further memo of 25 August 1949.   **31** NAI S. 13384. Norton's Labour party colleague (Labour and National Labour re-united in 1950), James Everett, Minister for Posts and Telegraphs, subsequently assured Norton that he personally supported the inclusion of civil servants despite the views of his department, see Everett to Norton 15 September 1950, ILHA Norton papers 116.   **32** This related to a libel action against the *Irish Press*, see D. McCullagh, *A Makeshift Majority*, p. 70.

and by no means the wealthiest half. He expressed doubts as to whether unemployment was an insurable contingency and as to the two-tier insurance system. He expressed a preference for the promotion of employment through investment and proposed a universal social welfare system like that existing in New Zealand.[33] On 4 October, the Taoiseach indicated that the White Paper should not be taken at government as discussions were continuing. However, by the eight of that month, the Taoiseach was able to say that the outstanding points had been settled and on 11 October the proposals were approved generally with the final draft to be settled by a Cabinet Committee of the Taoiseach, Tánaiste, Minister for Finance and Minister for Defence (Fine Gael's T.F. O'Higgins). On 21 October the White Paper was finally approved and it was immediately published on 25 October before the Dáil resumed.

Despite the strong opposition from some Ministers, there were relatively few changes to the final version from the April draft. A sentence was inserted stating that the position of public servants was 'receiving further considera-tion'.[34] Contributions were reduced from the proposed 3*s*. 9*d*. for employees to 3*s*. 6*d*. and from 2*s*. 6*d*. for employers to 2*s*. 2*d*. and low wage contributions were also reduced.[35] A retirement condition was introduced for the old age pension and the marriage grant was dropped.[36] A new concluding part VI was added, taking some material from the draft's part V. The new conclusion attempted to address the argument that the scheme proposed was more suit-able to an industrial than an agricultural country and pointed to the benefits which farmers already received from mean tested payments.[37] The proposed rates of the main benefits were set at 24*s*. for a person, with a 50% increase (12*s*.) for a dependent adult and 7*s*. for the first two children (subsequent children would receive the children's allowance only). A lower rate of 18*s*. was payable to a married woman unless she was separated from her husband. Benefits at roughly this scale had been proposed in the February 1948 'Outline'. In contrast to the United Kingdom, there does not appear to have been any detailed study in Ireland as to what should be the appropriate level of social welfare benefits. For example, there is no evidence that data from the National Nutrition Survey published in 1950 was used to obtain an 'adequacy' standard from which social welfare rates could be derived.[38] In

33 William Honohan scathingly dismissed McBride's observations and suggested that his New Zealand proposal could 'hardly qualify even for the description "half-baked"' Honohan to Norton, 26 September 1949, ILHA Norton papers 118. **34** White Paper, paras 55 and 97. See NAI IA 132/53 for a last minute 'semi-official' exchange of views between William Honohan of Social Welfare and McElligott on this issue. **35** Paras 98, 102. **36** See UCDA P35d/46 for two heavily annotated copies of the draft White Paper including these changes. **37** Paras 131–134. **38** See G. Hughes, *Payroll Tax Incidence, the Direct Tax Burden and the Rate of*

March 1949 Keady had argued that 24*s*. was 'probably too high . . . for the rural areas and possibly not high enough for urban areas'.[39] However, given inflation these rates were becoming progressively less adequate as time wore on. While the Beveridge Report had argued for benefits sufficient to meet subsistence, the UK government had subsequently fudged the issue.[40] Consciously or unconsciously the White Paper echoed the words of the UK Labour Minister James Griffiths in this regard stating that benefits would be set at 'a level which would be justified broadly by reference to the cost-of-living'.[41] The adult dependant payment represented a significant improvement on the existing relativity. Hughes has drawn attention to the convergence of Irish policy on relativities towards that proposed by Beveridge and has surmised that Irish policy in this area was influenced by Beveridge.[42] The White Paper received extensive coverage in the newspapers, although the *Irish Independent* and *Irish Times* editorials were somewhat reserved and the *Irish Press* carefully refrained from other than descriptive coverage.[43] The reception of the White Paper seems to have split along fairly

Return on State Pension Contributions in Ireland (Economic and Social Research Institute, Dublin, 1985), p. 88. As Hughes points out reference was made to the Nutrition Survey in the Dáil. However, I have not found any evidence that this Survey was used in setting the rates of social welfare payments.   **39** Memorandum of conference held on 9 and 10 March 1949, ILHA, Norton papers 116.   **40** *Social Assistance and Allied Services*, HMSO, London, 1942, para 193.   **41** White Paper para 65. Griffiths had stated that UK benefit levels could 'be justified broadly in relation to the present cost-of-living' *Hansard*, vol. 418 col. 1740–1, 6 February 1946 quoted in J. Tomlinson, 'Why so Austere? The British Welfare State of the 1940s' *Journal of Social Policy* (1998) 27, pp. 63–77 at p. 72. Viet-Wilson has been highly critical of Beveridge arguing that the rates he proposed were not in fact sufficient for social participation and that this had serious consequences for the poor in Britain. This is perhaps somewhat unfair. Beveridge may have had good reason to retain the principle of subsistence while reducing the actual rates proposed in order to maintain the total cost within 'realistic' limits. More fundamental though to a refutation of Viet-Wilson's criticism is the fact that the UK White Paper on Social Insurance published by the Conservative government in 1944 explicitly rejected a subsistence basis and, as we have seen, Labour subsequently fudged the issue. So any political blame for inadequate rates can hardly be attached to Beveridge. J. Veit-Wilson, 'Muddle or Mendacity? The Beveridge Committee and the Poverty Line', *Journal of Social Policy* (1992) 21, pp. 269–301; id. 'Condemned to Deprivation? Beveridge's Responsibility for the Invisibility of Poverty' in J. Hills et al. (eds.), *Beveridge and Social Security*, op. cit.; *Social Insurance* (HMSO, London, 1944), para. 12–13.   **42** G. Hughes 'The Irish Payroll Tax: Effects on Labour Supply and Incidence' (Ph.D. thesis, TCD, 1982), Appendix F. At the time of the White Paper, the adult dependant payment was 33% of the adult (male) payment for disability and unemployment payments. The White Paper proposed an increase to 50% compared to Beveridge's proposed 66% (which was accepted in the UK White Paper). While I have not found any documentary evidence in this regard it seems likely that Hughes is correct and that the improved relativities were influenced by the Beveridge proposals.   **43** *Irish Times, Irish Independent, Irish Press*, 26 October 1949.

predictable lines with trade unions supporting the proposals and business interests and sections of the agricultural community opposing them.[44] Leading exponents of Catholic social thinking also expressed their concerns but nothing like sustained opposition from the Catholic Church emerged.[45]

THE NORTON BILL (1950–51)

Before proceeding with the main bill, it was decided to get the NHIS issue out of the way. On 13 December 1949, the Minster for Social Welfare sought authority to introduce a bill to dissolve the NHIS and this was approved on 13 January 1950.[46] Legislation was subsequently enacted with (more-or-less) all party support in 1950.[47] On 12 May 1950, the Department circulated the heads of the Social Welfare bill to implement the White Paper. Despite the commitments given in the White Paper to give further consideration to the position of public servants, the Minister reaffirmed his conviction that there should be no departure from the principle of comprehensiveness of coverage of employees. On 27 June, Norton brought a memorandum to government including the observations of departments.[48] Finance objected somewhat half-heartedly on the basis that the scheme proposed was too costly and should be modified to reduce the burden of non-productive State expenditure which it would involve. Specifically they objected to the extent of the proposed State subvention to the social insurance fund and sought increased contributions and/or reduced benefits. They proposed reducing or dropping the proposals on maternity and attendance allowance, retirement pension, death grants and the transitional provisions. They objected again to the inclusion of public servants and sought total exemption for established civil servants earning £500 p.a. or more and those in a similar position (defence forces, Gardaí, teachers, etc.).[49] If such persons were to be included, it should

---

44 See, for example, extensive local and national newspaper reports and correspondence to an Taoiseach on NAI S. 11109 and to Norton on ILHA Norton papers 114. For the (somewhat unfavourable) reaction of the 'great and good' see the symposium reported in the *Journal of the Statistical and Social Inquiry Society of Ireland* (1949–50) XVIII, p. 247 *et seq.* 45 See J. Whyte, *Church and State in Modern Ireland, 1923–1979* (Gill and Macmillan, Dublin, 1980), pp. 179–83. Norton, himself a Knight of Columbanus, had on 25 October 1950 sent the Catholic bishops advance copies of the White Paper, ILHA, 114 Norton papers. 46 NAI S. 13384. 47 *Dáil Debates*, vol. CXX col. 223 *et seq.* 29 March 1950. MacEntee, with his characteristic approach to consistency, vigorously opposed the proposal, ibid. col. 246 *et seq.* 48 NAI S. 13384 and see NAI IA 136/53. 49 The objection was made on the basis either that the State would be required to pay double benefit to groups who already had sick pay/superannuation cover, or that public servants would object to having to pay contributions in respect of contingencies which did not affect them (unemployment) or for which they were already

be on the basis that they would pay contributions in respect of contingencies which might affect them and for which they were not already covered (in effect widows' and orphans' cover). Other Departments, including Education, Justice and Defence, also strongly objected to the inclusion of specific categories of public servant in the scheme.[50]

On 30 June, a decision to allow the bill to be drafted was withheld by government pending the completing of inter-departmental discussions between Social Welfare and Education, Justice and Defence. However, on 6 July Norton introduced the bill – the Social Welfare (Insurance) Bill, 1950 – in the Dáil without formal government approval. On 14 July a further Cabinet Committee was established consisting of the Taoiseach, Tánaiste and Ministers for Agriculture, Finance, Defence and Industry and Commerce to consider any points of controversy which might arise concerning the bill. It would appear that discussions were continuing between Ministers although there is a lack of any information about the content of these discussions. It seems that the Taoiseach was being strongly supportive of the Tánaiste. On 25 September 1950, Maurice Moynihan informed the Taoiseach that he had learnt that the Tánaiste had arranged for the drafting of the Social Welfare bill – without authority – only to be told by Costello that this was with his (Costello's) concurrence. In September 1950, the Civil Service General Council Staff Panel sought inclusion of civil servants in the scheme but with full entitlement to all benefits. If this was not forthcoming, they argued that there should be a reduction in the relevant contribution.[51] And on 5 October, Costello met with representatives of the Irish Conference of Professional and Service Associations (including the INTO, Railway Clerks Association, IBOA, Assurance Representatives Organisation and Civil Service Alliance) who reiterated their concerns about inclusion in the scheme.[52] Unsurprisingly, given the strength of opposition, Norton eventually lost the battle, at least in principle, to have comprehensive coverage of all employees and on 13 October the Cabinet Committee reported to government that the bill should be amended so as to include a power to exclude from the bill such classes or groups as civil servants, teachers, Gardaí, defence forces, etc. or to apply it with modifications to them. On the same day, the draft text was circulated to departments.[53]

With the key issue of possible modification of the application of the bill to public servants having been conceded, the departments concerned did not

adequately covered. **50** At various stages, the Department of Industry and Commerce also expressed concerns about the inclusion of some workers of CIE and the ESB. See NAI E 107/49/1. **51** UCDA P35d/47. **52** See memo of the meeting on NAI Plan 11/50 and various documents on the issue on NAI S. 13384 and UCDA P35d/47. **53** NAI Plan 11/50.

oppose the bill. Finance continued to object without much conviction to various aspects of the bill and James Dillon again argued that the bill was open to 'fundamental objections', e.g. that it was inappropriate to a largely agricultural country. Dillon argued that the needs of self-employed people must be thoroughly examined and proposed reduced contributions for all agricultural workers. It would seem that Dillon's broad concerns were shared and on 1 December the bill was approved subject to the insertion of two additional sections providing, first, for the inclusion as insured contributors of farmer members of co-operatives[54] and, secondly, allowing farmers whose rateable valuation did not exceed £30 to become eligible for the old age pension on the transfer of the land to a child or children. These additions required an amendment to the long title of the bill and it was decided to withdraw the original bill and introduce a new bill – to be known as the Social Welfare (Insurance) (No. 2) Bill, 1950. This was done on 7 December 1950. However, concerns about the focus of the bill clearly remained. In addition, recurrent concerns about old age pensions were also resurfacing. On 30 January 1951 the Labour party wrote to Costello seeking a meeting to discuss an immediate increase in the old age pension and improvements in the means test.[55] On 9 February, Con Lehane of Clann na Poblachta wrote to Costello expressing his concerns about pensions and seeking a meeting.[56] On 2 March, the Taoiseach reported to the government that the Cabinet Committee on Estimates for Public Services had agreed that the Minister for Social Welfare should announce that the bill would be amended to increase the rates of old age pension and to modify the pension means test.[57] However, on 7 March a petition was submitted to the Taoiseach by four independent Deputies, Cogan, P.D. Lehane, O'Reilly and Sheldon,[58] calling for the government to introduce the pensions improvements immediately rather than in the Social Welfare bill which contained 'many objectionable provisions'.[59]

The bill received its second stage reading in the Dáil beginning in March. Norton outlined the proposals it contained.[60] On the two late additional

54 The *Irish Times* estimated that it was doubtful if half of all farmers belonged to co-ops and those who did were 'apt to be the wealthier of their kind', 11 December 1950. In fact, total membership of agricultural societies in 1949 was just under 100,000, ILHA Norton papers 118. 55 NAI S. 11036B. 56 Ibid. 57 NAI S. 13384E. 58 All four had previously supported the government. In December 1951, Sheldon had informed Costello that he could no longer support the government; Cogan also indicated his inability to support the government at that time arising from the 'Battle of Baltinglass'; and Lehane left Clann na Talmhan and withdrew his support for the government, McCullagh, *Makeshift Majority*, p. 238. Both O'Reilly and Cogan were former Clann na Talmhan deputies. 59 NAI S. 13384. 60 *Dáil Debates*, vol. 124 col. 1069 *et seq.* 2 March 1951. Preparation for this final stage of the legislation may not have been helped by the fact that, following a prolonged dispute with Norton, the secretary D.J. O'Donovan, was dismissed by government for failure to obey a direct order (and replaced as

sections concerning farmers, he explained that the intention was that farmer co-op members would come in on the basis of eligibility for all payments except unemployment and disability benefit. On the pension transfer section, Norton stated that 86% of farmers were living on farms of under £30 PLV and estimated the costs of the proposal to the exchequer as £150,000–200,000 p.a. The increase of the old age pension by 2s. 6d. would cost a further £1,050,000 while the means test improvements would cost £250,000. In an unusually constructive second stage speech, Ryan opposed the bill on the basis that it was neither comprehensive nor balanced and that it would greatly increase the burdens on employers and employees.[61] While accepting that it would not be possible to collect contributions from the self-employed and ruling out a system of voluntary insurance, Ryan proposed an alternative approach to ensure comprehensive coverage for the self-employed. He argued that 'wherever a scheme is applicable to practically the whole population, the only fair way to finance it is through taxation and where it is applicable to a certain class, we should try to get that scheme financed through a particular scheme applicable only to that class.'[62] He identified old age pensions and widow's and orphan's pensions as being general schemes needed by all but the very wealthy. He argued that these payments should be made practically universal and be payable to all insured persons, to landholders of up to £25 PLV and to persons with an income up to £100 p.a.[63] However, he argued against the reduction of the pension age which he felt should be left at 70 because people were able to work up to that age and

secretary by William Maguire). This saga deserves its own telling, see McCullagh, *Makeshift Majority*, pp. 57–59. O'Donovan was subsequently re-appointed by the incoming Fianna Fáil government in August 1951 as special adviser to Ryan on a secretary's salary and on the understanding that on Maguire's retirement, O'Donovan would become Secretary which he did in January 1953. However, by October 1953, MacEntee had threatened to resign as Minister for Finance if O'Donovan continued as Secretary arising from his failure to notify Finance of an anticipated spending overrun. One of the first acts of the second Inter-party government was to suspend O'Donovan in June 1954 (to be replaced as secretary of the Department by P.J. Keady) and he was subsequently made Secretary to the President. See NAI S. 13988; *Irish Press*, 14 March 1951; *Dáil Debates*, vol. 124 col. 422, 767, 902, 1057, 1328, 1495, 1499, 1501, 1661, 1858, 21 February – 19 March 1951; UCDA P67/222. **61** *Dáil Debates*, vol. 124 col. 1072 *et seq.* 2 March 1951. **62** Ibid. 1107. See also Lemass' speech along these lines in late 1950, *Irish Times*, 7 October 1950. Lemass, reconsidering his earlier commitment to insurance pensions for workers, had suggested such an approach in July 1948, questioning whether it was 'really justifiable to talk of insuring against old age' and proposing that the costs of new social services be defrayed from taxation rather than insurance, *Dáil Debates*, vol. CXII col. 1677–9, 28 July 1948. **63** However, by the time Ryan came to put down amendments for the committee stage of the bill, this had been changed – at the instance of his party colleagues – to a full pension for any person with means of £55 p.a. or less reducing to a minimum pension for a person with means of £100, *Dáil Debates*, vol. 126 col.1053, 5 July 1951.

a lowering of the age was inappropriate given the anticipated increase in the numbers of older people.[64] Ryan expressed his doubts about the two-tier contribution system and about bringing in domestic workers given that there was, he claimed, no unemployment for such workers. As nutritional surveys carried out by the Department of Health had identified two classes not making ends meet as the long term unemployed and large families, he proposed improvements in family allowances.[65] Lemass who spoke on the bill also followed the Ryan line and this was published in the *Irish Press* as the Fianna Fáil Plan (see appendix).[66] MacEntee however favoured a scheme which would 'encourage voluntary adherence' and 'enable us to relinquish altogether the use of compulsion'.[67] The bill passed the second stage by 71 votes to 67 with the four independent deputies who had petitioned Costello voting against. Almost immediately after the completion of the second stage, Noel Browne resigned from government and, although the government survived for some further weeks, it looked increasingly unlikely to have a long-term future. Although committee stage amendments were put down for the bill, it seemed likely that the government would have had difficulties in getting it passed in its then form and committee stage had not been taken when the government decided to call an election without having been defeated on a vote.[68]

THE RETURN OF FIANNA FÁIL (1951)

The 1951 election campaign was lacklustre in the extreme and neither government nor opposition appeared to have any clear programme.[69] In the event, the Clann vote collapsed and Fianna Fáil, with only a slightly improved electoral performance, resumed office as a minority government with the support of independents. The new government published a government programme which ran to 17 points: point 12 was 'to secure the early enactment of a comprehensive Social Welfare bill on the general lines already

64 Ibid., 1113. 65 Ibid., 1119. See Department of Health, *National Nutrition Survey Parts I–VII*, Stationery Office, Dublin, 1953. 66 *Dáil Debates*, vol. 125 col. 60 et seq. 4 April 1951. 67 *Dáil Debates*, vol. 125 col. 592–603, 11 April 1951. 68 McCullagh, *Makeshift Majority*, pp. 239–240. The editorial of the *Leader* in March 1951 stated that 'some pundits . . . seriously entertain the possibility of a Government reverse' on the measure. It estimated that there were 70 definite votes for and 69 against with the balance being held by a handful of Independents. However, the editorial ultimately felt that the bill was unlikely to be rejected, *The Leader*, 3 March 1951. 69 The *Irish Times* identified an 'absence of any real political issue between the main parties' and referred to an 'indeterminate and unsatisfying election campaign' 26 and 28 May 1951.

indicated, to implement the raising of old age pension, increasing children's allowances for larger families, improving widow's pensions, and the avoidance of the heavy increased contributions proposed by the previous Government.'[70] James Ryan was again appointed Minister for Social Welfare. One of the first acts of the new government was to implement the pensions improvements proposed by the previous government in the Social Welfare Act, 1951 increasing the pension by 2*s*. 6*d*. to 20*s*., modifying the means test and introducing the transfer clause.[71] The bill was passed by both houses in July 1951.

THE RYAN BILL (1951–52)

On 28 June 1951, Ryan met with his senior Departmental officials to outline his new proposals and in the following weeks and months the Department worked to clarify the changes required and the issues arising.[72] It is clear that several senior officials had serious reservations about aspects of the new proposals, in particular the move away from an actuarial insurance approach and the dropping of the contributory widow's scheme. Indeed, these reservations were shared by Ryan's then special adviser, D.J. O'Donovan.[73]

However, Ryan largely stuck to his original proposals. At the end of November, he circulated a draft memo to the Minister for Finance setting out his proposals and on 10 December, he sought government approval for short and long titles for co-ordinating legislation. This was granted on the following day and introduced on 12 December. On 28 December, Ryan submitted his proposals for a social welfare scheme largely following the approach outlined in his second stage speech. He argued that where a service, such as unemployment or disability benefit, was mainly needed by employed persons, it should be on a contributory basis but there should be no extension outside that class. Where a service was needed by all, it should be on a non-contributory basis funded entirely by taxation. Ryan's proposals contained several significant differences to the Norton bill . He proposed a contribution limit of £600 p.a. and lower contribution levels, especially for the low paid. In particular, he proposed that widow's and orphan's pensions should be paid on a completely non-contributory basis with the contributory pension being dropped. Insured persons would be entitled without a means test, persons

<hr>

70 *Irish Press*, 5 June 1951.   71 See NAI S. 13884. Ryan resisted Finance pressure to reduce the £30 PLV to £25, NAI S. 11036.   72 NAI Plan 13/50. See, in particular, Honohan to Ryan 'Memorandum on Minister's New Proposals for Social Welfare', 8 August 1951.   73 NAI Plan 3/51. O'Donovan to Ryan 'Social Welfare Schemes – Proposed Legislation', 20 October 1950.

not insured with a rateable valuation of £25 or less or annual income of up to £100 would also qualify. Old age pension would be payable on the same basis (from age 70 for men and 65 for women). However, insured persons would receive an old age pension 4s. higher than others on the basis that they were more dependent on cash income and as many lived in urban areas with a higher cost-of-living. He envisaged that treatment benefit would be taken over by the Department of Health. The proposals envisaged an additional exchequer cost of £6 million p.a. over the original estimate for 1952 of £13 million.[74]

Seán MacEntee, the new Minister for Finance, replied on 5 January 1952. In contrast to the half-hearted stuff of the Inter-party government, this was a scathing performance. Things were bad and would only get worse. Finance argued that the 1952 Budget 'must be balanced in order to put the State's finances in order'. Public expenditure was 'already extended far beyond the capacity to finance it without serious inflationary consequences.' Ryan's proposal to transfer some funding from an insurance basis to general taxation was rubbished on the basis that it was not desirable to abolish the existing system and that all classes did not pay an appropriate amount of tax. MacEntee was, no doubt, influenced by the unfavourable economic position both nationally and internationally.[75] Economic growth had slowed to 1–2% in 1950–1 compared to 5% in previous years and very significant balance of payments and trade deficits had developed. The Central Bank report, published in October 1951, expressed grave fears about the financial state of the nation and generated a 'medley of noise and heat' seldom equalled by a slim volume since the publication of the Communist Manifesto – according to *The Leader*.[76] And in December MacEntee's UK counterpart, R.A. Butler, had written to him warning of the 'very grave economic crisis' facing the Sterling area and the need for all countries to prove that the economy was sound, in particular by establishing a current account surplus.[77] Fanning has shown how Finance used the Sterling crisis to support its own views on the need for, inter alia, budgetary balance. The Fianna Fáil government strongly supported the Finance line of retrenchment and the alacrity with which Ryan backed down from his well-publicised proposals indicates that he had little if any political support for them.[78] On 17 January he circulated a further memo indicating that he was now prepared to allow widow's and orphan's pension

74 NAI S. 13384.   75 See MacEntee's Budget speech, *Dáil Debates*, vol. 130 col. 1113 et seq., 2 April 1952 and Fanning, *Finance*, pp. 468–84.   76 Quoted in Fanning, *op. cit.*, p. 469. 77 Butler to MacEntee, 14 December 1951, UCDA P67/218.   78 Indeed, even Lemass opposed (or allowed his Department to oppose) several aspects of the proposals, 10 January 1952, S. 13384.

to remain on a contributory basis; to postpone his old age pension proposals;[79] and to exclude domestic servants from unemployment benefit and charge a lower contribution. This significantly reduced the costs involved[80] and was approved by government on 18 January.

On 4 March the draft bill was circulated. On 10 March McElligott wrote complaining that section 16(2) of the bill – which allowed for extended unemployment benefit for persons over 65 – was, in effect, a substitute form of retirement pension but his objections were not taken on board. He also opposed the level of increase in the pension means test limits and he was somewhat more successful with the maximum limit being reduced from £65 10s. to £52 5s. The text was approved on 11 March. The bill contained a number of significant changes to the Norton bill. The bill was far from universal in scope of insurance coverage for employees. While Norton had already conceded the principle of modification of insurance for public servants, Ryan also excluded the higher paid private sector employees (estimated to exclude 20 to 30,000 persons). Contributions in the Ryan bill were significantly lower, e.g. employee contributions of 2s. 4d. as opposed to 3s. 6d. in the earlier legislation. Conversely, benefits were more limited in the Ryan bill. The retirement pension was dropped entirely and pension age remained at 70, although improvements were made in the means test. The proposed maternity package was cut back and death grants were dropped. A marriage benefit was introduced but this was in effect a way of breaking married women's connection with the insurance system rather than a positive benefit. Improvements were also introduced in children's allowances in the Social Welfare (Children's Allowances) Act, 1952 which shortly followed the main legislation. This provided for increases in the allowance and for payment to the second child (previously payment had only been made to the third child and up). While these measures represented significant improvements in the scheme, they were largely intended to compensate for the withdrawal of food subsidies following the report of the Interdepartmental Committee on Food Subsidies: a measure announced in the 1952 Budget in April of that year.[81] The Ryan bill came before the House for second stage in March 1951 just before the April 1951 Budget – a Budget described as the harshest in the history of the state.[82] Ryan outlined his reasons for not proceeding with his

---

79 In fact, Ryan proposed to retain the pension 'free of means test' but this does not appear to have been proceeded with. 80 The additional amount to be met by the state was £4.5 million or £3 million when account was taken of the increase in pensions already provided for in the Social Welfare Act, 1951. 81 NAI S. 13965D. 82 P. Bew and H. Patterson *Sean Lemass and the making of Modern Ireland 1945–66* (Gill and Macmillan, Dublin), p. 65. A more neutral review describes it as 'inappropriate in the prevailing economic condition': K. Kennedy and B. Dowling, *Economic Growth in Ireland* (Gill and Macmillan, Dublin, 1975), p. 216.

original plans on more universal pensions, i.e. basically due to Finance opposition. In relation to the scope of insurance he stated that he could not see 'either the justice or necessity for the inclusion of classes that can never benefit' in the scheme and stated that he could not approve of 'hidden' taxation on such classes by the imposition of social insurance contributions.[83] He also explained that, despite his vulnerability to accusations of bias (Ryan was director of an insurance company), he had decided to drop the proposals for a death grant on the basis that it was unnecessary.[84] The final cost of the bill was estimated at £4.25 million of which £2.75 million would be met by the state.[85] There was limited opposition to the proposals and on 14 June the Social Welfare Act, 1952 was signed into law by the President. It came into effect at various dates later in 1952 and in January 1953. After a long gestation period, the social welfare system had finally been born.[86]

GENDER AND THE BIRTH OF SOCIAL WELFARE

Gender has not featured strongly in this analysis of either the establishment of the department or, perhaps more surprisingly, the unification of the social welfare system. The social welfare system was, of course, based on a particular understanding of gender roles – as we have seen in preceding chapters. However, the different political parties largely shared this understanding and, for this reason, there was relatively little public debate about gender issues (either explicitly or implicitly) in the late 1940s and the early 1950s. As we have seen women featured strongly in some areas of social welfare but were discriminated against or excluded in others. The White Paper and the 1952 Act changed this relatively little. Neither Fianna Fáil nor the Inter-Party government proposed to extend social insurance to the estimated 350,000 married women on 'home duties' who were seen as being properly covered by their husband's insurance nor to other women engaged in home duties (estimated at about 140,000) and there was little change in the numbers or proportion of women insured for sickness and widows' payments.[87] Women made up about 54% of old age pensioners though the period from 1947 to 1954 (compared to about 52% of the population over 70) although the

83 *Dáil Debates* vol. 130 col. 633, 27 March 1952. 84 Ibid., 633–4. 85 Ibid., 641–2. 86 Interestingly on 6 March, Ryan submitted a memo to government on a proposed bill to consolidate the law on social assistance payments (old age pension, unemployment assistance, widow's and orphan's pensions and children's allowances). This was intended as a no-cost operation. The proposal was approved by government on 13 March 1953 but was not proceeded with. See NAI S. 13384. Consolidation of the social assistance payments did not take place until the consolidation legislation of 1981 and 1993. 87 White Paper para 51.

number of women entitled to a pension increased in line with the general increase in pension coverage from an estimated 70% of the population (over 70) in 1947 to 78% in 1954. The number of widows entitled to a pension also increased from 35,400 in 1947 to 46,700 in 1954 (although most of this increase predated the 1952 Act and arose from the 1948 Act changes). Both these groups obviously benefited from the significant increases in the rates of old age and widow's pensions over the period. In 1947 women were very largely excluded from access to unemployment assistance, domestic workers were not covered by unemployment insurance and women received lower rates of payment of unemployment insurance. While, despite the opposition of Finance, the social insurance rates of payment for men and single women were equalised in the 1952 Act,[88] most married women still received lower rates of benefit on the basis that if the higher rates applied to them 'the degree of malingering would be even worse than it has been'.[89] And most women remained excluded from entitlement to UA.

As we have seen, Norton had proposed to extend unemployment insurance coverage to domestic workers. However, Ryan had opposed this and the 1952 Act continued to exclude them from entitlement to UB (albeit it that contributions were also reduced for this group). Despite this there was a significant increase of over 20% in the numbers of women insured against the risk of unemployment and, consequently, the numbers of women in receipt of unemployment insurance also increased significantly.[90] However, women remained a tiny proportion of those entitled to UA (3–4%) and the total number of women claiming actually fell over the period (possibly because a number of UA claimants now qualified for UB). The number of women on home assistance also fell but women actually increased slightly as a proportion of adults on this payment (63–67%). The other area in which Ryan reduced somewhat the supports which Norton had proposed was in relation to maternity and marriage benefits. The 1952 Act did provide for a maternity benefit of 12 weeks as proposed by Norton although additional measures proposed in the White Paper were dropped and replaced by a means-tested grant (in the 1953 Health Act).[91] Norton had proposed to reform the existing NHI marriage benefit, claimed by about 6,000 women per year, by introducing a new marriage grant. However, this was dropped from the White Paper. Ryan reinstated the marriage benefit but this functioned, as it had previously, as compensation for women who left insurable employment on marriage, as

88 See the brief discussion in the White Paper para 70 *et seq.* 89 Ibid., para 72. 90 Although women reminded roughly the same proportion of those insured for and claiming unemployment benefits. 91 See White Paper para 93; Cousins, *Irish Social Welfare System* (Round Hall, Dublin, 1995), p. 108.

women who married were disqualified from social insurance payments until they worked for a further six months after marriage. On the other hand, Ryan's scraping of the retirement pension avoided the introduction of the proposed different retirement ages for men and women – something which has created major difficulties in the UK social security system in recent years. In summary, women benefited – as did men – from the major changes in the social welfare system. However, neither the White Paper nor the 1952 Act marked any radical change in women's position nor was this a matter of major debate in the unification of the social welfare system. While there was relatively little difference between the views of Fianna Fáil and the Inter-Party government, the more restricted scheme introduced by Jim Ryan did make a number of changes which reinforced a construct of women as dependent.

ANALYSIS

On the one hand, the establishment of the Department of Social Welfare in 1947 and of a (more-or-less) unified social welfare system in 1952 was a major achievement of social policy in Ireland. It has very much shaped the type of welfare system we have today. Indeed, many of the proposals which were not accepted in 1952 were subsequently incorporated into the current system.[92] Expenditure increased significantly from £11 million in 1946 to £26.6 million in 1954. On the other hand, however, I would suggest that the establishment of a unified social welfare system – rather than reflecting a social democratic tendency inspired by Labour party participation in government or Fianna Fáil's 'traditional expansionary approach'[93] to social issues – represented a failure of politics (or, politics without a project). The Inter-party government and, in particular, the Labour party failed in its attempt to enact the Norton bill and all the parties involved (except Fine Gael) lost seats in the 1951 election. The Social Welfare Act, 1952 did not represent the project of any particular party and reflected a series of compromises. Its passage did not grant electoral benefits to the Fianna Fáil party which lost the subsequent general election in 1954. Nor did the incoming Inter-party government attempt to restore the measures which had been removed from the Norton bill by Fianna Fáil.

The policy structure within which the details of the operation of the social welfare system were designed was tightly constrained and only civil servants

---

92 In terms of benefits these included death grant (1970), contributory old age pension (1960), retirement pension (1970); in terms of scope, the self-employed (1988) and new civil servants (1994) are now included.   93 B. Girvin's phrase.

and politicians were directly involved. The initial establishment of the Department (thereby confining initial debate intradepartmentally as opposed to the inter-departmental discussion arising in relation to children's allowances) and the decision to publish a White Paper both increased the importance of the civil service. In contrast, for example, to the UK where the Beveridge committee received advice and submissions from about 130 individuals and groups, few submissions from outside groups were received in relation to the White Paper and there appears to have been few official meetings between politicians or civil servants and outside groupings.[94] Despite Norton's trade union background, there is little indication of any trade union input to proposals and Norton met the national executive of the ITUC in January 1950 *after* publication of the White Paper. Despite the objections raised by Catholic social thinkers, including the bishop of Clonfert, there is also a striking absence of opposition from the Catholic hierarchy as a body (particularly in comparison the contemporaneous Mother and Child scheme).

The civil service played a key role in formulating the proposals, particularly in relation to the White Paper. From the start, the Departmental officials tended heavily towards a social insurance approach. This was similar to the approach proposed by Beveridge and subsequently enacted (with modifications) in the UK.[95] Key officials in the Department such as Keady and Maguire (both future secretaries of the Department) came from an insurance background in the Departments of Local Government and Industry and Commerce while Honohan (also to become secretary) was qualified as an actuary and had worked in the UK government actuary's office which was favourably disposed to an insurance based approach. Given the closed nature of the Irish civil service, once a particular set of ideas became adopted, it would be particularly difficult to shift them[96] and in the context of the system of public finances, there were (and are) major advantages to having one's own social insurance income which reduces dependence on Exchequer funds. International influences, such as membership of the International Social

---

94 In addition, a social welfare advisory council which had been proposed in Norton's Bill was dropped from the final 1952 Act. 96 M. Weir, 'Ideas and Politics: The Acceptance of Keynesianism in Britain and the United States' in P. Hall (ed.), *The Political Power of Economic Ideas* (Princeton University Press, Princeton, 1989). 95 I would hesitate to call the Irish approach Beveridgean. Firstly, it is not clear that the Irish approach was underpinned by the same principles (e.g. full employment) as in the UK. Secondly, given the largely self-employed nature of the Irish workforce, the approach adopted was far from universal. Perhaps a Beveridgean approach in Ireland would have taken a different approach to his UK report. While the Irish drafters used the same technology (unified social insurance) it is not clear that they drew on the same principles or had the same objectives.

Security Association which promoted a social insurance approach and contact with their UK counterparts, may also have been influential. It is noteworthy that the White Paper presents the proposed improvements in the context of historical developments and 'principles of modern thought' as an evolutionary development towards a 'modern' state – rather than as a political process. Indeed, this is a feature of earlier drafts and of P.J. Keady's 1946 memorandum to government.

Ryan appears to have had relatively little input into the policy process in 1947, perhaps being preoccupied with events in the Department of Health. There is little indication of any input from him on early files and no sign of his subsequent 'Fianna Fáil Plan'. Although the social insurance approach was endorsed by Lemass and in Fianna Fáil advertising in the 1948 election, it is unclear if this approach would have found favour with a Fianna Fáil government.

Norton was strongly supportive of a social insurance based approach, and conversely, opposed to the mean-test. Reflecting opposition to the mean-test from the UK Labour party,[97] Norton, as late as July 1948, remained 'convinced of the desirability of doing away [with the mean test] altogether' and was hopeful that this would be possible 'in the not too distant future'.[98] However, this was obviously not feasible and by the time of publication of the White Paper, he could only point out that the introduction of social insurance payments meant the 'abolition of means test' for those classes covered. His social insurance approach was welcomed by the trade union movement. However, this very fact and the absence of similar benefits for the self-employed, allowed it to be presented as 'class legislation'.[99] While the initial departmental draft at least recognised the importance of the self-employed and proposed to include most non-employee categories over time, the final White Paper had effectively nothing new to offer the self-employed. It may well have been true that the self-employed were 'getting more than their fair share from the assistance schemes.'[100] However, this was hardly a selling point for the scheme in a country where about half the workers were self-employed. The subsequent addition of measures to benefit the self-employed was not sufficient to win over opposition to the bill. Costello was clearly quite supportive of his Tanaiste, perhaps too supportive, and did not sufficiently take account of the need to reflect the interests of other government parties (including his own Fine Gael party).

97 See generally A. Deacon and J. Bradshaw, *Reserved for the Poor: The Means Test in British Social Policy* (Blackwell, London, 1983).   98 *Dáil Debates*, vol. 112 col. 1627, 28 July 1948.
99 Norton's failure to make any sort of alliance with Clann na Talmhan, a party largely representative of small farmers, is striking.   100 Honohan to Norton, 26 September 1949, ILHA Norton papers 118. And see para 131 of the White Paper.

In many ways (and with the benefit of hindsight) one can argue that Norton erred tactically in his approach. He could have decided not to defer the White Paper in order to introduce the 1948 bill . He could have included the 1948 (and proposed 1951) pension improvements in the White Paper as measures for the self-employed. He could have bowed to the very strong opposition to the full inclusion of civil servants at an earlier date. Had he done these things, it is at least possible that he could have had legislation passed in 1950 which would have extended social insurance to all private employees and to a certain extent to civil servants; which would have established a wider range of benefits than the 1952 Act; and which would have provided significant increases for the self-employed. However, this was not to be. Ryan and Fianna Fáil put forward alternative proposals to provide additional benefits to the self-employed and to cut the cost of contributions to employers and employees by having a much more limited insurance element. Rather than the (at least notional) actuarial calculation of funding with costs divided in a tri-partite manner between state, employers and employees, Ryan's plan envisaged the State picking up the shortfall.[101] This proposal was a reasonably credible alternative to the Norton approach and had clear attractions for farmers and other self-employed persons. While not as comprehensive as the Norton bill (e.g. pensions would only be payable from the age of 70 rather than 60/65), it did not require any increase in contributions. Overall, the proposal was quite similar in approach to the 1947 White Paper on health which had proposed entitlement to GP and hospital care for all insured persons, farmers up to £25 PLV and persons with an income of up to £250 (subject to token payments).[102] However, holding down the contributions meant an increased Exchequer cost. In addition, a number of policy difficulties, such as Ryan's proposal to pay 4s. extra to 'insured' pensioners (on the basis of their additional costs but in the absence of any evidence that such persons, as a class, had extra costs) and to phase out the widow's contributory pension, were not dealt with in a satisfactory manner.

The passage of time meant that economic and budgetary difficulties which were only becoming apparent in the late 1940s were clearly visible by 1951. Opposition from MacEntee and Finance was vehement, Ryan's own Department was lukewarm at best about diluting the insurance principle; and Lemass' support appeared to evaporate. Ultimately, it is difficult to present the Ryan Act as other than a modified and less extensive version of the original

101 However, while the White Paper showed balanced costings over an initial five-year period, figures showing a longer-term imbalance over 20 years were removed from the final draft of the White Paper, NAI Plan 13/50. 102 Entitlement to health care was not introduced in precisely this form in the Health Act, 1954.

White Paper proposals. It is true that several groups benefited from the change introduced by Ryan including those earning over £600 who did not have to pay insurance, public servants who perhaps achieved modified status more easily than they would have from Norton, employers who had to pay significantly lower contributions and both agricultural labourers and their employers who received full insurance cover at subsidised rates. However, with the exception of the latter group, Ryan's changes involved the removal of proposed additional charges rather than implying positive benefits. His original proposals for tax-financed hybrid payments which might have favoured the self-employed disappeared entirely and the improvements in assistance payments and children's allowances related largely to compensation for the reduction in food subsidisation. Ryan specifically argued for the exclusion of higher earners who would not benefit from welfare payments in a deliberately non-solidaristic approach.[103] In addition, while all the proposals assumed a traditional family model (with wives giving up work to care for their family), several of Ryan's changes (e.g. treatment of domestic servants, marriage grant) reinforced the patriarchal nature of an already patriarchal system. In many ways the passage of time alone from the beginning of planning for the White Paper in 1947 to the passage of the bill in 1952, contributed to a scaling down of the final measure. The Ireland of 1952 was fully aware of the economic problems which were only becoming apparent in 1947. Thus although the final implementation of the 1952 Act did establish a reasonably comprehensive and unified social welfare system and result in significant increases in expenditure, it did not reflect a clear Fianna Fáil project and, of course, Fianna Fáil lost the subsequent 1954 election.

Overall I would argue that, while of crucial importance to the development of social welfare in the longer term, in the short-term the implementation of the social welfare proposals represented a failure of politics which was linked to the broader crisis of politics in the late 1940s and early 1950s. While, in the early 1940s, Fianna Fáil were still confident in their ability to solve Ireland's wrongs, by the end of that decade their inability to come up with a coherent economic project was becoming clear. Government discussions on post-war reconstruction and full employment failed to resolve the gap between Lemass' politically unrealistic statist plans for full employment and Finance's tradition fiscal liberalism. Despite MacEntee's penetrating ability to identify the weakness in other people's proposals, his own great weakness was his inability to develop a coherent project which could combine 'sound

103 Data from the first Household Budget Survey for 1951–2 (which applied to towns and villages only) show the regressive nature of insurance contributions at that time with semi-skilled and unskilled wage earners paying the highest proportionate contribution.

economics' with public demands for employment and social policy improvements. Other Ministers had little more to suggest than public works. Even if Fianna Fáil could think of a way of improving economic output, it could not (yet) bring itself to disturb the agricultural and industrial sectors – which included its supporters – to increase national output. Yet key Fianna Fáil figures were realistic enough to know that their social, and ultimately political, project was dependent on economic growth. The Inter-party government, delivering on the Clann's election slogan "Put Them Out," reflected diverse political viewpoints and was much less clear about what it wanted to do once it got elected. It too had neither a coherent economic nor social project. And this state of affairs lasted until the late 1950s.

In conclusion, major reform in the area of social welfare was probably inevitable in the late 1940s given popular expectations and measures in the UK. While it appears that much of the work on the White Paper was done in Ryan's first term, the White Paper itself owes much to Norton and, in particular, to the departmental officials who drafted it. While Norton's proposals arguably reflected a social-democratic shift, they did not build a broad enough coalition of support with a result that, despite significant modification, the final proposals fell in mid 1951 with the fall of government. While Fianna Fáil's original decision to establish a unified scheme and Ryan's Fianna Fáil Plan were consistent with the party's traditional expansionary approach, these proposals were blocked by MacEntee and Finance given the changed position of the early 1950s. The ultimate combination of 'mild social reform with financial orthodoxy' was perhaps more desperation than a complementary approach.[104] Fianna Fáil, in the early 1950s, was a party without a project which wanted to prevent the economy getting worse by tight fiscal control and, at the same time, tried to meet the public's social expectations. In the short-term it achieved neither objective.

---

104 As Bew and Patterson had suggested: *Sean Lemass and the Making of Modern Ireland, 1945–66* (Gill and Macmillan, Dublin), p. 63.

APPENDIX: PRINCIPAL DIFFERENCES BETWEEN VARIOUS PROPOSALS, 1948–52

	DSW "Outline" 1948	White Paper 1949	Norton Bill 1950	FF Plan 1951	Ryan Act 1952
Scope	Not considered	All employees. Application to public service to be considered. Self-employed excluded	All employees. Modified application to public service and farmer members of co-ops	Not specified	Non-manual employees > £600 p.a. excluded. Modified application to public service. Self-employed excluded
Contributions					
i) employee (m/f)	3s. 5d. (2s. 8d.)	H) 3s. 6d. (2s. 2d.)[1] L1) 2s. 6d. (1s. 2d.) L2) not specified	H) 3s. 6d. (2s. 2d.) L1) 2s. 6d. (1s. 2d.) L2) 4s. 6d. (2s. 8d.)	As existing Gen) 1s. 11d. (1s. 2d.) Ag) 9d. (5d.)	Gen) 2s. 4d. (1s. 4d.) Ag) 1s. 3d. (9d.)
ii) employer (m/f)	3s. 5d. (2s. 8d.)	H) 3s. 6d. (2s. 2d.) L1) 3s. 6d. (1s/2d.) L2) not specified	H) 3s. 6d. (2s. 2d.) L1) 3s. 6d. (1s. 2d.) L2) 4s. 6d. (2s. 8d.)	Gen) 2s. (1s. 10d.) Ag) 10d. (10d.)	Gen) 2s. 4d. (2s. 0d.) Ag) 1s. 3d. (1s. 3d.)
DB & UB rates					
personal married woman	24s.	24s. -1d.[1]	24s. -2d.[2]	24s.	24s.
		18s.	18s.	not specified	18s.
adult	12s.	12s.	12s.	12s.	12s.
child	6s.	7s.	7s.	7s.	7s.
New benefits	Contributory old age pension at age 65/60 @ 20s.	Contributory retirement pension at age 65/60 @ 24s.	Contributory retirement pension at age 65/60 @ 24s.	Pension at age 70 for insured persons, farmers < £25 PLV, persons with means < £100 p.a. @ 24s.	Continued UB/DB for those 65–70
Death Grant	Grant of £20	Grant of £10	Grant of £10	Not specified	No death grant
Workman's compensation	Integrated	Further consideration	Not included	Not specified	Not included
Maternity benefit	12 weeks	12 weeks	12 weeks	Not specified	12 weeks

[1] Benefits reduced for low paid group.
[2] Benefits reduced for low paid group.

	DSW 'Outline' 1948	White Paper 1949	Norton Bill 1950	FF Plan 1951	Ryan Act 1952
Maternity grant	£4	£5 grant + £4 attendance allowance	£5 grant + £4 attendance allowance	Not specified	£2 grant[3]
Marriage grant	£50	None	None	Not specified	£10 grant
Assistance issues	Not considered	Not considered			
Transfer of land to qualify for OAP			Land up to £30 PLV		Enacted in SW Act 1951
Increase in OAP			Extra increase to be introduced on Committee	As Norton Bill	Increases in SW Act 1951 and SW Act 1952[4]
OAP Means Test			Improvements to be introduced on Committee	Major improvements in means test	SW Acts 1951 and 1952
Children's allowance			Not included	Extra £500,000 in increases to larger families	Extended to second child[5]
Unemployment Assistance			Not included	Not included	Increases in 1952 Act[6]

[3] Further grant introduced under Health legislation.
[4] Linked to modification of food subsidisation.
[5] Linked to modification of food subsidisation.
[6] Do.

8

State *and* society

'I have a particular case in mind . . .'[1]

In this final chapter, we outline the key developments in the establishment of the social welfare system in an independent Ireland and look at some of the main factors which influenced that development. We also look at how this study can inform some of the current key social policy debates about the interaction of state and society and what this can tell us about the broader issues of welfare regime formation.

THE IMPACT OF CHANGE

While the initial measures which helped to shape the Irish social welfare system pre-date Irish independence, as we have seen, these policies (the Poor Law, workmen's compensation, etc.) did not form a coherent system and it was not until 1952 that the social welfare system, as we now call it,[2] was 'born'. The period from the early 1920s to 1952 saw a significant increase in spending on social welfare schemes both in cash terms and as a percentage of national income. Spending on the major schemes increased from just over £5 million in the early 1920s to over £26 million in 1954. Spending as a proportion of national income increased from just over 3% in 1926 to almost 6% in 1953. This was not, however, a linear growth pattern. While caution is required as no official data for national income are available for before 1938, it would appear that social welfare expenditure remained at about 3% of national income from the mid 1920s to the early 1930s. There was a signifi-

1 Senator J.C. Counihan, *Report of the Select Committee on the National Health Insurance Bill, 1933*, p. 6. 2 In this chapter I use the term 'social welfare' to refer to the range of policies discussed in this book even in those periods when the term itself was not commonly used. While anachronistic, it avoids clumsy circumlocution.

cant rise during the Fianna Fáil expansionary period in the 1930s – although the early rise is partially due to the (possibly overstated) fall in national income estimates during the economic war. Having reached a peak of 5% in the late 1930s, spending fell back significantly during the war, in line with public spending generally.[3] After the war, expenditure rose rapidly both in terms of current spending and, despite a drop in 1950–2, as a percentage of national income to 6% by 1953–4 when the 1952 legislation was fully in effect.[4] As several authors have shown, the post-war period was one of rapid growth of public expenditure – both generally and on social services in particular. Overall public expenditure increased from 26% of GNP in 1947 to 37% by 1954 while social expenditure rose from 35% to 46% of total public expenditure over the period from 1947 to 1955.[5] This was, in part, a 'catch-up' spurt after the suppression of expenditure during the War period. And it was also part of, and influenced by, the general European expansionary period after the War which saw a number of European countries embark on expansionary social security reform.[6]

The level of industrialisation certainly increased in Ireland over that period with industrial employment increasing from 13% of employment in 1926 to 23% by 1951 and agricultural employment falling from over half to 41%.[7] To this extent, the growth of social welfare certainly reflects the 'logic of industrialisation' and 'logic of modernisation'[8] arguments which suggest that welfare state growth is related to the industrialisation and modernisation of society.[9] However, this does not, of course, explain the precise shape which the system took.

How did this increased funding impact on the people of Ireland? Unfortunately, the limited statistical data for the period means that we can only speculate about the impact on poverty and income distribution.[10] We

3 M. O'Donoghue and A.A. Tait, 'The Growth of Public Revenue and Expenditure in Ireland' in J.A. Bristow and A.A. Tait (eds.), *Economic Policy in Ireland* (Institute of Public Administration, Dublin, 1968). 4 Expenditure data are for the year to 31 March while national income data are for the calendar year. 5 O'Donoghue and Tait, op. cit.; F. Kennedy, *Public Social Expenditure in Ireland* (ESRI, Dublin, 1975); M. Maguire 'Ireland' in P. Flora (ed.), *Growth to Limits: The Western European Welfare States since World War Two*, vol. 2 (de Gruyter, Berlin, 1986). Both total public expenditure and social expenditure did not increase further in the later 1950s. 6 P. Baldwin, *The Politics of Social Solidarity* (Cambridge University Press, Cambridge, 1990); K. Van Kersbergen, *Social Capitalism* (Routledge, London, 1995). 7 K. Kennedy et al., *Economic Development* (Routledge, London, 1998), Table 7.2. 8 C. Kerr et al., *Industrialism and Industrial Man* (New York: Oxford University Press, 1964). 9 P. Flora and A. Heidenheimer, *The Development of Welfare States in Europe and America* (Transaction 1981, New Brunswick). 10 The census data which are available on 'quality of life' indicators such as health, longevity and housing status are only loosely related to income. For example, while there was a dramatic improvement in infant mortality after 1944,

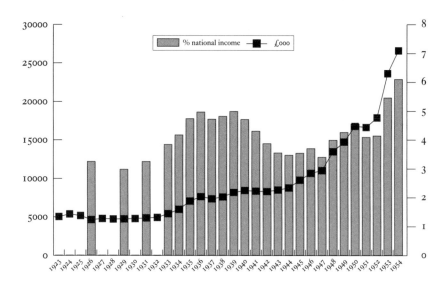

1 Social welfare expenditure, 1923–1954

can, however, look at the coverage of social welfare payments and at their 'generosity'. In the case of pensioners, the proportion of the population over 70 in receipt of a pension fell significantly in the 1920s from over three-quarters to under two-thirds. This returned to a peak of 75% in the mid 1930s and thereafter remained between 70 and 74%. In contrast, less than one in ten of the working age population (15–70) were in receipt of a social welfare payments at any time.[11] While there was a significant increase in the proportion of the working age population in receipt of a social welfare payment from about 4% in 1926 to 9% by 1936, this did not increase further in the period to 1951 (or indeed to 1961) and the rise in numbers in areas such as widows and disability payments was balanced by a fall in unemployment payments.

While the number of people in insurable employment increased steadily over the period, numbers on the Live Register fell back steadily despite rises in the pre-war period and again in 1951. Following a rise in the mid 1930s, numbers on employment schemes fell away rapidly.

it would be hard to prove a causative link between this and the introduction of children's allowances. The first, limited, Household Budget Inquiry was in 1951 but reports only expenditure data. 11 Due to data limitations this figure does not include the adult 'dependants' of persons on unemployment payments but these numbers would not significantly alter the picture.

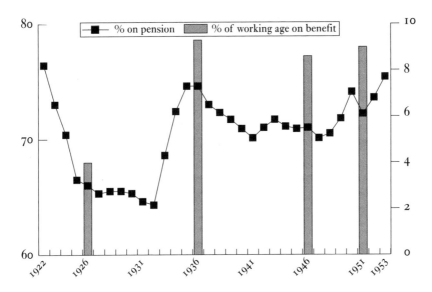

2 Percentage of population on welfare benefits, 1922–1952

In terms of the level of benefits, international studies indicate that Irish social welfare rates fell back in comparative terms over the period. Korpi estimates that in 1930 the old age pension represented over 30% of average industrial earnings – comparing favourably with the average for European countries of about 25%.[12] However, while average replacement rates in other European countries increased to 35% up to the mid 1950s, the Irish replacement stagnated at about 30%. And a similar tendency can be seen in relation to sickness and unemployment benefits. In comparison with prices, the value of old age pensions fell sharply in the period after 1924, although a decline in the cost-of-living index in the period after 1925 lessened the impact of the reduction in the pension. The 1932 pension improvements, combined with a further fall in the index in the mid 1930s, meant that pensioners benefited significantly although these benefits were eventually reduced by rising cost-of-living in the late 1930s. During the war years pensions and unemployment assistance (the two biggest payments for most of the period) broadly kept pace with earnings – taking account of the various supplementary cash and non-cash benefits – but both welfare payments and earnings fell well behind

12 W. Korpi, *Ireland in a Comparative Perspective*, pp. 4–8. Considerable caution must be expressed in relation to the use of hypothetical replacement rates in this period – both in relation to the general limitations of such an approach and the additional data limitations which apply in the period.

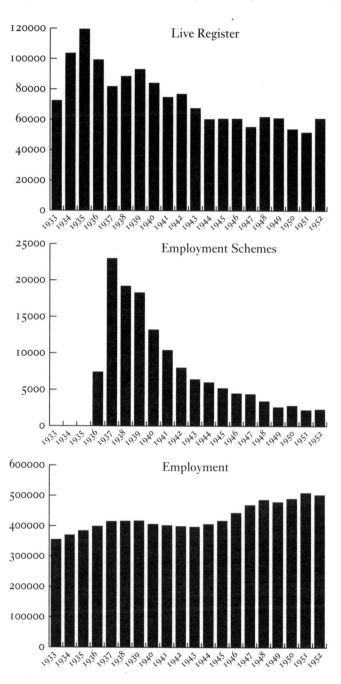

3 Employment and unemployment, 1933–52

the cost-of-living. Hughes has pointed out that there was a significant shift in the distribution of income during the period 1938–46 in favour of the agricultural sector and company profits and away from employees. He suggests that this was due to the freeze on wages and salaries imposed from 1942 to 1946 together with the rapid rise in consumer and agricultural prices.[13] Those on social welfare were obviously also affected by this relative shift in income distribution. In the immediate post-war period (1946–52), earnings rose rapidly in real terms.[14] Social welfare rates after the war also rose significantly in real terms but it would appear that, in general, only old age pensions gained as against wages (and then only after 1948).

An analysis of the growth in social welfare expenditure in terms of the influence of demographic changes, changes in eligibility and changes in average benefits for old age pensions, sickness and unemployment payments (which make up about two thirds of total expenditure in the early 1950s) support the picture of growing coverage but declining relative generosity (see Appendix at pages 204–8, below). In the case of old age pensions and unemployment payments, while the 'eligibility ratio' (the ratio of beneficiaries to the potential claimant population) increased in both cases (with increases concentrated in the period to 1936), the 'transfer ratio' (the ratio of the average payment per beneficiary to per capita national income) declined over time.[15] In the case of sickness benefits we see a significant increase in both spending and the eligibility ratio both before and after the 1952 Act but a long-term fall in the transfer ratio.

The funding structure of the system changed relatively little over the period. Despite the emphasis in the White Paper on social insurance, in the short-term there was relatively little change in the level of total expenditure which came from social insurance. In 1924, one-third of total expenditure was funded from this source. Notwithstanding the significant broadening of social insurance schemes over the period, the establishment of tax-funded schemes such as unemployment assistance and children's allowances meant that this balance shifted in favour of non-insurance schemes so that by 1955 only 28% of social welfare spending was funded from social insurance. Taking account of the fact that in the 1920s and 1930s about one quarter of social insurance funding came from the state, this meant that employers and employees contributed about 26% of total social welfare expenditure in 1930 by way of social insurance contributions. In comparative terms, the level of

13 J.G. Hughes, *The Functional Distribution on Income in Ireland, 1938–70* (ESRI, Dublin, 1972), pp. 17–20. 14 E. Nevin, *Wages in Ireland* (ESRI, Dublin, 1963), table A. 15 Following the methodology set out in M. Maguire, 'Components of Growth of Income Maintenance Expenditure in Ireland 1951–1979', *Economic and Social Review* (1984) 15, pp. 75–85.

funding from social insurance was originally broadly in line with the average found in a study of 18 OECD countries in the period from 1930.[16] By the later 1940s, social insurance contributions from employers and employees had fallen to about one-fifth of total expenditure in Ireland, in contrast to the position in other countries where there had been a significant increase in the proportion of total funding coming from employers and employees to about 50%. There was a shift in the period from local to central exchequer funding with local funding declining from 7% of total expenditure in 1924 to 3% in 1954.[17] The growth in non-agricultural employment,[18] the increase in the scope of social insurance and the insurantial logic of the White Paper meant that the total numbers insured increased significantly from 418,000 in 1923 to 726,000 in 1955 – at a time when the total numbers in employment fell slightly from 1,220,000 in the 1920s to about 1,150,000 in the mid 1950s.[19] The numbers insured for all contingencies increased even more significantly from 214,000 in 1923 (the number for those insured for unemployment insurance the smallest of the insurance schemes) to 639,000 in 1955. The range of contingencies covered increased very significantly with the inclusion of the new risks of widowhood and of low income in large families, the extension of unemployment cover, and the rationalisation of sickness benefits. But, of course, the major initiative of the White Paper and the 1952 Act was to bring all the disparate systems of income support together in one reasonably coherent system – one which, despite the significant changes which have taken place, still underpins the Irish social welfare system today fifty years on.

POLICY LEGACIES

What were the factors which shaped the social welfare system established in 1952? Firstly, we must acknowledge the vital role played by Ireland's membership of the United Kingdom in the period to 1922. The basis of what became our social welfare system was established in the short century between the establishment of the Poor Law in 1838 and the introduction of national insurance in 1911–13. It seems unlikely that an independent Ireland

16 O. Sjøberg, *Paying for Social Rights* (Swedish Institute for Social Research, Stockholm, 1999).   17 In 1924, this related to home assistance; in 1954 to home assistance and the local authority contribution to unemployment assistance.   18 Agricultural employment (largely uninsured) made up over 50% of all employment in 1926, but fell to about 40% by the 1950s.   19 K. Kennedy et al., *The Economic Development of Ireland in the Twentieth Century* (Routledge, London, 1988), table 7.2. It is *not* advisable to express the numbers insured as a percentage of the total in employment, other than as an indication of trends in coverage, as the two involve quite different measures.

would have introduced such an extensive system of benefits. Unlike England and Wales, the Irish parliament had not introduced any national system of Poor Law before the Union in 1801. Indeed, in adopting this approach they followed the European rule to which England and Wales were very much the exception. It seems unlikely, had some form of political independence been obtained in the late nineteenth century, that the Irish Party would have strong exponents of an extensive system of income payments. As we have seen, the policies which were applied to Ireland were, with limited exceptions, those developed for the much more industrialised remainder of the UK. Accordingly Ireland inherited a generous but inconsistent coverage. For example, while a means-tested old age pension of 10s. may seem limited today, comparative studies have shown that this left Ireland with one of the higher and more comprehensive pensions coverages.[20] However, the insurance based nature of the unemployment scheme meant that the very significant unemployment and underemployment in Ireland was largely unaffected by this scheme (although it did again provide relatively generous benefits to the limited numbers who did qualify for unemployment insurance).[21] The same limitation also applied to health insurance and workmen's compensation again leaving well over half the population unprotected against sickness related risks.[22] After Independence the Irish state and Irish society was to be responsible for the further development of the system. But, and leaving aside the influence on state structures and the economic relationship which are dealt with below, the UK remained a formative influence of social welfare developments. The basic similarity of both schemes, the common language, and the fact that the UK scheme broadly applied in Northern Ireland meant that developments in the UK were highly influential both for policy makers and the general public. This is not to say that UK developments were slavishly followed – they often were not followed at all and even when a similar scheme (such as unemployment assistance or children's allowances) was introduced in both countries the rationale or the detail was often quite different. But, for example, it is clear that the publication of the Beveridge

20 Palme has estimated that close to 70% of the Irish population over pension age received a pension in 1930 compared to an average for countries with 'citizenship' based pensions of about one-third while the Irish old age pension also constituted a much higher than average proportion of average industrial earnings. See J. Palme, *Pension Rights in Welfare Capitalism* (Swedish Institute for Social Research, Stockholm, 1990), pp. 47 and 50. See also W. Korpi, *Welfare State Development in Europe Since 1930: Ireland in a Comparative Perspective* (ESRI, Dublin, 1992). 21 E. Carroll, *Emergence and Structuring of Social Insurance Institutions* (Swedish Institute for Social Research, Stockholm, 1999), p. 141–3. 22 O. Kangas, *The Politics of Social Rights: Studies of Sickness Insurance in OECD Countries* (Swedish Institute for Social Research, Stockholm, 1991), p. 69.

report had an impact in Ireland not far short of that produced in the UK
itself.

BRINGING SOCIETY BACK IN

Much social policy writing in recent decades has focussed on the role of the
state arguing both that the state can (at least potentially) be an autonomous
actor with its own interests to pursue and that states as 'configurations of
organization and action . . . influence the meanings and methods of politics
for all groups and classes in society'.[23] More recently Skocpol has broadened
this state-centred approach in her study of the political origins of social
policy in the United State of America. Here she utilises a 'polity-centred'
approach which includes not only the state but also 'party organisations' and
'politically active groups' as part of the polity.[24] Skocpol's analysis provides a
complex and convincing analysis of the way in which politics and policies
interrelate. I suggest that this polity-centred approach has much to offer the
study on the development of welfare in Ireland but that we also need to bring
societal institutions to the forefront of the equation. Looking at the role of
Irish civil society can help us to understand both specific events in the development of the social welfare system and also can help to account for the
structure of decision making.[25]

In the Irish context, societal organisations relevant to the area of 'social
welfare' payments were weak and fragmented. This had numerous implications for the development of the Irish social welfare system. As we have seen,
friendly societies in Ireland had a very limited coverage (with only 40,000
members before 1911) and, unlike the situation in the UK where the national
insurance system was grafted on to the existing system of friendly and industrial societies, a network of societies had, in effect, to be created in Ireland to
fulfil this role. This led to a highly dispersed and fragmented system with
474,000 members in 65 different societies.[26] This was inefficient in many

23 T. Skocpol, 'Bringing the State Back In: Strategies of Analysis in Current Research' in P.
Evans et al., *Bringing the State Back In* (Cambridge University Press, Cambridge, 1985).   24 T.
Skocpol, *Protecting Soldiers and Mothers: The Political Origins of Social Policy in the United
States* (Belknap Press, Harvard, 1992), pp. 41 *et seq.*   25 For present purposes, I am using the
term 'society' to refer to all structures outside the formal remit of the public sector, including
market-based actors such as employers.   26 While there were also a large number of societies
in the UK, Gilbert makes the point that 90% were members of less than 12 societies, B.
Gilbert, *British Social Policy*, p. 301. In contrast, while the Ancient Order of Hibernians
dominated the Irish scene with over 20% of all membership, the largest six Irish societies – each
with 20,000 or more members (Slainte, the Liver, Irish Amalgamated, Prudential, Irish
National Foresters and the AOH) – represented only 50% of total membership with the

cases and was unable to withstand the political pressure brought to bear on it by Fianna Fáil in 1933. Accordingly the running of the existing system of national health insurance was transferred from a set of private organisations to what was, in effect, a quasi-state body which was, in turn, absorbed into the departmental structure in 1951. In contrast, friendly and industrial societies in the UK remained responsible for the administration of health insurance until 1948.[27] Trade unions were also highly fragmented with over 100 trade unions in 1930 with a total membership of only 100,000. The Irish Trade Union Congress (and, after the split in 1945, the Congress of Irish Unions) had relatively little centralised power and neither individual unions nor the ITUC showed much interest in taking on responsibility for social welfare matters.[28] Unlike the UK, there was no strong trade union confederation to insist on the inclusion of public servants and the higher paid in social insurance to benefit lower-paid, private sector employees.[29] The small size of employers, the fragmentation of trade unions, and the lack of strong co-ordinating mechanisms on the part of both trade unions and employers certainly weakened the possibility of adopting a corporatist approach to policy. For example, as we have seen in relation to children's allowance, MacEntee had argued strongly for a more corporatist type approach with an allowance to be paid by employers, as happened in many other European countries. But this had already been rejected by the interdepartmental committee on family allowances on the basis of the small size of most Irish employers. Of course, in many cases there was also strong political and administrative hostility to developing the role of 'civil society' – seen, for example, in the political and administrative dismissal of the report of the Commission on Vocational Organisation.

No doubt the weakness of civil society contributed to, although it does not completely explain, the Fianna Fáil approach to policy formation. As we saw in chapter 2, Cumann na nGaedheal retained a pluralist approach to policy formation (an aspect of its politics which has received little attention to date). It established a myriad of public committees and commissions on pensions, the Poor Law, unemployment, workmen's compensation and national health insurance all of which received lengthy evidence from the public and inter-

remainder scattered through many small societies.   **27** On the position in the UK see Gilbert, *British Social Policy* chapter 6; N. Whiteside, 'Private Agencies for Public Purposes: Some New Perspectives on Policy Making in Health Insurance Between the Wars', *Journal of Social Policy* (1983) 12, pp. 165–94; id. 'Private Provision and Public Welfare: Health Insurance between the Wars' in D. Gladstone (ed.), *Before Beveridge* (Institute of Economic Affairs, London, 2000). **28** See, for example, the fact that very few trade unions took up the possibility of paying unemployment insurance under the 1911 legislation. In 1944 trade unions paid only 3% of all unemployment insurance, NAI EB 280602.   **29** Baldwin, *Politics of Social Solidarity*, p. 119.

ested bodies and all of which published reports. In contrast, Fianna Fáil established the Widows Pensions Committee and never established one other public investigation solely related to any area considered in this book in the period to 1952 (and indeed for some decades after that).[30] This was not because Fianna Fáil administrations did not carry out important studies of issues such as unemployment assistance, public works, family allowances, and the establishment of a department of social welfare. These were carried out by interdepartmental committees which generally took no evidence (other than from public service bodies) and none of which were subsequently published (indeed all remain unpublished to this day). This approach was generally continued by the first Inter-party government in 1948. The classic example of this approach to policy formulation is the White Paper on Social Security. In the UK, the White Paper on Social Insurance and the subsequent 1946 legislation was preceded by the Beveridge report. Beveridge received written and oral evidence from about 130 organisations and individuals representing a very wide range of interests. In contrast, there was no formal public consultation whatsoever in relation to the drafting of the Irish White Paper and the consultation with non-civil servants in any form was minimal. And we have seen that there was little substantive consultation with trade unions or employers in relation to the White Paper or subsequent legislation even though Norton himself had a strong trade union background.[31]

THE ROLE OF THE STATE

So the weakness of Irish civil society – and the related fact that Fianna Fáil (and the Inter-party government) did not operate through a pluralist decision-making structure – meant that the state played a crucial role in the development of the Irish social welfare system. Ireland's colonial history had left it with a strong and centralised state with a civil service modelled on the British approach, a feature it had in common with other colonial administrations.[32] One example of this is the influence and policy stance of the

30 The NHIS might, of course, be seen as a corporatist body. But, as we have seen, its membership was structured in such a way as to be subject to effective political control – assuming, of course, that political appointees did not fall out with their appointers. And in the Society's one major initiative – the Dignan plan – the lead role was clearly taken by Bishop Dignan himself with the trade union and employer representatives relegated to onlookers. 31 Nor was this contrast between the early pluralist and subsequent statist approaches confined to the social policy area. P. and G. Ford (eds.), *Select List of Reports of Inquiries of the Irish Dáil and Senate 1922–1972* (Irish Academic Press, Dublin, 1974). 32 S. MacPherson and J. Midgley, *Comparative Social Policy and the Third World* (Wheatsheaf, London, 1987).

Department of Finance. O'Connell and Rottman have argued that the Department of Finance 'following the Treasury model inherited from the British administrative system played a dominant role in state policy formation for much of Ireland's post-Independence history'.[33] Thus the key players in the period in question were the government and the civil service. Because of the centralised nature of Irish government and the tendency over the period to greater centralisation, local government, which in the early decades had been an important player, had little impact on developments from the 1930s on. Secondly, governments were, for the vast majority of the period, in an effective majority position in the Oireachtas which meant that initiatives came only from the government party.[34] The strict system of party allegiances and the lack of any real committee system meant that policy proposals came almost invariable from the executive itself.[35]

While there was obviously a considerable commingling of influences in the adoption of any policy measure, a number of clear trends can be identified. In the first decade of independence, few major policy measures were adopted and the commitment of both government and the Department of Finance to economy was so shared that it is difficult to allocate individual responsibility for this overall approach. Finance was clearly the dominant department in this period and the ambitions of other departments were kept well in check for most of the period. The arrival of Fianna Fáil in power signalled a dramatic change. Firstly, ministers now took the initiative in pushing forward measures which had been promised in their election manifesto such as reform of old age pensions, widows' and orphans' pensions and unemployment support. Secondly, departments now had the opportunity to support these measures and to advance measures, such as unification of national health insurance, which had been resisted by the previous government. However, it is clear that, while the details of proposals were generally

33 P.J. O'Connell and D. Rottman, 'The Irish Social Welfare in Comparative Perspective' in J.H. Goldthorpe and C.T. Wheland (eds.), *The Development of Industrial Society in Ireland* (Oxford University Press, Oxford, 1992). 34 On the role of political institutions in shaping policy, see E. Immergut, *Health Politics: Interests and Institutions in Western Europe* (Cambridge University Press, Cambridge, 1992); S. Steinmo et al. (eds.), *Structuring Politics: Historical Institutionalism in Comparative Analysis* (Cambridge University Press, Cambridge, 1992); E. Amenta, *Bold Relief* (Princeton University Press, Princeton, 1998). 35 The only two significant exceptions to this rule were the Labour bill on Poor Law reform in Dublin introduced in the Senate which was passed by the Senate but subsequently replaced by a government prepared measure to similar effect and the Fianna Fáil old age pensions bill which led to the defeat of the Cumann na nGaedheal government and its resignation (and immediate re-election). Both significantly were in the first decade of Cumann na nGeadheal rule when the party was a nominal minority government and when the party system was less rigid than it later became.

thrashed out by departments or interdepartmental groups, individual Fianna Fáil figures (in particular Lemass and de Valera) played a very significant role in advancing social policy measures up to and including children's allowances in the 1940s.

The establishment of the Department of Social Welfare marks a significant turning point here. Firstly, although the establishment of the department was a response to the political imperative to 'do something' in reply to the Beveridge and Dignan reports and the general sense of a need for postwar reconstruction, the decision to establish a department was in essence a technocratic response. One gets the strong impression that Lemass would have seen the establishment of a contributory old age pension as a politically more attractive alternative. Secondly, once the department was established, it meant that much of the debate about policy measures was carried out *intra* rather than inter-departmentally. It ended the fascinating, if hardly efficient, debates which had taken place between ministers and departments on issues such as children's allowances and increased the influence of the civil service as opposed to politicians. It meant that the key experts on social welfare matters were now concentrated in one department so that ministers no longer had the time or resources to develop alternative proposals and that social welfare officials could dismiss objections from dissenting ministers as 'half-baked'. This can be seen in the White Paper where the basic shape of the proposed system, perhaps to the detriment of its political prospects, was decided in the Department of Social Welfare and where discussion on the draft White Paper focussed on relatively minor matters of direct interest to departments such as insurability of public servants and, of course, the cost of the scheme. Key issues such as the relevance of the scheme to the agricultural community received only belated and limited discussion.

ECONOMY AND SOCIAL CLASS

The economy and economic policy played an important – but not determinant – role in shaping discussions on social welfare issues. In particular Ireland's continued relationship of economic dependency on the UK[36] influenced both the economic context in which social welfare policies were set and, more indirectly, social policies themselves. In the first decade of independence, Cumann na nGaedheal focused largely on a policy of agricultural development and free trade which was consistent with limiting public expen-

---

36 L. Mjøset, *The Irish Economy in a Comparative Institutional Perspective* (NESC, Dublin, 1992), chapter 12.

diture and social services to keep down costs to farmers and employers. Cumann na nGaedheal ministers were determined to establish Ireland's reputation for fiscal responsibility and were, if necessary, prepared to inflict pain on the population to do so. In contrast, Fianna Fáil embarked on both the economic war with the UK and a policy of protection and import substitution industrialisation (ISI). Such an approach could have been consistent with a Keynesian development of the welfare state as in Sweden. However, I have argued that, whatever the occasionally heterodox economic views of Fianna Fáil ministers and although their social policies may in fact have had a demand creation effect, nothing could have been further from their thoughts. In fact, policies such as unemployment assistance had more to do with compensating groups affected by the economic war than with supporting ISI. While ISI was a limited success, the advent of the Second World War meant that the government had to operate on a 'war economy' footing. Ireland was saved from mass unemployment by very high levels of emigration to the UK while the government struggled to control prices and, somewhat more successfully, to limit wages and social welfare rates. The end of the war found a Fianna Fáil government which was, in many way, surprisingly resilient but whose key members clearly realised that they had no economic policy. And they had been in power long enough to know that social policy could not be sustained without a successful economy. Lemass' plans for a controlled economy (more Beveridge than Keynes) were not acceptable to his colleagues (nor, if they had known about them, to the general public). Fianna Fáil had not (yet) envisaged taking on the native bourgeoisie by changing its policies to export led industrialisation, as it was to do a decade later. Finance remained committed to a failed *laissez faire* approach.[37] Nor had the Inter-party government the time to develop more coherent economic proposals. The 1952 Act was, to some extent, a victim of the 'balance of payments crisis' and economic slowdown of 1951 as the delay in bringing the measure into law meant that the concerns about the economy in 1951–2 and the 'crisis' facing the sterling area reinforced the perceived need for economy.

The development of the social welfare system also reflected social class interests. However, the social-democratic or labourist interpretation,[38] which

---

37 The failure of any key interest to develop a coherent alternative economic viewpoint which might have been acceptable to the general public at a time when even the (normally influential) UK government had adopted a broadly Keynesian approach remains to be explained.
38 Most recently restated in Hicks' interesting qualitative and quantitative study: A. Hicks, *Social Democracy and Welfare Capitalism* (Ithaca: Cornell University Press 1999). Unfortunately, Hicks (incorrectly) excludes Ireland from his analysis in the period from 1920 to after World War II 'for excessively mimicking British social policy'. This is doubly unfortunate in that the Irish case does not appear to support the general social democratic trend he identifies.

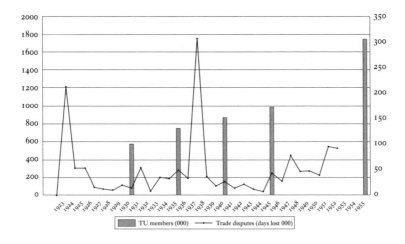

4 Trade union membership and trade disputes, 1923–55

sees welfare states being influenced by working class strength as represented through social democratic parties, receives little support from the Irish case. It should be noted that this is not because Ireland had a comparatively undeveloped welfare state at that time. Indeed, comparative studies indicate that in relation to the scope and level of coverage of old age pensions and unemployment payments, Ireland in the mid 1950s compared not unfavourably with the average of 18 OECD countries (and indeed with some of the Nordic countries at that time).[39]

The Labour party was only in government (and then in coalition with more conservative parties) for a very short period of the three decades involved. Nor is there any clear relationship between either trade union membership or the level of trade disputes and the growth in social welfare.

The growth in trade union membership in the 1930s followed the Fianna Fáil industrialisation programme and appears to have taken place *after* rather than before the expansion of social welfare schemes. And while there was a 'dramatic acceleration' in trade union membership and density after 1945,[40] this did not convert into increased support for the Labour party (or parties). The political impact of this significant increase in trade union membership

39 J. Palme, *Pension Rights in Welfare Capitalism* (Swedish Institute for Social Research, Stockholm, 1990); E. Carroll, *Emergence and Structuring of Social Insurance Institutions* (Swedish Institute for Social Research, Stockholm, 1990). Albeit that sickness benefits were somewhat below average: O. Kangas *The Politics of Social Rights* (Swedish Institute for Social Research, Stockholm, 1991). 40 W.K. Roche, 'The Trend of Unionisation' in T.V. Murphy and W.K. Roche (eds.), *Irish Industrial Relations in Practice* (Oak Tree, Dublin, 1997).

was further weakened by the long-term fragmentation of the membership into a large number of unions and by the schism in the trade union movement which led to the formation of two rival Congresses (the Irish Trade Union Congress and the Congress of Irish Unions) in 1945 (a split which lasted to 1959).[41] While trade disputes increased after the War, the main focus of trade union activity was on wages rather than welfare. Tellingly, Norton, shortly after losing office, was highly critical of the trade union movement which 'during the past three years' had been 'overtaken by a form of social paralysis in the matter of advocating an effective Social Security Scheme'.[42]

Government policy in the initial decade clearly favoured large farmers and, at least in the earlier part of the decade, many sections of business. But the economic crisis of the late 20s undermined that relationship and many businesses favoured protectionism and were not averse to greater social spending. Fianna Fáil adopted a policy of strategic incorporation of various class interests. Its policies of protectionism and its significant building programme for public housing and hospitals clearly helped create employment. It is likely that the significant expansion in social welfare schemes in the 1930s would have had a demand creation effect on the economy. The expansion or introduction of schemes such as old age and widows' pensions, public works and unemployment assistance helped to support the 'small man' to whom Fianna Fáil looked for support. In particular, public works and unemployment assistance helped to provide support to small farmers and their families who were hard hit by the economic war until the recovery of agricultural prices in the late 1930s.[43] And the introduction of children's allowances was certainly aimed at key Fianna Fáil supporters: workers and farmers who were the most fertile social groups. However, there was a limit to the extent to which Fianna Fáil would go in redistributing income and the party was always conscious of the need to build a coalition of both business and workers. Thus, for example, Fianna Fáil ministers had little sympathy for the 'work-shy' and were prepared to use effective compulsory enlistment in the Construction Corps to keep down recorded unemployment.

Norton's White Paper and subsequent bill was a document which heavily reflected the interests of employed workers and which drew on the UK precedents set by Beveridge and subsequent legislation.[44] Norton sought to

41 E. O'Connor, *A Labour History of Ireland* (Gill and Macmillan, Dublin, 1992). 42 ITUC, *Fifty Seventh Annual Report 1950–1*, pp. 95–7. 43 In December 1934, of the 94,000 applicants for UA, 66,000 had means of whom 59% were farmers or farmer's relatives, *The Trend of Employment and Unemployment in the Saorstat*, appendix D. 44 However, it is clear from the work done before Norton came to office that this was the general direction in which the White Paper was heading in any event. One can only speculate as to whether a White Paper published in 1948 by a Fianna Fáil government would have toned down the heavy emphasis on

have a 'universal' approach to social insurance but, crucially, only so far as employees were concerned. Perhaps fatally for his project, he made insufficient attempts to build an alliance with other social classes and the concerns of representatives of agricultural interests such as James Dillon were only taken on board too little and too late. Ryan's 'Fianna Fáil Plan' was an interesting alternative to Norton's 'workerist' approach – a coherent attempt to provide support to both workers and farmers at a lesser cost than Norton's plan. But Fianna Fáil did not implement its plan. Becoming more fundamentally conservative, affected by the economic downturn of the early 50s, with MacEntee in control of Finance and Lemass temporarily sidelined, Fianna Fáil abandoned Ryan's plan, cut back Norton's proposals and implemented what was left. Ryan's 1952 Act as finally implemented was explicitly *not* comprehensive. Ryan stated that he could see neither the justice nor the necessity in including classes in social insurance who could never benefit and he could not approve of what he described as the 'hidden taxation' of such classes through social insurance contributions.[45] And the 1952 Act left room for private insurance. The White Paper had rejected pay-related benefits on a number of grounds including the need to leave room for voluntary private insurance. Fianna Fáil subsequently dropped the proposed death grant which would have been in competition with private life insurance.[46]

Ironically, given that much of the criticism of the White Paper and the Norton bill was in relation to its failure to provide additional support to farmers, farmers generally did well out of the social welfare system. As the White Paper somewhat defensively pointed out, farmers already received 'in relation to their numbers far more than their proportionate share from the assistance schemes'.[47] It estimated that more than 75% of old age pensions were paid in rural areas implying that a very large part of the expenditure of almost £7 million went 'free of any contribution' to non-employee classes.[48] The comparative predominance of general (as opposed to social insurance) funding for the Irish welfare system, outlined above, reflected this bias in support towards the self-employed. As we have seen, policy makers were well aware of both the political and administrative issues involved in asking farmers to pay directly for welfare improvements. MacEntee and Ó Ceallaigh

employees. 45 *Dáil Debates*, vol. 130 col. 633, 27 March 1952. This reflected the position in some other European countries at this time where the opposition of the middle classes or self-employed prevented the establishment of a universal system; see Baldwin, *Politics of Social Solidarity*. 46 Ryan himself, as critics pointed out, was a director of an insurance company. 47 White Paper para 131. 48 Norton's failure was perhaps that he did not get this message across both by decoupling the 1948 improvements (which benefited mainly assistance schemes) from the White Paper and by allowing the White Paper to be presented as though social insurance was the only plank of policy.

had quickly dismissed the notion of collecting social insurance contributions by adding them to the agricultural rates. And de Valera had been very cognisant of the interests of farmers and the self-employed in the drawing up of the children's allowance scheme. Fahey has made the point that in the first half of the century 'the state in Ireland engaged in an extensive range of interventions in social and economic life in rural Ireland'.[49] These included land reform and rural housing programmes which were highly redistributive, although Fahey argues that they may have benefited the middle ranks in rural Ireland rather than those at the bottom. These policies were consistent with de Valera's vision of the small family farm as a social ideal. The social welfare policies which Fianna Fáil pursued in the 1930s and 1940s were largely consistent with this approach. And the 'Fianna Fáil Plan' advanced by Ryan and, perhaps surprisingly, Lemass would have brought a more agrarian dimension to the social welfare system. But it was not to be. Contemporary observers, including Senator Joseph Connolly, Minister for Lands from 1932 to 1936, have suggested that 'the interest in 'The Land' ha[d] waned' and that de Valera had, privately, changed his policy.[50] In any case, Ireland's employment structure would have inevitably changed and a more agrarian welfare system might well have hindered rather than favoured economic development in the longer-term.

GENDER

Women made up about half of those in receipt of social welfare payments over the period covered by this study. If, as I have argued, the weakness of societal organisations was an important issue in the development of social welfare policy, then the gendered structure of Irish society was equally important. And, of course, the State had an important role to play in shaping that gendered structure. There is no doubt that the social welfare system was built around assumptions as to different roles for men and women. But this view was broadly shared by all political parties and, unlike the position in the UK, there was little public debate about an alternative approach. While it may be interesting to know, for example, that women's organisations proposed to de Valera that the first Minister for Social Welfare be a woman, there is no sign that anybody in government paid the slightest attention to this proposal.[51]

49 T. Fahey, 'The Agrarian Dimension in the History of the Irish Welfare State' seminar paper, ESRI May 1998. 50 J.A. Gaughan (ed.), *Memoirs of Senator Joseph Connolly* (Irish Academic Press, Dublin, 1996), pp. 365, 381. And see Fahey op. cit. pp. 3–7. 51 See NAI S.

As we have seen, the precursor schemes established in the early twentieth century did not always adopt a coherent approach to gender. The old age pension scheme tended to favour women as it paid the same amount to all pensioners, men and women, and also paid two full pensions to a pensioner couple rather than assuming economies of scale. The National Insurance Act was a much more gendered measure as the primary risks it aimed to address (sickness and unemployment) were, in a male dominated labour market, predominantly male whereas the risk of maternity received much more cursory treatment. The majority of those insured for both main contingencies and the majority of those in receipt of sickness and unemployment benefits were, of course, men.[52] The 1911 Act provided for higher rates of sickness benefit for men (10s. compared to 7s. 6d. for women) but the same rate of disablement benefit (5s.) and unemployment benefit (7s.). National health and unemployment benefits did not originally include increases in respect of 'dependants' but, as we have seen, these were added in a somewhat ad hoc fashion for some benefits in 1920. The Poor Law, in contrast, had always been a predominantly 'female' scheme in that the majority of adult claimants were women. Thus the insurantial logic of the patchwork of social welfare schemes in the early twentieth century meant that the focus of protection for those of working age was on the risk of exclusion from the workforce through sickness and unemployment. There was an assumption that the working population was mainly male, that single women received lower rates of pay and should, therefore, generally receive lower benefits, and that women would quite likely leave work on marriage. People who were not in employment but were poor, such as single mothers with children, had to rely on the Poor Law. Older people were, however, to be entitled to a payment which, despite the original 'merits' tests soon became effectively universal (subject to means). In the 1920s there was little change to this approach. The only significant policy change in that period which had specific reference to women was the termination of married women's membership of national health insurance – a move which was not opposed by any of the major parties. Over the decade to 1932, there was relatively little change in the proportion of women insured or the proportion of women claiming most social welfare payments.

Fianna Fáil if anything strengthened the gendered approach to welfare policy in line with its overall views on family policy and encouragement of

11036. All senior politicians and almost all key civil servants were men. A meeting of 18 'higher officials' in the Department of Social Welfare to finalise the draft White Paper included one woman, ILHA Norton papers 116. **52** In 1923, only 30% of those insured under national health insurance and 21% of those insured under unemployment insurance were women.

male (as opposed to female) employment.[53] As we have seen, both the introduction of widows' pensions and unemployment assistance were highly
gendered with 'deserving' women without male support being lifted off
home assistance but many women being excluded from entitlement to unemployment support. The numbers of women insured for national health insurance grew significantly from 1932 to 1938 but fell slightly as a proportion of
the total numbers insured. During the war, female unemployment rose
sharply while male unemployment fell – largely due to emigration. And
female unemployment remained volatile in the post-war years. But in most
other areas there was relatively little change. Women made up about 30% of
those insured for national health benefits from 1933 to the 1950s although the
overall numbers insured increased by almost half in that period. Similarly,
having fallen back during the 1930s, the proportion of pensioners who were
women remained at about 54% from 1938 to the 1950s. The one significant
policy change in the War years was the introduction of children's allowances.
But as we have seen, unlike the UK, these were made to the father rather than
the mother and were explicitly intended *not* to affect the existing relationship
within the family.

The White Paper and the subsequent legislation made some small moves
in the direction of gender equality with the introduction of uniform benefit
(but not contribution) rates for men and women (other than married women).
But like the Beveridge report, it was again based on the assumption that men
and women had fundamentally different roles in society. Dependency
increases were extended to all social welfare schemes and there was no real
question of extending insurance to women on 'home duties'. Again differences between the parties were on the details of this approach rather than
being of a more fundamental nature as is evidenced by the relatively narrow
differences on gender issues between the White Paper and the 1952 Act.
Overall, the political parties produced a unified social welfare system which
was built around the notion of the family headed by a male breadwinner. And
in doing so they very largely reflected a widespread consensus in Irish society.
Thus, as in most European countries, social welfare reform 'had an important
meaning for, and impact on, mothers and maternity' and its 'indirect impact

---

53 Clear has made the point that much of the decline in women's employment after 1926 was
due to a secular decline in domestic and agricultural employment (assisting relatives) and
argues on that basis that 'women were patently not being chased out of the work-force and
"back into" the home', see C. Clear, *Women of the House: Women's Household Work in Ireland
1922–1961* (Irish Academic Press, Dublin, 2000), chapter 1. This, however, does not take
account of the fact that women leaving traditional work were not being re-employed in the
developing areas of employment. As quoted in this book, senior Fianna Fáil figures explicitly
acknowledged their policy of favouring male over female employment.

was to reinforce women's dependency on husbands who benefited from the welfare measures'. However, unlike a number of other countries, the absence of a strong women's movement meant that women had little direct impact on the structure of welfare reforms.[54]

THE ROLE OF THE CATHOLIC CHURCH

In the development of the social welfare system, the Catholic Church is the dog which does not bark. Given the important role it played in social policy areas such as education and health, it appears to have had very little direct impact on the social welfare system. Clearly, most policy makers were Catholics and could be assumed to share common values about, for example, appropriate family structures. Norton, to take just one example, famously said in relation to the Mother and Child scheme that there would be 'no flouting of the authority of the Bishops in the matter of Catholic social or Catholic moral teaching'.[55] In addition, the Church obviously helped to shape the demands of the general public.[56] Over the period in question, the general approach of the Church to social policy in that period relied on the principles of 'Subsidiarity and Supplementation' and opposed extensive state intervention.[57] The State did

> 'not exist to do for individuals and families and other organisations what they can do reasonably well themselves; the State should not supplant them when they can partly do things but should supplement them; finally, the State is there to do for them what they cannot at all do for themselves'.[58]

But the Church itself played no direct role in the provision of social welfare policies – unlike its important role in education and health. And Catholic lay organisations – such as the Society of St Vincent de Paul which played an important role in providing support to the poor – explicitly rejected suggestions that it become more directly involved in state support on the

---

54 G. Bock and P. Thane (eds.), *Maternity and Gender Policies: Women and the Rise of the European Welfare States, 1880s–1950s* (Routledge, London, 1991), chapter 1.   55 *Dáil Debates*, vol. 125 col. 952, 17 April 1951.   56 F.G. Castles, 'On Religion and Public Policy: Does Catholicism Make a Difference?', *European Journal of Political Research* (1994) 25, p.19.   57 J. Kavanagh, *Manual of Social Ethics* (Gill, Dublin, 1954), p. 54 drawing on the encyclical *Quadragesimo Anno*. On Catholic social thought in the period see Kelly 'Social Security in Independent Ireland', pp. 43–61.   58 For a practical invocation of these principles, see the Hierarchy's criticism of the Mother and Child scheme quoted in J.H. Whyte, *Church and State in Modern Ireland, 1923–1979* (Gill & Macmillan, Dublin, 1980), pp. 424–5.

grounds that its primary purpose was not one of providing relief but the 'moral uplifting' of the poor.[59] Individual clergy did play a significant part either as members of commissions and committees in the first decade and, subsequently, as social commentators. And, of course, Bishop Dignan played an important role as the chair of the NHIS for a decade. There does not appear to have been any formal consultation with the Hierarchy on the White Paper, although Whyte does suggest that Norton sought informal approval from representatives of Catholic social thought.[60] Several clerical commentators were quite critical of the flat rate, social insurance based, departmental approach to reform of social welfare in an Irish context preferring a more corporatist, pay related approach.[61] But, unlike the Mother and Child scheme, this never became an issue for the hierarchy itself as opposed to individual members of the clergy. It is worth noting that Bishop Dignan himself explicitly stated that his original proposals were not sacroscant: he wrote as chairman of the NHIS and not as bishop of Clonfert.[62] Nor did his subsequent criticism of Norton's proposals suggest that they were contrary to Catholic teaching.[63] Dignan's reluctance to make his proposals an issue of 'church or state' may have contributed to the fact they did not, in fact, become an issue of conflict between the two. In contrast to the much touted Mother and Child scheme, MacEntee's harsh treatment of Dignan and the lack of any public Church response show the significant degree of separation between church and state which could exist at the time.

RATIONALITIES OF GOVERNANCE

If the concept of a unified system of social welfare, which was brought to fruition in 1952, was a new one, then the rationalities underlying the relationship between the individual and the state dated back some decades at least. Much recent work has examined the rationalities which underlie such

59 Commission on the Relief of the Poor, *Report*, p. 59.   60 J.H. Whyte, op. cit. pp. 181–2. 61 In addition to Dignan, *Social Security*, op. cit.; id. 'The Government Proposals for Social Security' *Christus Rex* (1950) IV, 103; C. Lucey, 'The Beveridge Report and Eire', *Studies* (1943) XXXII 36, P. McKevitt, 'The Beveridge Plan Revisited', *Irish Ecclesiastical Record* (1943) LXI, p. 145.   62 Foreword to *Social Security*.   63 Most Rev. J. Dignan, 'The Government Proposals for Social Security' op cit. Indeed Dignan had argued, in a letter read to the Hierarchy's meeting on 4 April 1951 which he was unable to attend, that in his view there was 'nothing in the [Mother and Child] Scheme opposed to Catholic teaching', Clonfert Diocessan Archives and see Whyte, *Church and State*, p. 219. To this extent, Whyte's assertion that the hierarchy's decision on the Mother and Child scheme was 'unanimous' may be slightly misleading.

relationships – the *hows* rather than the *whys* of policy.[64] In the case of the Irish social welfare system, the relationship between the state and the individual was an amalgam of at least three, sometimes conflicting, approaches. First there is the 'welfarist' approach perhaps best outlined in the first minority report of the Widows' Pensions Committee. The report argued for a social insurance based approach because it would encourage thrift, forethought and prudence, would recognise the responsibilities of workers and the duties of employers, and would safeguard the self-respect of beneficiaries. A means-tested approach, in contrast, discouraged thrift, removed responsibility and sapped and destroyed self-respect and self-reliance. This approach envisaged the state having an active role in 'making up' responsible, thrifty, prudent workers. It is also shown in the work of the approved societies and subsequently the National Health Insurance Society with their local agents and sick visitation staff. Local agents were to establish 'personal and immediate contact' between the organisation and the workers – workers who were to be seen as 'a neighbour, a living entity – the *industrious* head of a family, or the *helpful* son or daughter . . .'.[65] And the NHIS believed it had the technology to support this approach. Amalgamation of the societies had resulted in an organisation 'capable of providing improved facilities and *more perfect control* than heretofore'. 'Control' it was argued, involved 'much more than mere direction', it implied 'a capacity for adapting the organisation to suit the requirements of dynamic conditions'. The science of statistics had been so developed as to allow 'practically every alteration in human circumstances' to be measured.[66] The extent to which the Society played an important role in shaping the day-to-day life of Irish people in the 1930s and 40s is, of course, more difficult to judge but the objective is clear.

A second approach was the fiscal liberalism of the Department of Finance (and McElligott in particular). The state was not responsible for the relief of poverty in all its degrees and should only intervene in 'extreme cases where employment and the minimum necessities of existence are lacking'. Unlike both liberalism in its original form and more recent neo-liberalism, fiscal liberalism saw little role for the state in making up citizens and wished

---

64 On welfare policy, see F. Ewald, *Histoire de l'état providence* (Grasset, Paris, 1996); M. Dean, 'A genealogy of the government of poverty', *Economy and Society* (1992) 21, pp. 215–51; *id*, 'Governing the unemployed self in an active society', *Economy and Society* (1995) 24, pp. 559–83; W. Walters, 'The discovery of "unemployment": new forms of the government of poverty', *Economy and Society* (1994) 23, pp. 265–90.   65 *Sláinte 1935*, p. 78, my emphasis. 66 A.A. McPhie 'Statistics' in *Sláinte 1936*, p. 80, my emphasis. The Society had installed Powers-Samas punch-card statistical machines which would allow them 'to extract a mine of information and to control the claims[,] contributions and movement of every member of the Society'.

to leave this almost entirely to the market and to society. Finally, there was the 'familialism' advocated by a range of Catholic social thinkers. While their detailed proposals were sometimes inconsistent, they did cohere around a familial model based on that outlined in *Quadragesimo Anno*. Dignan, for example, argued that it was the family, and not the individual, that 'deserves prior place in our planning'. By natural and divine law, the father of the family was bound to maintain his home for himself, his wife and his family. The state should not attempt to relieve him of this duty and privilege but should assist him so that he could better meet these obligations. A family wage was the ideal solution to the social problems of the worker but in its absence (due to an accepted contingency) a pay-related, insurance-based 'indemnity' must be provided.[67] Thus the 'familialist' approach is not inconsistent with the welfarist approach outlined above but puts more emphasis on the family and on specifically Catholic ethics. The White Paper, as we have seen, is based primarily on a welfarist concept. It is family based but its emphasis on the family comes as much from Beveridge as from Catholic social thought. Insurance was advocated as it 'safeguards the self-respect of the beneficiary' and did not penalise thrift. But it was a much less ambitious approach than that advocated by the NHIS and more narrowly focussed on payment of benefits.[68] And there is little sense in the subsequent publications of the new department that it saw its role in the holistic manner of the NHIS.[69] One could argue that the new department operated a 'benefitist' variant of welfarism whereby its main relationship with the 'claimant' was via the payment or non-payment of a benefit – rather than through broader activities such as finding employment.[70]

A PARTICULARISTIC WELFARE SYSTEM

In conclusion, I return to the role of society, its interaction with the state and what this can tell us about the broader issues of welfare state formation.

Civil society and policy formation
I have argued that the societal organisations in the area of social welfare policy were weak and played little role in the formation of policy in the period

---

67 *Social Security*, *passim*. 68 For example, the White Paper explicitly excluded the employment-seeking role of employment exchanges from its definition of 'social security', *Social Security* para 1. 69 By the 1954–8 report, for example, the role of the local agent was simply to 'accept claims for . . . benefits and deliver cheques to claimants in receipt of those benefits.' 70 The number of vacancies filled by employment exchanges and offices declined from a peak of 130,000 in 1937–8 to only 40,000 in 1952.

in question.[71] However, this does not mean that social classes and their interests did not exist. The weakness of civil society means that the demands of particular social classes and groups were not mediated by an interest group *per se* but rather came to the attention of policy makers through particularistic interchanges. In the case of ministers, for example, such exchanges came about through the party organisation, meetings with businessmen, in their 'clinics' and role in making representations of behalf of constituents, and through contact with backbenchers.[72] I would suggest that, for much of the period covered in this book, this was one of the primary methods of conveying interests to the attention of policy makers. In the case of children's allowances, for example, politicians clearly knew that different policies would favour different groups and proposals were altered to ensure that the needs of particular groups were met, although representative groups had almost no formal input into the establishment of policy.

State autonomy

But if the state played an important role in shaping policy, did it act autonomously in the development of policy, as argued by authors like Skocpol in the 'state-centred' approach, or was in acting with relative autonomy to reflect class interests as argued for by neo-Marxists like Poulantzas?[73] To give a concrete example, in shaping children's allowances which favoured farmers and workers, was the Fianna Fáil government acting autonomously in its own interests to maximise votes or was in acting in a relatively autonomous manner to mediate the interests of those social classes such as farmers and workers who wanted more support with the interests of other groups which did not wish to see an excessive increase in taxation. The same question applies to applies to the foundation of the Department of Social Welfare. Was this a state (civil servant) driven plan to create a new department with consequent benefits to the public (better planning) but also promotional prospects for the civil servants involved or was it a state planned response to popular demands after the hardships of the Emergency period?

71 This analysis may clearly be less relevant in other social policy areas such as health or education where societal actors played a much more important role. 72 Given the relative abundance of departmental archival material and the paucity of private political material (much of the material in the archives of key politicians is retained departmental material) it is, of course, difficult to locate documentary traces of these types of contacts. 73 N. Poulantzas, *Pouvoir politique et classes sociales* (Maspero, Paris, 1968). In a social policy context, see J. Quadagno, *The Transformation of Old Age Security* (University of Chicago, Chicago, 1988); id., 'Welfare Capitalism and the Social Security Act of 1935' *American Sociological Review* (1984), p. 632; J. Melling, 'Welfare capitalism and the origins of welfare states: British industry, workplace welfare and social reform, *c*.1870–1914', *Social History* (1992) 17, pp. 453–78.

These type of questions can only be answered by a detailed empirical study of how policy was formed. But even then there can be very significant differences in the interpretation of events[74] and indeed conceptual differences as to the understanding of the political process in which outcomes are determined. One of the difficulties is that, as Quadagno has pointed out, analysis tends to focus on the 'arena of decision making' which is most visible and where the viewpoint tends to emphasise the role of the state decision makers.[75] But as Offe has argued, 'the space of possible decisions of political elites is determined by societal forces that, on a far less visible level, shape and change the politicians' view and perception of reality'.[76] At this level, it is more difficult to identify specific actor and 'the forces operating here are most often the aggregate outcome of a multitude of anonymous actors and actions. . .'. In addition, the focus on the initial decision making arena hides the fact that, once adopted, policies often take on a life of their own: expanding or contracting for reasons which have little to do with the ostensible reasons for which they were originally introduced. Thus, for example, unemployment assistance played an important role in supporting small farmers and their families affected by the economic war although there is no indication that this was a role envisaged for the payment when it was being planned.

My interpretation, based on the analysis in this book is that, at a macro level, those who argue for the relative autonomy of the state are correct. States and bureaucracies are ultimately constrained by social interests in formulating and implementing policy. Cumann na nGaedheal lost power because they could not (arguably they did not even try very hard to) build a sufficiently broad political alliance to support their policies. Fianna Fáil, in contrast, while implementing relatively radical policies in the 1930s, was always aware of the need to build a cross-class alliance of business, workers and small farmers.[77] Had Irish business withdrawn its support from the party in the course of 1932, it is not conceivable that it would have won a plurality of votes in 1933. But deterministic analyses do not find support in this inquiry. Unemployment policy was not simply shaped by the needs of business at any given time. To take the example of unemployment assistance again, it is clear that many employers felt that the state was providing support which was, in modern terms, insufficiently active in requiring unemployed

74 See for example the debate between Quadagno on the one hand and Skocpol and Amenta on the other on the origins of the USA 'New Deal' social security measures: Quadagno, op. cit.; T. Skocpol and E. Amenta, 'Did Capitalists Shape Social Security?', *American Sociology Review* (1985), p. 572; J. Quadagno, 'Two Models of Welfare State Development', *American Sociology Review* (1985), p. 575. 75 Op. cit. at p. 576. 76 C. Offe, *Contradictions of the Welfare State* (MIT Press, Cambridge, 1984), p. 159. 77 For an early example of this see Fianna Fáil's subtle approach to the introduction of broader Poor relief in Dublin in 1929.

claimants to seek work. But despite the efforts of Seán Lemass, there was little change in the way in which UA was administered. In practical terms, the analyses of the state-centred approach have a lot to tell us about how policies are developed and what institutional factors constrain and encourage such development. Clearly, states as 'configurations of organization and action' *do* influence the meanings and methods of politics for all groups and classes in society. The state does have its own (differing) interests and these can certainly influence policy as, arguably, in the establishment of new departments.[78]

THE LEGACY FOR THE FUTURE

I have argued, perhaps harshly, that the ultimate enactment of the 1952 Act was a failure of politics – a political project which ultimately pleased few people at the time and certainly did little to rebound to the credit of the Fianna Fáil government. However, the real merit of the White Paper and the 1952 legislation can only be seen in the longer term. One of the criticisms one can make of the White Paper is that it was before its time. Influenced by Beveridge and the subsequent UK legislation, it opted for a heavily insurance-based approach but excluded from that the self-employed who still made up almost half the working population. But this very 'out-of-timeness' meant that the White Paper was more relevant as Ireland's employment structure changed away from agriculture in the 1960s. Indeed the long decade after 1952 can be seen as dominated by dealing with the issues outlined or proposed in the White Paper.[79] A contributory old age pension was introduced, largely at Lemass' (by then Taoiseach) instigation in 1960. The workmen's compensation scheme, parked by the White Paper, was considered by a Commission established in 1955 and ultimately, in line with the minority report of that Commission, a system of occupational injuries benefits was introduced as part of the overall social welfare scheme in 1966.[80] A retirement pension and death grant were introduced in 1970. And the social

78 The use of the singular 'state' suggests that there is one monolithic state view. Clearly this is not correct and, as this study has shown there is endless debate between and within departments, between politicians and between politicians and administrators as to appropriate policies. 79 This may have been as much luck as judgement on the part of the policymakers as there is little indication in the White Paper or the archives that any great consideration was given to future employment trends. 80 Commission on Workmen's Compensation, *Reports*, Dublin, 1962. The Commission was appointed by the second Inter-party government. The Fianna Fáil government had proposed in 1953 to establish a parliamentary committee to consider the issue.

insurance system was finally extended to all fulltime employees in 1974. The 1952 legislation provided a necessary unified basis for the future expansion of the welfare state. The social insurance-based structure which it established continues to underpin the system we have today.

Appendix: Analysis in growth of social welfare expenditure, 1926-1961

This note sets out an analysis of the growth in social welfare expenditure in terms of the influence of demographic changes, changes in eligibility and changes in average benefits for old age pensions, sickness and unemployment payments (which make up about two thirds of total expenditure in the early 1950s) over the period 1926 to 1961.[1] It utilises the methodology drawn up by the OECD and previously used by Maguire in her study of social welfare spending in the period 1951-1981.[2] It uses the data in relation to the Census years of 1926, 1936, 1946, 1951 and 1961.[3] While some of this data is highly reliable (e.g. the population statistics), it should be recalled that official data in relation to national income was not available until the 1940s and that there may be variations in the administrative data over the period. Considerable caution should be utilised in interpreting this data other than in relation to general trends.

The variation in the share of national income spent on a particular payment are the product of changes in demography (i.e. the size of the relevant population group), eligibility (the proportion of the relevant population who actually receive the payment), and the level of benefit (i.e. the average payment per person). Thus changes in the share of expenditure as a percentage of national income can be decomposed into

- a demographic ratio (the ratio of the relevant population to the total population)

---

1 Children's allowances were not included in the analysis as data is only available for part of the overall period. 2 M. Maguire, 'Components of Growth of Income Maintenance Expenditure in Ireland 1951–1979' *Economic and Social Review* (1984) 15, pp. 75–85 and updated to 1981 in M, Maguire, 'Ireland' in P. Flora ed., *Growth to Limits: The Western European Welfare States Since World War II. Volume 2* (de Gruyter, Berlin, 1986). 3 The 1961 data is the closest available to end of the period under examination here. Given that there were few major changes in the structure of payments, the 1961 data probably provides a reasonable indication of the outcomes of the 1952 reforms in relation to eligibility for payments. However, changes in the transfer ratio in the period from 1951 to 1961 clearly owe much to decisions taken after 1952.

- an eligibility ratio (the ratio of the beneficiaries to the relevant population), and
- a transfer ratio (the ratio of the average payment per beneficiary to national income per capita).

OLD AGE PENSIONS

The analysis presented here supports the picture of growing coverage but declining relative generosity referred to in the chapter. In the case of old age pensions (see figure A8.1), there was little change in the proportion of national income going on old age pensions (about 2%) over the period.

There was a steady increase in the demographic ratio (the ratio of the potential claimant population to the total population) in the case of old age pensions from 5.7% in 1926 to 7.5% in 1961.

The 'eligibility ratio' increased from two thirds of the relevant population in 1926 to 80% in 1961 – increasing in the period to 1936, falling back somewhat during the war years and increasing again after 1951.

The 'transfer ratio' declined over time from 44% of national income in 1926 to 36% in 1951 and 31% in 1961.[4] So we see a broadening of eligibility but a decline in the relative level of payment.

UNEMPLOYMENT PAYMENTS

Unemployment payments (unemployment assistance and benefit) are another area in which there was little change in the overall level of spending as a percentage of national income from 1926 to 1961. With the exception of 1936, when spending almost tripled to 1.7% of national income, it remained at about 0.6-0.7% of national income over the period.[5] The concept of a demographic ratio is not particularly relevant to unemployment so no data are quoted here.

Again the 'eligibility ratio' (the ratio of beneficiaries to the labour force) increased in the case of unemployment payments from only 1.3% in 1926, rising dramatically to 7% in 1936 and falling back thereafter to about 4%.[6]

---

4 The fall in 1946 is somewhat overstated as it does not take account of other income supports such as food vouchers in this period.   5 The 1936 peak no doubt reflects the major increase in spending with the introduction of unemployment assistance but also reflects the (possibly overstated) fall in national income in this period.   6 The activity rate (i.e. the ratio of the labour force to the total population) fell slightly over the period from 44% in 1926 to 39% in 1961.

Table A8.1: Old age pensions, 1926–61

	Expenditure ratio	Demographic ratio	Eligibility ratio	Transfer ratio
1926	0.017	0.057	0.660	0.441
1936	0.022	0.059	0.746	0.511
1946	0.012	0.068	0.710	0.260
1951	0.018	0.071	0.722	0.361
1961	0.019	0.075	0.795	0.312

Note: 61 figures includes WP over 70 and OACP ADAs.

Table A8.2: Unemployment benefits

	Expenditure ratio	Eligibility ratio	Transfer ratio
1926	0.006	0.013	0.995
1936	0.017	0.071	0.523
1946	0.007	0.045	0.378
1951	0.007	0.039	0.424
1961	0.006	0.042	0.356

Note: Kennedy et al. table 7.2

Table A8.3: Sickness benefits

	Expenditure ratio	Eligibility ratio	Transfer ratio	B/L	I/L
1926	0.005	0.017	0.601	0.4935	38.0
1936	0.006	0.019	0.688	0.5719	43.0
1946	0.003	0.019	0.365	0.6458	50.1
1951	0.004	0.030	0.345	0.6769	53.6
1961	0.007	0.041	0.426	0.6588	59.5

Note: E excludes mat and other bens but includes all administration costs

The 'transfer ratio' declined over time from a peak of 100% of per capita income in 1926 to 52% in 1936 reflecting the fact that unemployment assistance was paid at a significantly lower level than unemployment benefit. Thereafter it continued to fall more slowly to 42% in 1951 and 36% by 1961.

Again we see a broadening of eligibility but a decline in the relative level of payment.

SICKNESS BENEFITS

Finally, in the case of sickness benefits (sickness and disablement benefit and, after 1952, disability benefit) we see a slight overall increase in the expendi-

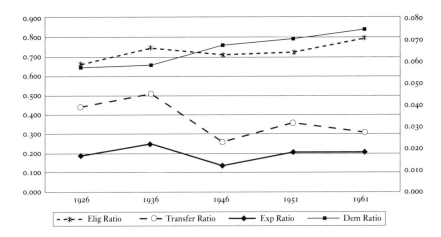

Figure A8.1 Old age pensions, 1926–61

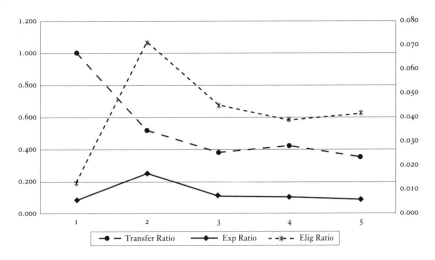

Figure A8.2 Unemployment payments, 1926–61

ture ratio from 0.5% of national income in 1926 to 0.7% in 1961. Again we see an increase in 1936, a fall in 1946 but only a partial recovery to 0.4% by 1951 with most of the increase coming after 1951 and – at least partially – as a result of the changes in sickness payments introduced in 1952. The demographic ratio is again not clearly defined for this payment and no data is reported.

There is little change in the eligibility ratio (i.e. the beneficiaries as

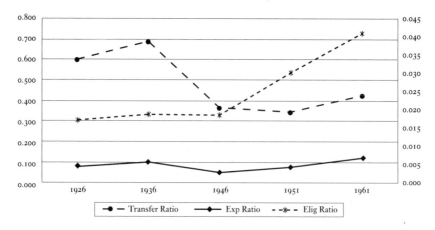

Figure A8.3 Sickness payments, 1926–61

proportion of the labour force) up to the 1940s remaining just under 2%. After that there is a significant increase the eligibility ratio to 3% in 1951 and 4% by 1961. The eligibility ratio can be broken down into the ratio of the insured population to the labour force which increased steadily over the period from 38% in 1926 to 60% in 1961 and the ratio of beneficiaries to the insured population which remained at about 4% up to 1946 and increased sharply thereafter to 7% by 1961.

However, there is a long-term fall in the transfer ratio from 60% in 1926 (followed by a slight increase to 69% in 1936) to 35% in 1951 rising slightly to 42% in 1961.

Thus we again see a broadening of eligibility arising both from increased insurability (itself resulting both from policy changes to broaden the scope of insurability and a increase in non-agricultural employment) and a higher claiming rate perhaps related both to changes in employment conditions and to the 1952 reforms. And again we see a decline in the relative level of benefits.

Overall these findings are in striking contrast to Maguire's findings in the later period which generally found significant increases in the transfer ratio.[7]

7 Maguire, op cit. fn 1.

Index